The Parent's Guide to Oppositional Defiant Disorder

Other titles for parents by Jessica Kingsley Publishers

Step by Step Help for Children with ADHD
A Self-Help Manual for Parents
Cathy Laver-Bradbury, Margaret Thompson, Anne Weeks,
David Daley and Edmund J. S. Sonuga-Barke
ISBN 978 1 84905 070 8
eISBN 978 0 85700 235 8

Sulky, Rowdy, Rude?
Why kids really act out and what to do about it
Bo Hejlskov Elven and Tina Wiman
ISBN 978 1 78592 213 8
eISBN 978 1 78450 492 2

Parenting OCD
Down to Earth Advice from One Parent to Another
Claire Sanders
ISBN 978 1 84905 478 2
eISBN 978 0 8570 0916 6

Stay Cool and In Control with the Keep-Calm Guru
Wise Ways for Children to Regulate their Emotions and Senses
Lauren Brukner
Illustrated by Apsley
ISBN 978 1 78592 714 0
eISBN 978 1 78450 300 0

More Creative Coping Skills for Children
Activities, Games, Stories, and Handouts to Help Children Self-regulate
Bonnie Thomas
ISBN 978 1 78592 021 9
eISBN 978 1 78450 267 6

The Parent's Guide to
OPPOSITIONAL
DEFIANT DISORDER

Your Questions Answered

AMELIA BOWLER

ILLUSTRATED BY AMELIA BOWLER

Jessica Kingsley Publishers
London and Philadelphia

First published in Great Britain in 2020 by Jessica Kingsley Publishers

An Hachette Company

1

Copyright © Amelia Bowler 2020

Front cover image source: Unsplash. The cover image is for
illustrative purposes only, and any person featuring is a model.

A CIP catalogue record for this title is available from the
British Library and the Library of Congress

ISBN 978 1 78775 238 2
eISBN 978 1 78775 239 9

Printed and bound in the United States by LSC Communications

Jessica Kingsley Publishers' policy is to use papers that are natural,
renewable and recyclable products and made from wood grown in
sustainable forests. The logging and manufacturing processes are expected
to conform to the environmental regulations of the country of origin.

Jessica Kingsley Publishers
73 Collier Street
London N1 9BE, UK

www.jkp.com

This book is dedicated to my children, Rufus and Malcolm.

You are my best teachers.

Thank you for loving me, being honest with me, and being gracious with me. It's an honor to be your mom.

Contents

Preface

This book began, years ago, when I looked at the results of a psychological assessment and realised that my own son fit the profile for Oppositional Defiant Disorder (ODD). His psychologist, teachers, and instructors all agreed: He was charming and bright, but disruptive, prone to conflict with other children, and hard to manage.

I started digging for some answers. I read textbooks, research papers, public health websites, and personal stories. The experts seemed to be saying that my son's behavior was caused by some kind of brain damage; or perhaps it was due to my own failings as a parent. Other parents told me to remove certain ingredients from his diet or try a range of supplements and oils. Psychologists recommended treatments such as parent training and psychotherapy.

Meanwhile, I was already a Board Certified Behavior Analyst, and my job description included teaching parents how to address problem behavior. I knew how to give clear instructions and positive feedback, maintain consistency, and build motivation. I prided myself on being a dedicated, affectionate, and creative parent. Still, I was clearly missing something. I could help other families but I couldn't help my own.

In other words, the label "Oppositional Defiant Disorder" only told me what I already knew: My son was frustrated, angry, and struggling to follow the rules. There was nothing to tell me what to do next, and no map to tell me what my child needed most. I felt alone and discouraged, as if I was standing in the centre of a maze, trying to lead my family out.

I wrote this book to help other parents who have found themselves in that same difficult maze. In my research I realized that for each family the answer will be a little bit different, even if the behavior looks similar. I learned about how shame, despair and stress can shape behavior, both for parents and children. I learned that there is no single path to treating the symptoms of ODD, because there is no single cause.

After sifting through the most up-to-date research and looking at disruptive behavior from a physiological, psychological, neurological, social, and behavioral perspective, I was able to draw five possible maps that parents can use to find help. In this book, I have described:

- what we know about these maps from the best available research evidence

- how to use each of the maps to find the possible causes of disruptive behavior

- practical ideas that parents can try straightaway

- suggestions for where to find professional support in this area of need.

Acknowledgments

This book could not have been written without the help of:

My family, who gave me time to write, endless inspiration, and refreshingly honest feedback on my behavioral interventions.

My fellow clinicians, especially those who agreed to read the book and offer feedback from many disciplines.

Dayna and Jason Abraham, creators of the Calm the Chaos Framework, who challenged me to look deeper within myself and within my children, and find a richer empathy, acceptance, and understanding.

Disclaimer

This book is not intended to be a substitute for clinical advice. It includes general information and recommendations, based on the available evidence.

According to the Behavior Analyst Certification Board's Ethics and Standards of practice, any behavior intervention should be individualized and based on a comprehensive assessment of your child's needs.

Behavior interventions should also be sensitive to culture and context, and although this book was written using research sources from around the world, the author acknowledges that this book was written from her own racial and gender perspective, and not all cultures and populations have been equally represented in the research.

PART 1

WHAT IS OPPOSITIONAL DEFIANT DISORDER?

CHAPTER 1

What Does It Mean to Have a Diagnosis of Oppositional Defiant Disorder?

Oppositional Defiant Disorder: What's in a name?

The very first thing to understand about a diagnosis of ODD is that the term "Oppositional Defiant Disorder" describes what is happening on the outside. The diagnosis does not point to a specific emotional or cognitive problem.

If your child has been tested, and diagnosed with ODD, your psychologist, psychiatrist, or pediatrician is simply agreeing that your child's behavior is more disruptive, angry, and unpleasant than they would typically expect. The behavior you are seeing matches a description in a diagnostic manual. The label "Oppositional Defiant Disorder" is a quick way for mental health professionals to summarize your child's behavioral symptoms, and note that they are causing problems.

And that's all.

What are the requirements for a diagnosis of Oppositional Defiant Disorder?

A psychiatric diagnosis such as ODD should only be given by a qualified mental health expert, such as a psychiatrist, a psychologist, or a general medical practitioner with appropriate training. Accordingly, this book should not be used for the purposes of self-diagnosis.

The requirements for a diagnosis of ODD will vary, depending on where you live. ODD is listed in both the World Health Organization's *International Classification of Diseases for Mortality and Morbidity*

Statistics (ICD-10)[1] and the American Psychiatric Association's *Diagnostic and Statistical Manual of Mental Disorders (DSM-5)*.[2] There are some subtle differences between the two descriptions, but they have some key factors in common. Both diagnostic criteria describe:

- a pattern of disobedience that begins in childhood
- defiant and angry behavior, especially toward adults in authority
- an easily offended, *irritable* temperament
- a tendency to blame others or carry out retribution.

A close reading of the full diagnostic criteria suggests that a child who is diagnosed with ODD may be struggling on a number of different fronts, including emotional self-regulation, self-control, and interpersonal skills. You may recognize one particular area of need in your own child, or you may see that most of your child's struggles are concentrated in one particular area, such as:

1. **Difficulty regulating intense emotions.** From the outside, these children often seem to have an "angry and *irritable* mood." They appear to be easily annoyed and quickly lose their temper when things don't go their way. Emotionally, these children are very sensitive, but they have difficulty expressing their feelings to others. They may express sadness, worry, and even loneliness in a hostile and abrupt way that does not attract much sympathy.

2. **Difficulty moderating goal-directed behavior.** From an adult perspective, these children are considered "argumentative and defiant." They seem almost immune to punishment or scolding, ignoring rules and warnings as they persist toward their goals. These children tend to be very strong-willed and independent, even impulsive or reckless.

3. **Difficulty cooperating with other people.** Sometimes described as "*vindictive*" or "aggressive," these children struggle to problem-solve and negotiate in a socially acceptable way. In disagreements, these children are more likely to use physical force or simple refusal to get their own way. They may have difficulty understanding the perspective of other people, so instead of resolving interpersonal

---

1   World Health Organization (2018) *International Classification of Diseases for Mortality and Morbidity Statistics* (10th Revision). Geneva: WHO.

2   American Psychiatric Association (2013) *Diagnostic and Statistical Manual of Mental Disorders* (5th edition). Washington, DC: American Psychiatric Association Publishing.

problems with compromise or forgiveness, they may resort to lashing out or escalating the conflict.

Understanding psychiatric labels

When it comes to mental health and behavior, the language of diagnosis can be misleading. While the medical field can often link a symptom with a particular injury or imbalance, a psychiatric diagnosis does not imply a particular biological problem. Although the field of mental health often speaks in the language of diseases and treatments, a behavioral disorder such as ODD does not point to a specific physical problem.

Saying "My child has Oppositional Defiant Disorder" is not the same as saying "My child has a specific medical condition with a known cause." It is more like saying "My child's arm is often swollen" or "My daughter has a persistent rash on her skin."

Furthermore, words like "oppositional" and "defiant" are not medical terms; they are subjective. Babies are not considered "defiant" and neither are most adults. A child can only be considered "oppositional" when confronted with an adult who expects to be obeyed. There is no known medical disorder that compels a child to do the opposite of what is expected, so terms like "oppositional" and "defiant" tell us more about how parents and teachers are feeling than about the child who refuses to cooperate.

Even the word "disorder" may sound like it helps to explain something, but as far as psychiatric labels go, a disorder is only a description. The disorder is not the cause, just like a headache is not an illness but a symptom.

Psychiatric diagnoses change over time, as social norms change and scientists shed more light on what kind of social, biological, and developmental pressures shape behavior. The diagnosis of ODD is a relatively recent addition to the field of psychiatry, and it has already been edited and revised several times.

A psychiatric label can change the way a behavior is treated. For example, the term "male hysteria" was used in the 18th and 19th centuries to label men who had emotional outbursts or "nervous conditions," especially after coming home from a war. In the present day, those same behaviors could be described and explained as post-traumatic stress disorder. The wrong label can assign blame and weakness or suggest a misleading cause. A properly-labeled psychiatric disorder helps others to understand what may be triggering the behavior and accurately describes the symptoms.

The term "Oppositional Defiant Disorder" can be misleading. It's a pattern of behavior, not a condition, a trait, a neurological defect, a chemical imbalance, or a genetic fault. It's not that your child has a "contrary quality" or a "delinquent personality." In fact, it would be dangerous to assume that your child is simply defying you for defiance's sake.

When your child argues or says "no," he or she might be trying to meet a legitimate need or might be showing you that he or she lacks coping skills. Children refuse and protest for many reasons, including:

- avoiding a frightening social situation

- attempting to follow a rigid self-imposed rule

- feeling triggered by past trauma

- expressing emotional distress when sensory needs are not met

- signaling confusion and feelings of overwhelm.

In other words, the term "Oppositional Defiant Disorder" summarizes how your child might be behaving but does not help you to understand why your child is behaving that way.

Future editions of diagnostic manuals may be able to describe challenging behavior in a way that takes a child's history, development, and cognitive skills into account, which would allow clinicians to recommend treatment according to the child's specific need. In the meantime, the diagnosis can only point to a broad set of problems, and doctors and clinicians must look at each child individually to decide what treatments and supports will help the most.

Psychiatric labels are created based on cultural norms and expectations. This diagnosis doesn't mean that your child is inherently mean, unpleasant, or cruel. It simply means that your child is currently struggling to meet expectations and is probably struggling with emotional self-regulation, self-control, and social skills.

Additional sources of physiological, sensory, emotional, cognitive, relational, or situational stress can put pressure on children and their ability to cope with expectations. You will read more about these factors as you progress through this book.

Oppositional Defiant Disorder and the nature of optimism

There is one more thing to note: A diagnosis of ODD takes a lot of different struggles and lumps them all together into one category.

Children who have disruptive and challenging behavior are still whole, complex, and full of amazing potential. They have specific needs and struggles, but when those children get the right kind of help, they can start to express their gifts and interests in a much healthier way.

The word "disorder" does not leave room for an appreciation of your child's strengths. In a different context, your child's behavior could be interpreted as determined, creative, passionate, independent, and brave. The world needs rebels, free-thinkers, warriors, and leaders.

When you hear all of your child's most frustrating, disruptive, and dangerous behaviors heaped together under one banner, you may feel overwhelmed. It is hard to be hopeful when the problem seems to be huge, permanent, and innate.

Remember that your child's abilities are growing. Just because your child struggles with emotional self-regulation right now, that does not mean he or she has a lifelong "emotional self-regulation disorder." It could mean that your child is missing some important skills, but with the right learning opportunities and support, progress is possible.

Fortunately, behavior happens one moment at a time, and as you read this book, you will see opportunities to make a significant difference in your child's behavior and his or her life.

What do we know about Oppositional Defiant Disorder?

If you dive into the research on ODD and start reading articles published in journals such as *Clinical Child and Family Psychological Review*, you will find a sea of conflicting opinions and findings. Some researchers point to the importance of genetics and family histories, while others say there is no such connection. Some researchers focus on the relationship between "negative parenting practices" and ODD, while other researchers say there is only a small predictive relationship. You will find hundreds of articles on trauma, neglect, depression, anxiety, parental mental health, and socioeconomic status. The only thing they all agree on is this that *we need more research*.

Still, there are some self-dubbed experts who say they have it all figured out. You will find books on the shelf at your local library, assuring you that they know exactly what is to blame for all this challenging behavior, including:

- "problems with brain chemistry"
- "planned, purposeful behavior"

- "well-defined temperament traits…not brain damaged, emotionally disturbed, or defective"

- "because they've gotten away with it!"

Even among the most respected names in the field of child behavior, there is very little consensus. For instance, Dr. Ross Greene has been an influential voice encouraging families to look beneath the surface of challenging behavior to find "unmet needs and lagging skills," while the venerable Dr. Alan Kazdin advises parents to "[s]tart by changing the behavior, not by trying to get to the root causes of your child's misbehavior."

Oppositional Defiant Disorder: Different from the inside out

When you read statistics on ODD, you are seeing the stories of thousands of children and families, all compressed and processed into a few easily digestible statistics. However, as you know, any two children diagnosed with ODD can have different behavior patterns and different struggles. They may even have different brain patterns and physiological reactions from typical children, or from one another.

These children have different motivations, different families, different genetic profiles, different emotional difficulties, and even different measurements of resting heart rate and skin conductivity, according to some researchers. What unites them all is that they are struggling to meet adult expectations.

What is this book about and who is it for?

This book is for you. You may be a parent of a child already diagnosed with ODD, or you may recognize some of the symptoms in your child.

In this book, you will find a summary of the latest research on ODD, gathered from journals in the fields of psychology, nursing, education, behavior science, psychiatry, social work, genetics, and neurology.

This book exists to do three things. First, it is to *inform*. Accurate information on ODD is scarce, and an internet search tends to yield information that is superficial at best, misleading at worst. Next, the book is written to help you gain *insight and empathy*. Children diagnosed with ODD are often judged harshly and badly misunderstood. The same can often be said for parents facing negative judgment from their communities and even from themselves. Finally, the book is written to *equip and empower* you as a parent, so you can make practical changes in your parenting approach and find qualified outside help wherever it is needed.

Oppositional Defiant Disorder: What research tells us

ODD is not a diagnosis that describes a specific medical condition or a single mental health issue. It describes a set of behaviors that tend to get your child "into trouble" but *it does not point to one root cause*. Children diagnosed with ODD struggle in emotional, cognitive, and behavioral ways. Experts have disagreed over whether this is the result of "nature" or "nurture," but in the first section of this book, you will get a balanced view of what research has been able to uncover so far, including:

- What does it mean to have a diagnosis of ODD?

- What are the known causes of ODD?

- What else could be going on?

- What kind of treatment is effective?

No one-size-fits-all solutions

In this book, you will *not* find a list of behaviors and how to fix them. There is no one single "solution" for arguing, tantrums, swearing, stealing, refusing to complete chores, or eye-rolling. A one-size-fits-all approach to behavior ignores the fact that all behavior happens *in context*. People will behave differently depending on their relationships, their moods, what they had for breakfast, or even the weather. If your child is yelling on a daily basis, there may be a different underlying reason for the yelling every day of the week. What "works" for your neighbor's child may not work for yours. The strategy that "works" on Monday may not work on Thursday.

Support where you need it most

Parenting is not a simple task, and your child's needs might be hard to discern at first. As you read this book, you will find five sections that describe five different ways that families struggle when a child's behavior is "oppositional" and "defiant." As you explore these sections and reflect on them, you will see opportunities to grow and pitfalls to avoid.

These sections cover your family from many different angles, including: your perspective as a parent, the ways in which you and your child relate to one another, how to support your child's emotional and cognitive development, and your child's values and motivation.

Finding behavior solutions: A proactive approach versus reactive approach

As you read through the chapters, you will see positive, proactive strategies that you can use every day. Most of these strategies are not designed to be used when the conflict is already raging and tempers are flaring. In order to help your child build healthy behavior habits, you will need to set up learning opportunities throughout the day and plan ahead in order to set your family up for success.

Of course, there will be times when a strategy falls through when your child is still learning to cope, and life will get messy. Your child's best learning does not happen when the mistakes have already occurred. Success is a much more powerful teacher than failure, so keep your focus on the proactive ways you can meet your child's needs and build up those important life skills.

One diagnosis, many different struggles

When psychologists test large groups of children and average out the results, important information can sometimes get lost. For example, children diagnosed with ODD may come from very different families, with different skills and levels of maturity. They may even have different physiological reactions to stress.

Subtypes within the Oppositional Defiant Disorder diagnosis

When giving a diagnosis of "Oppositional Defiant Disorder," psychologists look for patterns of behavior that fall into three major categories: *irritable, headstrong,* and *vindictive*.[3] These categories are sometimes called "dimensions," and they describe groups of behaviors that might have the same underlying cause. Just a reminder: These labels describe the way the behavior appears to an outside observer. It does not mean that your child has an *irritable* or *headstrong* or *vindictive*

3   Stringaris, A. & Goodman, R. (2009) Three dimensions of oppositionality in youth. *Journal of Child Psychology and Psychiatry, 50*(3), 216–223.

personality or character trait. These labels simply describe a pattern of behavior:

1. *Irritable,*[4] meaning easily provoked to anger, often suspicious of others, resentful, and annoyed. These children are extra-sensitive and may have difficulty letting go of anger. They are also prone to holding a grudge or expressing anger in the form of verbal or physical attacks.

2. *Headstrong,* meaning that conflict tends to happen when others impose authority, redirect the child's activity, or ask the child to stop unexpected and inappropriate behavior. These children are very goal-oriented and seem to be able to tune out reminders and threats while in pursuit of their goal.

3. *Vindictive* behavior could be described as deliberately hurtful to others (e.g., teasing, laughing when someone gets hurt, provoking others with the apparent intent to annoy). These children also have a keen sense of justice and fairness, so they may intervene on behalf of others and look for a leadership role.

Your child's behavior may fit into every one of these categories, or you might find one particular category stands out to you as a major reason for conflict. To give you a better sense of how these subtypes might be handled differently, this chapter contains a brief overview of the three subtypes/dimensions of ODD: *irritable, headstrong,* or *vindictive.* For each subtype, you will find:

- examples of typical behavior
- possible underlying reasons
- related cognitive and emotional struggles
- how to help this kind of child
- parenting styles that best suit this kind of struggle.

You will be able to find much more detailed advice on how to tailor your parenting approach, explore in-depth information on cognitive and emotional struggles, and choose possible treatment interventions

---

4   Zastrow, B. L., Martel, M. M. & Widiger, T. A. (2018) Preschool oppositional defiant disorder: A disorder of negative affect, surgency, and disagreeableness. *Journal of Clinical Child & Adolescent Psychology, 47*(6), 967–977.

later in this book, but for now, here is a summary of how each category might be handled differently.

Irritable behavior: Why is this happening and what should you do?

Children who are often angry and easily upset are hard to be around. They may complain frequently, criticize others, give up easily, and create explosive scenes with their outbursts. Family members, teachers, friends, and classmates may become frustrated and vent their annoyance at the child or start to avoid contact with the child who seems to create so much drama. These reactions usually trigger more angry outbursts from the child, and escalate into family arguments, broken friendships, and exclusion from community activities.

Irritable children are also likely to say that they are unhappy and angry a lot of the time. These children are at higher risk of developing anxiety and mood disorders[5] later in life.

If you are seeing mostly *irritable* behavior, then your child might be struggling in the following areas:

- emotional awareness, emotional coping skills, self-regulation

- cognitive skills related to sequencing and planning (e.g., setting priorities)

- flexibility, perspective-taking, and problem-solving.

HOW DO YOU HELP A VERY *IRRITABLE* CHILD?

- Build up your own emotional self-regulation skills, so you can limit your negative and stressful reactions.

- Look for possible sources of stress and overwhelm that may lead to outbursts, including sensory overload such as noise, crowds, and light.

- Teach proactive problem-solving skills within the family, so you can plan to avoid disappointment, confusion, and conflicting interests.

- Provide emotion coaching and self-regulation tools, to support healthy expression of anger and other emotions that might be expressed as hostility (e.g., anxiety, poor self-esteem).

---

5   Kolko, D. J. & Pardini, D. A. (2010) ODD dimensions, ADHD, and callous–unemotional traits as predictors of treatment response in children with disruptive behavior disorders. *Journal of Abnormal Psychology, 119*(4), 713.

- Appreciate your child's sensitivity and passion. Accept it as part of what makes him or her unique.

PARENTING STYLES AND THE *IRRITABLE* CHILD

If your child is having frequent emotional outbursts, you might find it very difficult to balance your family's need to observe rules and etiquette, while also trying to react to your child's dramatic highs and lows in a calm, supportive way. The more offensive, disruptive, rude, and hurtful these outbursts are, the harder it is for parents to show sensitivity and kindness.

It's only human to feel angry, worried, offended, and overwhelmed when children react in a negative and hostile way. It's understandable to feel stressed out when any situation could quickly spin out of control, when your physical safety is threatened, or when other family members suffer as a result of these outbursts.

Often, parents and teachers try to reduce these outbursts by using systems of rewards and punishments, in the hope that a punishment will discourage the child from being so offensive in the future, or assuming that a tempting reward will remind the child to use more self-control.

Some parents assume that being stricter or having more consistent systems of discipline will convince an *irritable* child to follow the rules and make better choices. However, if your child is overreacting to stress, and has difficulty controlling his or her emotions, then a warm, attachment-based approach will be more effective in teaching those missing emotional self-regulation skills.

Headstrong behavior: Why is this happening and what should you do?

Children who tend to argue, defy authority, and provoke others are often very intense and determined, especially when they are focused on their own priorities. They may interact with other people in unexpected ways (e.g., laughing when they are scolded, or ignoring social etiquette).

Headstrong children are likely to struggle in situations that require rule-following and self-control. Defiant and rule-breaking patterns of behavior can be simply oppositional and difficult, or they can escalate to more hurtful and dangerous types of behavior, at which point these behaviors would be reclassified as symptoms of Conduct Disorder (CD).

If you are seeing mostly *headstrong* behaviour, then your child might be struggling in the following areas:

- delaying gratification and resisting impulses

- changing plans and problem-solving
- switching attention and prioritizing
- predicting and planning, using logic
- accepting help and adapting to suggestions.

HOW DO YOU HELP A VERY *HEADSTRONG* CHILD?

- Communicate expectations as simply and gently as possible.
- Plan ahead, using visuals and checklists to help stay on task.
- Set up predictable reminders and consequences for desirable and undesirable behaviour.
- Collaborate to create a comfortable routine to start difficult tasks.
- Celebrate your child's determination and focus. Accept it as part of what makes him or her unique.

PARENTING STYLES AND THE *HEADSTRONG* CHILD

If your child's *headstrong* behavior is related to difficulty with impulsivity and inflexibility, then a firm, logical, and predictable parenting approach will create a more manageable structure than a loose, improvisational approach to the daily routine.

Inconsistent reactions to your child's *headstrong* behavior can also make the situation worse by setting up the expectation that loud, insistent or aggressive behavior "gets results."

Vindictive behavior: Why is this happening and what should you do?

Children who get angry and lash out at others in retribution are often referred to as "*vindictive*." *Vindictive* behavior often happens when children are lacking the skills to understand the behavior of others, and so they misjudge people as hostile, mean, or deliberately hurtful.[6] *Vindictive* behavior may also be a form of emotional processing; if the child does not know how to emotionally self-regulate or problem-solve, then simple revenge may take the place of problem-solving, empathy, and reconciliation.

---

6   Lochman, J. E. & Wells, K. C. (2002) Contextual social–cognitive mediators and child outcome: A test of the theoretical model in the Coping Power program. *Development and Psychopathology, 14*(4), 945–967.

If you are seeing mostly *vindictive* behavior, then your child might be struggling in the following areas:

- understanding logical consequences
- letting go of angry thoughts and plans for "pay-back"
- self-calming, flexibility, and acceptance
- attachment and trust.

HOW DO YOU HELP A VERY *VINDICTIVE* CHILD?

To help a child to handle situations without resorting to *vindictive* behaviour such as revenge and payback:

- Offer emotion coaching, including labeling thoughts and emotions, recognizing the difference between thoughts and reality.
- Teach collaborative problem-solving skills and perspective-taking.
- Look for increased opportunities for positive interactions.
- Model alternatives to punishment, and strategies for reconciliation.
- Address past trauma and the need for safety.
- Validate your child's desire for fairness and encourage your child to help others who are suffering.

PARENTING STYLES AND THE *VINDICTIVE* CHILD

If your child has a tendency to deliver "payback" for perceived wrongs, it is important to think carefully through your own concept of discipline in your home. If you have tried to maintain order with a set of planned penalties for misdeeds, your child may be following suit. If your child frequently hears criticism, or if your child has a harsh and unforgiving attitude toward mistakes, he or she may assume the responsibility of settling the score when others step out of line.

The best way to teach flexibility, forgiveness, and grace to a *vindictive* child is to lead by example. When you can discuss your own mistakes with self-compassion, and offer empathy to others despite their mistakes, your child will start to understand the alternative to vengeance and judgment.

If and when you do need to lay down a consequence following

a mistake, be sure to explain your decision in the most benevolent terms possible. If possible, help your child to understand how the consequence is for his or her benefit, and how learning can take place in the future. For example, instead of telling a child, "You've lost the privilege of using a knife at the table," you can say instead, "I need to keep you safe, so I have to take this away for now. Let's talk about how to use it safely when you're ready."

An important warning

So often, psychological labels describe children as having traits, personalities, or mental illnesses. For example, when children are categorized as simply "*irritable,*" "*headstrong,*" or "*vindictive,*" these labels create expectations and assumptions. These expectations will shape the behavior of teachers and caregivers. Just remember that these labels describe what children look like from the outside. Thinking of your child as actually "irritable," "headstrong," or "vindictive" might make it hard for you to feel hopeful about the future, or to be sympathetic when your child is struggling with a big emotion.

Labels can also hurt children by creating low expectations, and even changing the adult's ability to see a child's performance for what it really is. Researchers call this "confirmation bias," and studies have shown that parents and teachers who label children as "difficult" often overlook the child's successes because the behavior doesn't fit in with the expectations. The label starts to become self-fulfilling, as caregivers with low expectations give less positive feedback and avoid challenging situations, so the child misses out on learning opportunities. Without challenges, encouragement, and learning opportunities, the child stays stuck at the same level.

Contrary to popular belief, emotional self-regulation is a skill that can be learned. "Accepting no" is a skill that can be learned. Following a routine and waiting before interrupting is a skill that can be learned. Your child may learn at his or her own pace, and in unexpected ways, but growth and development are always possible. It is so important for you as a parent to keep looking for the process that works best for your child.

The behavior that you see today is not the whole story. Your child's behavior is telling the story of what has happened so far, based on his or her development, relationships, and learning opportunities up to this moment. As you discover ways to improve your child's relationships and learning opportunities, you will see your child's development start to tell a different story.

What are the benefits of getting an official diagnosis of Oppositional Defiant Disorder?

If you are reading this book because you've noticed that your child's behavior seems to match the criteria for ODD, and you're wondering whether a formal diagnosis from a psychologist would be worth the time and expense, here are some questions to consider:

- *Is ODD considered a legal disability in the country you live in?*

  If your child currently needs extra support with behavior, especially in areas such as following instructions calmly or regulating emotions in a school or childcare setting, a formal diagnosis of ODD may help you to apply for accommodations.

- *Would a diagnosis help you to access support programs, medication, and treatment for your family?*

  Some treatment programs are designed specifically for children with a diagnosis of ODD, so a formal diagnosis would be required. A psychological diagnosis may also be helpful if psychological treatment is covered under your family or work health insurance policy.

- *Would a diagnosis help others understand that your child needs extra support and understanding?*

  One of the most frustrating aspects of finding support for your child is that his or her struggles are often an "invisible disability." Your child may appear to be "normal" at school or when visiting relatives, which makes it hard for teachers or family members to acknowledge the very real struggles you are facing at home.

  For some families, a formal diagnosis of ODD can be a positive experience. A diagnosis can help to validate the difficulty you are facing and help other people in your life to accept that your child may need extra help such as professional treatment, positive feedback, and patience.

- *Would a mental health diagnosis invite unwanted judgment or stigmatization?*

  Unfortunately, your community may not think of a psychological diagnosis as a valid or useful tool. If you live in a country or cultural community with traditional values, you may experience rejection or judgment from those who refuse to accept the existence of developmental differences.

CHAPTER 2

What Are the Causes of Oppositional Defiant Disorder?

Why do children obey?

To really understand the difference between children diagnosed with ODD and those children who seem to cope with life with less drama and strife, it's worth asking, *"Why do children obey?"*

Of course, no child is perfectly compliant, and some disobedience is just a developmentally appropriate part of learning. Still, why do some children navigate the world so successfully, following parent and teacher instructions often enough to stay out of trouble? What do these typical kids do that helps them succeed? What's different about them, compared to children diagnosed with ODD?

It would be over-simplifying to say that children obey simply because they are "obedient." Both nature and nurture have a part to play in shaping a child who can cope with adult expectations. So, what makes a child "obedient"?

The role of temperament and personality

As you have probably noticed, children raised in the same family can have wildly different responses to the same set of parents. Children are born with some unique qualities, preferences, and sensitivities, and psychologists refer to this as "temperament." Temperaments and personality traits are considered to be somewhat stable across the lifetime, although not every "high-needs" infant grows into an *irritable* child, and some agreeable toddlers grow up into very independent and outspoken children. Research suggests that even newborns have differing biological responses to stress; some infants can settle down easily after being startled, while others struggle to recover from an uncomfortable moment. Scientists disagree about exactly which aspects of personality are learned and which are innate,[1] but children do appear to have consistent preferences for how much risk, social interaction, sensory input, and novelty they can tolerate.

Maturity and rule-following

Maturity and physical development also help to determine how well a child can handle difficult everyday situations.

As children get older and more sophisticated, they gain experience and their brains continue to develop. They begin to apply "rules" to their own behavior, delaying short-term pleasures for more long-term or abstract gains. They learn to put off gratification and remind themselves of the benefits of waiting. They can accept parental limits such as "First we eat dinner, then we get dessert." When children understand the reasons behind the less enjoyable parts of their day, then they are more willing to tolerate them. For example, children can understand the logic when parents explain, "We don't want to get cavities, so we brush our teeth every day."

Children also follow rules in order to avoid punishment, or even the possibility of punishment. Sometimes these rules are articulated by parents, and then children privately repeat these rules to themselves. For instance, a child who remembers a rule may caution himself or herself: "Don't go in that closet or Mommy will be angry." In a sense, rule-following acts as its own reward because it helps the child to avoid unpleasant thoughts, even if no one is standing nearby and threatening to impose a punishment.

Opportunities for socialization

The process of shaping a child's behavior to meet cultural expectations is often called "socialization." Socialization is built on three processes:

1. **Modeling**: a consistent and clear model to follow and look up to.

2. **Positive feedback**: encouragement, attachment, and nurture.

3. **Negative feedback**: correction, and in some cases, rejection or coercion.

Some children adapt easily to this process, because they understand

---

1   Rettew, D. C. & McKee, L. (2005) Temperament and its role in developmental psychopathology. *Harvard Review of Psychiatry*, 13(1), 14–27.

and readily imitate their role models, they respond positively to their family's attempts to include them and encourage them, and they learn to control their behavior in order to avoid negative feedback.

Obedient behavior in context

To summarize, children tend to be cooperative when:

- They have close relationships with positive role-models.

- They have the skills to imitate desired behaviors.

- They have the skills to regulate unacceptable behaviors.

- They have the skills to understand social expectations.

- They are able to communicate their needs and have those needs met.

Clearly, socialization is a process of interaction between the child and the environment. A child's willingness to obey adult instructions depends on his or her capacities and skills, and the relationships he or she develops. When children are discouraged or losing trust in caregivers, they invest less in being cooperative and meeting social expectations. When children are stressed, in pain, or worried, they tend to prioritize their own needs over the needs of the group. When children are missing the skills to perform as expected, they become trapped in a cycle of negative feedback.

What are the "causes" of Oppositional Defiant Disorder?

Many parents make the understandable mistake of blaming ODD for causing their child's behavior. "It's just his ODD," they say.

Unfortunately, there is a circular logic to this and, ultimately, it makes no sense at all. If you ask this parent, "How do you know he has ODD?", they will reply, "Because he is oppositional." However, if you ask, "Why is he oppositional?", they may answer, "Because he has ODD."

It makes more sense to say, "He's been diagnosed with ODD because he has oppositional behavior, but we don't really know why he behaves like this just yet."

As you have certainly seen, some children struggle to be socialized. They ignore norms and expectations, they do not perform as expected when offered the usual set of rewards, and no amount of punishment and negative feedback seems to bring them back in line.

Why doesn't the process of "socialization" seem to be working for your child?

If your child doesn't respond as expected to the social contract, then it's worth looking at how the environment has been interacting with your child's particular set of needs and skills. The process often breaks down when:

- Social expectations are not in line with the child's developmental and relationship needs.

- Social expectations have not been taught or modeled consistently.

- Important relationships have been disrupted, so social acceptance is hard to access.

- The child's key needs are not being met or communicated.

- The child's key skills are missing, not yet developed.

- Stress or trauma overrides self-control.

- Self-regulation skills are lacking.

How environments and abilities interact

In any of these cases, you might be asking "Why?" and the answer would be a complicated tangle of cultural, social, genetic, developmental, psychological, biological, and neurological factors. *To put it simply, most defiant and oppositional behavior happens when a child's environment collides with his or her abilities.* Research has shown that there is no one single factor that "causes" oppositional and defiant behavior. Rather, children who are diagnosed with ODD have usually been living with a number of factors that interact with one another.

As you read this book, you will see examples of how many factors can interact in complex ways to increase the risk of challenging behavior, including:

- genetic vulnerability

- neurological differences including Attention Deficit Hyperactivity Disorder (ADHD)

- family history of behavior and mental health problems

- family socioeconomic status

- negative, critical parenting style

- exposure to abuse, neglect, and criminality
- exposure in-utero to drugs, alcohol, or environmental toxins
- history of trauma or brain injury[2]
- difficulty with executive functioning skills
- sensitivity to pain and stress
- rejection by peers.

Some factors can be positive and protective, so even if the child is living with some of the risk factors above, he or she may adapt well and develop healthy behavior patterns. These protective factors include:

- parental warmth and responsivity
- parental optimism and mental flexibility
- emotion coaching
- positive relationships with peers
- safe, well-supervised upbringing.

As you can see, some risk factors are outside your control as a parent. Fortunately, you don't have to go through this alone. Throughout this book, you will find a wealth of information on how to support your child's emotional and cognitive needs, how to provide a calm and stable environment (even when your child's behavior gets wild), and what kind of interventions have been shown to be effective for children diagnosed with ODD.

What is the relationship between Oppositional Defiant Disorder and parenting?

If you are a parent, you may be asking yourself questions such as: "Did I do this?", "Is this my fault?", "Can I make it better?", and "Am I making this worse?"

First of all, you have already taken a positive step toward helping your child, simply by picking up this book. You have probably already spent hours asking questions, consulting experts, and lying awake

---

2   Noordermeer, S. D., Luman, M. & Oosterlaan, J. (2016) A systematic review and meta-analysis of neuroimaging in oppositional defiant disorder (ODD) and conduct disorder (CD) taking attention-deficit hyperactivity disorder (ADHD) into account. *Neuropsychology Review*, 26(1), 44–72.

wondering what you could possibly do to help your child. Every parent does their best, and every parent has areas in which they can improve, so there is no need to assign blame, as long as you are committed to getting the support your family needs.

Parenting and Oppositional Defiant Disorder: Questions on cause and effect

Your parenting style[3] and your child's behavior is a bit of a chicken-and-egg situation.

First of all, let's look at the elephant in the room. You've probably heard that studies indicate that there is a relationship between children with "oppositional and defiant behavior" and parents who have a "harsh or withdrawn" parenting style.

However, this information can be interpreted in a few different ways. Even if your stomach lurched when you read that sentence, because your own parenting behavior is sometimes harsh or timid, this is not evidence that you *caused* your child to be oppositional with your parenting style.

After all, if your child's behavior was easy to manage, why would you ever be tempted to yell? You probably wouldn't feel as overwhelmed or depressed. You'd have more positive interactions,[4] because you wouldn't need to spend so much time trying to cope with arguments, refusal, and aggressive outbursts.

It's natural to be discouraged when your child ignores your reasonable and gentle approach. In fact, research has shown that parents do sometimes switch to a more aggressive or defeated style of parenting in response to their child's oppositional behavior.[5]

In other words: You are not alone. You and your child are responding to one another, and it can be very hard to change this dynamic.

How do these parent–child patterns develop?

One team of researchers set out to answer the question of how children

3 Darling, N. & Steinberg, L. (2017) Parenting Style as Context: An Integrative Model. In R. Zukauskiene (ed.) *Interpersonal Development*. London: Routledge.
4 Barkley, R. A. & Cunningham, C. E. (1979) The effects of methylphenidate on the mother–child interactions of hyperactive children. *Archives of General Psychiatry*, 36(2), 201–208.
5 Greene, R. W. & Doyle, A. E. (1999) Toward a transactional conceptualization of oppositional defiant disorder: Implications for assessment and treatment. *Clinical Child and Family Psychology Review*, 2(3), 129–148.

and parents influence each other.[6] They noted that, in previous studies, poor supervision and lack of warmth was a good predictor of oppositional behavior. They also pointed out that parents of children with oppositional behavior also reported higher levels of stress and difficulty with mental health. After studying 177 families of children with oppositional and defiant behavior for several years, they concluded that it is actually easier for children to change their parents' behavior than it is for parents to change their children.

Of course, every parent–child relationship has an emotional push–pull within it, starting on the day your child is born. You hear the sound of your child crying and you spring into action. The baby calls and you respond. Gradually, the baby learns to respond to you, too. You develop a way of responding to each other, and that pattern is shaped by each of you in turn.

Factors that shape the parent–child relationship

Your relationship with your child is influenced by your history, your personality, and your skills. However, the way you parent is also shaped by your child's personality and skills. The interplay between you and your child can be complicated, but this chapter will help you identify some of these factors, and how they fit together.

Parent's emotional reactivity triggers child's emotional reactivity

Child's emotional reactivity triggers parent's emotional reactivity

Figure 2.1: Parent and child emotional self-regulation

---

6   Burke, J. D., Pardini, D. A. & Loeber, R. (2008) Reciprocal relationships between parenting behavior and disruptive psychopathology from childhood through adolescence. *Journal of Abnormal Child Psychology, 36*(5), 679–692.

Parent reactivity and emotional self-regulation

The easier it is for your child to "push your buttons," the more likely it is that you will be pulled into conflicts and negative interactions.

Why are your buttons being pushed? The answer may lie in your personal history and your overall personality.

You may have a tendency toward emotional reactivity if:

- You have a general tendency to be impulsive and react quickly (e.g., if you have a diagnosis or family history of ADHD).

- You are already experiencing stress in other parts of your life (e.g., financial worries, a toxic relationship with your partner).

- You tend to feel easily overwhelmed, anxious, or sad.

- You have a family history of harsh or avoidant caregivers.

On the flip side, the better you are at self-regulation, the harder it will be for your child to "push your buttons."

You are boosting your self-regulation when:

- You can talk yourself through the problem in a positive way.

- You notice when you are starting to feel distressed, and you have some go-to strategies for reducing stress.

- You can stop yourself from saying or doing hurtful things.

- You can remember what's most important in the moment.

"Goodness of fit": How much self-regulation should a parent have?

If you would rate your ability to self-regulate as a solid B+, this might be absolutely adequate when raising a child who can manage emotions well most of the time and is not too persistent. Even if you struggle with sadness or have a hard time keeping your temper, this might not be a major issue if your child finds it easy to meet expectations at home and at school.

However, if you have a child with wild mood swings and violent outbursts, then your perfectly adequate ability to self-regulate might not be up to scratch. After all, any reasonable person would be overwhelmed and upset when confronted with these challenges daily. Your child's intensity might require you to find new ways to stay calm and manage stress.

Similarly, if you have a child who is very sensitive and easily upset, your normal range of emotions (including excitement, disapproval, frustration) can send your child into a spiral of worry or hostility, so your ability to self-regulate becomes a very important factor in maintaining a healthy relationship with your child.

The interplay between your child's needs and abilities and your capacity is what ultimately determines what your relationship will look like, and sometimes parents find themselves trying to play catch-up as a child's needs grow and change.

Child reactivity and emotional self-regulation

Your child's emotional reactions are partly shaped by biology, as some children are more physiologically vulnerable to stress and might take longer to self-regulate. Children who are very emotionally reactive often have other qualities in common, such as:

- becoming frustrated and overwhelmed very quickly

- waking up often at night

- staying angry for long periods

- having a diagnosis or family history of ADHD.

You are an important ingredient but you are not the whole recipe

When all is said and done, your parenting style might only account for a small percentage of what "causes" your child's oppositional behaviour. (One study estimated that parenting style accounts for only 11% of variability in cases where children have problems with disruptive behavior.) Still, the ability to keep cool and see the big picture will be a tremendous advantage when it comes to finding the rest of the pieces in the puzzle.

Research into the "cause" of oppositional and defiant behavior

In order to understand what "causes" the behaviors known as "Oppositional Defiant Disorder," most of the time all we can do is observe and say, "Okay, we're seeing a lot of ODD over here, and not as much over here."

Psychological research does not always help to find the "why" but it can offer some clues. Most research falls into two categories: observational studies and experimental studies. Observational studies can help to show patterns. Experimental studies can show that changing one thing has an important impact on something else. Sometimes, large numbers of studies are analyzed together, to see if the evidence all points in the same direction, and these are called meta-analyses.

What can we learn about parenting and Oppositional Defiant Disorder from observational studies?

Observational studies make comparisons. In order to learn more about why some children are diagnosed with ODD, researchers start by gathering information. They ask questions about gender, developmental history, life events, and other diagnoses, and collect the results from their behavior checklists. Next, they take a deep dive into the information to see what connections or patterns start to emerge. They might find that children with one particular diagnosis or behavioral pattern tend to have parents who use a specific style of parenting. This kind of research does not prove that one thing causes another. It just shows that those two variables are happening together.

For example, in an observational study, researchers noticed that harsh and inconsistent parenting styles were "positively associated" with oppositional and disruptive child behavior.[7] This means that parents who reported more harsh or inconsistent parenting habits also had children with more disruptive behavior. The study does not say what came first: Did the harsh and inconsistent parenting create the disruptive behavior, or did the disruptive behavior shape the parenting style? Similarly, studies have found that parents who have a history of substance abuse and depression are more likely to have children who are diagnosed with ODD. That's called a "correlation," but it's important to remember that correlation does not equal causation. Sometimes there are pieces of the puzzle that we don't see.

What can we learn about parenting and Oppositional Defiant Disorder from experimental studies?

Experimental studies are more hands-on. Researchers collect information about a group of people, and then they try to change something (e.g., adding a medicine, asking parents to attend a therapy group) to see if that change makes a difference in an important way (e.g., testing if parents discipline their children in a different way, or measuring if teachers notice an improvement in classroom behavior).

---

7   Tung, I. & Lee, S. S. (2014) Negative parenting behavior and childhood oppositional defiant disorder: Differential moderation by positive and negative peer regard. *Aggressive Behavior*, 40(1), 79–90.

It's not possible to set up an experiment that will prove what exactly *causes* high rates of oppositional defiant behaviour. (It would take some pretty mad science to directly experiment on parents and babies to see if we could cause them to grow up to be oppositional and defiant.)

However, experimental studies can reveal a lot about how parents and children influence each other. For example, Dr. Russell Barkley, a psychologist and specialist in ADHD, set up an experiment to look at the relationship between parent and child behavior. He recruited 20 families, and carefully observed their interactions across three sessions, under three different conditions. The children had previously been diagnosed with ADHD, and in each of the observations, Dr. Barkley's researchers made one small change: The children were given no medication in the first condition, medicated in the second condition, and given a placebo in the third condition.

As you might be able to guess, the children did behave differently when medicated (they were more likely to comply with their mothers' instructions), but the mothers behaved differently, too. When the children were more compliant, mothers were more likely to react in a positive way. By testing how the mothers' behavior changed in reaction to the child's levels of cooperation, this experimental study helps to show more than just a correlation.

What can we learn about parenting and Oppositional Defiant Disorder from meta-analysis?

Meta-analyses review large numbers of studies, testing each one for quality and measuring how strong the conclusions are. Some studies may have statistical errors, or draw broad conclusions based on a small sample. Some studies contradict each other or have never been replicated. Meta-analyses look at many studies at once and shine a light on the most reliable results.

For example, one meta-analysis collected 161 studies and sifted through the data to look at all the possible factors that may contribute to delinquent behavior. The meta-analysis found that some factors had a strong association with delinquency (e.g., boys were more likely to be delinquent compared to girls and living with an antisocial father was a very high risk factor). The authors found that a lack of parental support (e.g., neglectful, hostile, and rejecting) had quite a strong relationship to delinquent behavior. Still, when the researchers looked at the relationship between delinquent behavior and parenting (comparing all kinds of different approaches, including supportive, authoritative, and authoritarian), they found that "parenting accounted for 11% of the variance in delinquency."[8]

What research cannot tell us about children diagnosed with Oppositional Defiant Disorder

Studies track large groups of people, but intervention depends on finding exactly the right fit for individual families struggling with ODD.

To understand an individual child, studies alone do not offer a full picture. To understand what challenges the child is facing and to make an informed recommendation for treatment, a clinician should look at the individual, in depth and in context. Direct interviews can help to create a picture of how impulsive, how sensitive, and how fearless a child can be. IQ tests, brain scans, and social skills checklists can add to the picture and point out important strengths and needs.

A comprehensive assessment should also include information related to a child's:

- physical health
- emotional self-regulation skills
- home life
- relationships with friends
- access to mentors and role models
- community involvement.

Research studies with large groups of people increase our understanding of general trends and factors, but they do not help with our understanding of the individual child. It is important to keep in mind that each child's destiny is not written in his or her genes or set in stone at any particular age. There is always room for hope.

Is there a gene for Oppositional Defiant Disorder?

Well, no, not really.[9] At the time of writing this book, research on the

8   Hoeve, M., Dubas, J. S., Eichelsheim, V. I., Van der Laan, P. H., Smeenk, W. & Gerris, J. R. (2009) The relationship between parenting and delinquency: A meta-analysis. *Journal of Abnormal Child Psychology, 37*(6), 749–775.
9   Aebi, M., Van Donkelaar, M. M., Poelmans, G., Buitelaar, J. K. *et al.* (2016) Gene-set and multivariate genome-wide association analysis of oppositional defiant behavior subtypes in attention-deficit/hyperactivity disorder. *American Journal of Medical Genetics Part B: Neuropsychiatric Genetics, 171*(5), 573–588.

relationship between behavior and genetics is still at a very early stage and, so far, no single gene or gene set has been reliably associated with the diagnosis of ODD.

In the future, your family doctor may be able to order genetic testing that helps to predict risk factors for challenging behaviors, such as aggression, lack of inhibition, or novelty seeking, but for now, there are no genetic tests that can accurately predict oppositional and defiant behavior.

Still, studies do show that children diagnosed with ODD tend to have relatives with similar behavior patterns, which suggests that some heritability is likely. The heritability of ADHD has also been well-established, and since a diagnosis of ADHD often leads to a diagnosis of ODD, the heritability of ODD could depend on other known neurological differences.

Genetics and environment intertwined

The debate between "nature" and "nurture" has swung to the extremes over the last century, but current scientific research might finally put the debate to rest, albeit in a surprisingly complicated way.

Even as scientists have rummaged through the human genome and found specific deletions or duplications that might be associated with human traits, it has also become apparent that our environment has an effect on how our genes behave.

Yes, you read that correctly. The same genes can behave differently under different circumstances.[10] As you have seen over and over elsewhere, *context is everything*.

- Some genes seem to make children more vulnerable to the negative effects of a harsh or neglectful environment.

- Some environments seem to help mitigate the activity of genes associated with risk-taking or aggressive behavior.

In short: We can't change our genes, but sometimes we can change our behavior, which affects the way our genes behave.

---

10 Tuvblad, C., Zheng, M., Raine, A. & Baker, L. A. (2009) A common genetic factor explains the covariation among ADHD ODD and CD symptoms in 9–10 year old boys and girls. *Journal of Abnormal Child Psychology, 37*(2), 153–167.

CHAPTER 3

What Other Diagnoses Are Related to Oppositional Defiant Disorder?

What other problems are related to Oppositional Defiant Disorder?

For many children diagnosed with ODD, challenging behavior is not their only struggle. When a person is given more than one diagnosis, doctors call this a "comorbidity." Sometimes the two diagnoses describe problems that are independent of one another but just happen to have been identified at the same time. However, two different diagnoses can also point in the same direction. The relationship between the two (or more) diagnoses can be complex.

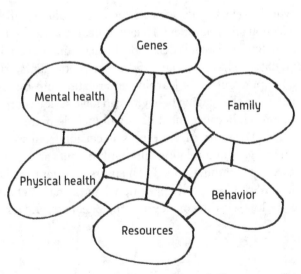

Figure 3.1: Example of interrelated factors involving both person and environment

A mental health problem can lead to a behavioral problem.

A behavioral problem can lead to a mental health problem.

A cognitive or learning problem can lead to a behavioral problem.

Behavioral problems can interfere with learning and testing.

Other problems can affect both behavior and mental health, such as family instability, trauma, illness, brain development, hormonal problems, and genetic differences.

For example, sometimes a child's life circumstances can put pressure on his/her mental health, school performance, and behavior. If a child is struggling to recover from trauma, this tends to show up as changes in behavior and mood. Similarly, a child who is grieving an important loss or adapting to a major transition will often struggle to meet expectations at home and at school. Medical issues, especially those related to pain, energy levels, and hormones, are sometimes at the root of difficult behavior and emotional disturbances.

If your child's behavior is disruptive and challenging, it is vital to look at his or her emotional and physical health as part of the picture, and, whenever possible, find a team of people who can help you support your child on all those fronts.

The impact of behavior on mental health or social struggles

Children who struggle to meet expectations face challenges that can lead to social rejection and poor mental health outcomes. If a child refuses to follow instructions and avoids demands throughout the school day or at home, each day will have its share of conflicts, complaints, frustration, and missed opportunities for learning and relationship-building.

This pattern of challenging behavior can have serious consequences for a child's mood, because most days will include more than a usual amount of angry responses from others, exclusion from social groups, and tension in important relationships with parents and mentors.

With fewer opportunities for adult mentorship, peer friendships, and social inclusion, children with oppositional and defiant behavior are at higher risk for low self-esteem, depression, loneliness, and anxiety.

Oppositional Defiant Disorder and anxiety

In the general population, anxiety disorders are diagnosed in about 10–12 percent of the population. However, among children diagnosed with ODD, the likelihood of being diagnosed with an anxiety disorder shoots up to 40 percent.[1]

At first, it might be hard to see the relationship between anxiety and defiant behavior. When you think of "anxiety," you might picture a child who is shy or downcast. Psychologists sometimes refer to anxiety as an "internalizing disorder" because a child's anxious thoughts often go unnoticed, and their behavior may appear to be withdrawn and avoidant, instead of loud and confrontational.

Likewise, ODD is considered to be an "externalizing" disorder because a child who is loudly disobedient is more noticeable and disruptive to others.

However, *there can certainly be a quiet reason for a loud behavior.* If your child is struggling with anxious thoughts, feelings of panic and worry can certainly be expressed in the form of arguing and aggressive behaviors.

Children with a diagnosis of anxiety and children with a diagnosis of ODD both tend to:

- have difficulty with emotional self-regulation

- react more quickly to a stressful situation

- take longer to recover their ability to self-regulate

- struggle with self-control

- be extra-sensitive to the possibility of a threat in their environment

- be more likely to rate something as dangerous, or to assume that another person has a hostile intent.

Children who struggle with anxiety often try to avoid situations that trigger feelings of panic and worry. When a child with anxiety successfully escapes a stressful situation, the feelings of panic and worry subside. As you can see, a child might also use oppositional and defiant behavior to get out of an anxiety-inducing situation or overreact to a potential threat.

---

1   Drabick, D. A., Ollendick, T. H. & Bubier, J. L. (2010) Co-occurrence of ODD and anxiety: Shared risk processes and evidence for a dual-pathway model. *Clinical Psychology: Science and Practice, 17*(4), 307–318.

This mother described how she discovered the anxious thoughts hiding behind her son's hostile and *irritable* behavior:

> My seven-year-old son and I made a plan to borrow a special book from the library. We searched the online directory and visited a nearby branch to pick it up. Unfortunately, when we arrived, the book was not on the shelf as expected. Ethan waited patiently as I searched other sections, but finally I had to tell him, "Sorry, honey, the book isn't here. There's another library near here, so let's head over there and check to see if they have it."
>
> Ethan started scowling, whining, and accusing. He said, "You lied. You said you were getting me that other comic book, too." I explained that I had already searched for the other comic he requested, but it wasn't there either. I asked: "Are you okay? Maybe you're getting a little hungry. Let's have a snack when we get home." On the way to the other library, Ethan kept fussing and complaining. He said, "Why won't you let me visit my friend? His house is right there. You're the worst mom. When I get home, I'm going to watch as much screens as I want. I don't have to listen to you." I tried to keep a cheerful tone in my voice and replied, "It sounds like you're not feeling well. Let's just try not to fight."
>
> At the next branch of the library, I was pleased to see that the book was available. As soon as my son picked up that book, his face relaxed and his mood completed changed. Finally, I could see why he was being so unpleasant. I said, "Aha! I think I know why you were so grumpy. You were worried this library wouldn't have the book."
>
> He actually smiled and then muttered, "Correct."

Oppositional Defiant Disorder and cognitive differences

If your child has a specific learning disability, brain injury, medical disorder, or genetic difference, the associated skill deficits can certainly lead to behavioral struggles.

Injuries and illnesses that affect behavior include (but are not limited to) genetic differences such as Fragile X Syndrome and Prader-Willi Syndrome, sleep disorders, severe anemia, seizure disorders, lead poisoning, foetal alcohol effects, hypoglycemia, head trauma, and prenatal exposure to drugs and other toxins.

Cognitive differences can affect your child's ability to stay calm and solve problems. Specifically, anything that affects the following skills will have an effect on your child's ability to meet adult expectations:

- accurately detecting threats

- predicting unwanted outcomes

- delaying gratification

- remembering rules

- perceiving social expectations

- resisting impulses

- self-calming when upset.

Oppositional Defiant Disorder and Attention Deficit Hyperactivity Disorder

How do Attention Deficit Hyperactivity Disorder and Oppositional Defiant Disorder overlap?

Attention Deficit Hyperactivity Disorder (ADHD) is classified as a neurodevelopmental disorder, rather than a behavioral disorder, but many children are diagnosed with both ADHD and ODD. In the general population, prevalence for both ADHD and ODD is around 10 percent, but about 50 percent of children who are diagnosed with ADHD also meet criteria for ODD, and vice versa.[2]

If you compare the symptoms of ADHD and ODD, you will see some similarities.[3] Children with ADHD tend to be easily frustrated and sometimes emotionally sensitive, and the same can be said for children diagnosed with the *irritable* subtype of ODD. Children with ADHD also tend to be impulsive and struggle to inhibit inappropriate behavior, much like children diagnosed with the *headstrong* subtype of ODD. The struggles that go along with ADHD can certainly make it difficult for a child to follow instructions and meet expectations.

How does Attention Deficit Hyperactivity Disorder contribute to problems with rule-following?

Children are often diagnosed with ODD when they consistently have difficulty with adult expectations, such as following rules.

---

2   Nock, M. K., Kazdin, A. E., Hiripi, E. & Kessler, R. C. (2007) Lifetime prevalence, correlates, and persistence of oppositional defiant disorder: Results from the National Comorbidity Survey Replication. *Journal of Child Psychology and Psychiatry, 48*(7), 703–713.

3   Harvey, E. A., Breaux, R. P. & Lugo-Candelas, C. I. (2016) Early development of comorbidity between symptoms of attention-deficit/hyperactivity disorder (ADHD) and oppositional defiant disorder (ODD). *Journal of Abnormal Psychology, 125*(2), 154.

Children with ADHD are likely to:

- be distracted when adults give instructions
- have difficulty staying focused during adult-led activities
- have poor time-management skills
- avoid tasks that seem dull or monotonous
- be disorganized, unprepared for class (having forgotten or misplaced materials)
- move around when asked to sit still
- interrupt or talk excessively
- use things without permission.

If a child is already struggling to stay focused, stay organized and sit still, they are much more likely to get into trouble at school and at home. This type of behavior can sometimes be interpreted as difficult, lazy, disrespectful, or rude, so adults may attribute these behaviors to the *headstrong* subtype of ODD.

How does Attention Deficit Hyperactivity Disorder contribute to problems with problem-solving?

Dr. Russell Barkley describes ADHD as a deficit across a range of "executive functioning" skills. Specifically, people with ADHD have difficulty with cognitive processes such as: coaching oneself through a problem, pausing to reflect, thinking about the past and future, and organizing ideas around time and priorities.

Similarly, oppositional defiant behavior can be understood as a maladaptive set of problem-solving skills. Some children with oppositional and defiant symptoms struggle to cope with instructions from adults because they have difficulty switching priorities, understanding the adult's point of view, prioritizing, or using past experience to make good choices. You will find more information in Chapter 8 about building your child's executive functioning skills.

How does Attention Deficit Hyperactivity Disorder contribute to problems with emotional self-regulation?

When children struggle to inhibit their behavior and they also have difficulty problem-solving, they may find themselves pushed to their emotional limits in the face of overwhelm, misunderstandings, stress, and confusion. Many children with ADHD struggle with self-esteem and even depression,[4] especially when the child's friends, family, and teachers can't understand why they behave differently.

To make matters worse, emotional coping requires perspective-taking and self-talk, which are also a challenge for children with ADHD. Children diagnosed with ODD, especially within the *irritable* subtype, also tend to behave in angry, argumentative, or even explosive ways. Your child's struggles with emotional self-regulation are explored in more detail in Chapter 6.

What's the difference between Oppositional Defiant Disorder and Attention Deficit Hyperactivity Disorder?

Despite their similarities, ADHD and ODD are still considered separate diagnostic categories. Not all children with ADHD are easily upset or frequently defiant. Also, when children diagnosed with ODD alone are tested, they perform well on measures of executive functioning, unlike children diagnosed with ADHD.

Some studies have examined the lives of children diagnosed with ADHD, to try to understand why some children grew up to exhibit oppositional and defiant behavior patterns, while others did not. In comparing how the children were raised and what life events they experienced, researchers found that children who were diagnosed with ODD as well as ADHD sometimes had more difficult life events, such as parental divorce and family conflict, or experienced more deviant peer behavior and parental criticism.

Interestingly, these studies found the biggest difference between ADHD only and ADHD and ODD was parenting style.[5] This finding suggests that a warm and responsive parenting style might be especially important for children with ADHD, because parents who used a negative, emotion-dismissing parenting style were more likely to raise children with both an ADHD and ODD diagnosis.

ADHD can help to explain certain behaviors associated with ODD, such as lack of impulse control. However, the symptoms of ADHD do not include the same specific social struggles as ODD, including being spiteful or deliberately upsetting toward others.

---

4   Deault, L. C. (2010) A systematic review of parenting in relation to the development of comorbidities and functional impairments in children with attention-deficit/hyperactivity disorder (ADHD). *Child Psychiatry & Human Development, 41*(2), 168–192.

5   Deault, L. C. (2010) A systematic review of parenting in relation to the development of comorbidities and functional impairments in children with attention-deficit/hyperactivity disorder (ADHD). *Child Psychiatry & Human Development, 41*(2), 168–192.

Children who struggle to understand the emotional perspective of others and have trouble with flexible thinking may be diagnosed with ODD without an ADHD diagnosis.

Why are Attention Deficit Hyperactivity Disorder and Oppositional Defiant Disorder so similar?

Some research suggests that the relationship between ADHD and ODD is a complicated one. Here's what we know so far:

- ADHD and ODD appear to have shared genetic factors.

- ADHD and ODD also have similar environmental factors.

- Studies have shown that an early diagnosis of ADHD often leads to a later diagnosis of ODD.[6] Research has shown that parents of children with ADHD sometimes use more negative parenting practices with their children. This may lead to a more conflict-prone and volatile family dynamic, which is a known risk factor for the development of oppositional and defiant behavior patterns.

- Children with ADHD are also at high risk of peer rejection,[7] which may increase the risk of developing oppositional and defiant behavior patterns.

- Children with ADHD may become argumentative and oppositional when asked to perform tasks that are difficult, due to difficulties with executive functioning.

- Children with ADHD tend to be more vulnerable to adverse life events and need parents who are quite warm and responsive in order to be successful.

Conduct Disorder (CD)
What is Conduct Disorder?

CD is a psychiatric diagnosis that is usually given to older children and teens, as rule-breaking and aggressive behavior starts to escalate to more serious social and legal violations.

---

6   Burke, J. D., Loeber, R., Lahey, B. B. & Rathouz, P. J. (2005) Developmental transitions among affective and behavioral disorders in adolescent boys. *Journal of Child Psychology and Psychiatry*, 46(11), 1200–1210.

7   Hoza, B. (2007) Peer functioning in children with ADHD. *Journal of Pediatric Psychology*, 32(6), 655–663.

What's the connection between Oppositional Defiant Disorder and Conduct Disorder?

Approximately 30 percent of children who are diagnosed with ODD will go on to be diagnosed with CD. ODD and CD are both descriptions of disruptive behavior patterns, also known as "externalizing behaviors" that negatively impact the lives of other people.

What is the difference between Oppositional Defiant Disorder and Conduct Disorder?

ODD and CD both describe disruptive behavior patterns, but the diagnoses involve different levels of severity and the diagnosis of CD is usually given to older children.

However, there is another important distinction between ODD and CD that is sometimes overlooked. The "symptoms" (or behaviors) associated with ODD tend to be confrontational, provocative, disruptive, and emotionally charged. It is simply not possible to be diagnosed with ODD without "rubbing others the wrong way" somehow. ODD is marked by a pattern of confrontation and conflict with others.

On the other hand, the "symptoms" of CD do not have the same emotional or conflict-prone quality. A person diagnosed with CD could appear to be calm and even pleasant, while quietly stealing valuable items and skipping school. Even the violent and aggressive behaviors associated with CD could be carried out calmly. Coercion, not emotion, is at the root of all the behaviors described in the diagnostic criteria.

What kind of children are most likely to be diagnosed with Conduct Disorder?

The symptoms of CD fall into two distinct groups: *aggressive* and *non-aggressive*.[8] If a person's symptoms tend to fall into one category or the other, then they are given a "subtype" of aggressive or non-aggressive.

1. **Aggressive** CD includes fighting, sexual assault, robbery, and bullying. Youth diagnosed with this subtype tend to have more challenges related to intelligence and self-control. For example, they tend to be more impulsive, and don't do as well on tests of working memory, planning, self-regulation, and verbal IQ.

2. **Non-aggressive** CD includes vandalism, arson, break-ins, and theft. Individuals diagnosed with this subtype are also more

---

8   Jusyte, A., Pfister, R., Gehrer, N. & Schönenberg, M. (2019) Risky business! Behavioral bias and motivational salience of rule-violations in children with conduct disorder. *Psychiatry Research, 271,* 740–746.

likely to be impulsive than the average person, with a tendency to make rule-breaking friends, and may become more anti-social as they get older.

What are the causes of Conduct Disorder?

As with ODD, the causes of CD are complex. A child's risk of developing a more harmful pattern of behavior often depends on how he or she interacts with the social community.

RULE-BREAKING ROOTED IN MISTRUST OF AUTHORITY

The process of socialization depends on warm, secure relationships with caregivers and community members. When children meet expectations and follow norms, they can usually expect to enjoy safety, approval, and positive feedback from the community.

Sometimes, this process goes wrong. If a child experiences low social acceptance and limited positive feedback for rule-following, then his or her motivation to follow social norms is likely to deteriorate. If acceptance and protection come from antisocial groups such as gangs or peers with high rates of delinquent behavior, then a child's behavior will follow suit, in order to gain this crucial bond.

RULE-BREAKING ROOTED IN DEPRIVATION

If there are relatively few opportunities to succeed "the right way" in a child's life, then the temptation to cut corners or skip the line becomes much higher. If rule-breaking is the most reliable way for a child to meet his or her basic needs, then it is much easier for a child to generalize rule-breaking in other areas. In other words, a child may learn that rule-breaking (as a general rule) is more rewarding than rule-following.

RULE-BREAKING BEHAVIOR AND THE ROLE OF CONSEQUENCES

Rules are usually enforced by the delivery of consequences, whether the consequences are informal in the shape of social disapproval or whether the penalties are systematized and formally handed down by an authority figure. If a child grows up in an environment where penalties are rare or hard to predict, then consequences will not have much effect on rule-breaking behavior.

Some systems of consequences are designed with the intention of discouraging rule-breaking behavior but inadvertently have the opposite effect and deliver a reward instead. For example, a child who is suspended from school may enjoy having the day off. An aggravated adult who delivers an impassioned lecture may have accidentally performed an entertaining solo for the child's benefit.

PUNISHMENT INSENSITIVITY

Finally, children do not all experience consequences in the same way. For some children with limited social skills, social disapproval is hard to interpret and does not have a punishing effect. Scientists have also found that some children appear to be less "sensitive to punishment information,"[9] so they take longer to adjust their behavior when they get negative feedback. If these "punishment insensitive" children do spend more time breaking the rules, then they will have more opportunities to discover the "rewards" of rule-breaking (e.g., peer approval, unlawful gains, emotional thrills), and more time to learn to tolerate the consequences doled out (e.g., yelling, detention, spanking, time-out, etc.). Children who get these mixed messages will certainly find it harder to adjust their behavior and follow social expectations.

How do I make sure my child doesn't go down this road?

ODD and CD are not diagnoses that last a lifetime. However, an early pattern of emotional dysregulation and negative social interactions can sometimes set the stage for more antisocial behavior later in life.

POSITIVE OPPORTUNITIES FOR BELONGING AND ACHIEVEMENT

Antisocial behavior may be connected to a lack of empathy, but also a lack of opportunity. A child needs many different experiences that teach the positive benefits of rule-following—that is, rule-following is generally easier, more enjoyable, and more beneficial than rule-breaking.[10] Also, remember that in the long run, positive experiences with rule-following and social approval will be much more powerful than unpleasant experiences with rule-breaking and social disapproval.

Here are some tips for creating positive social opportunities:

- Cultivate your child's role within your community in a positive way, such as using his or her strengths to help others in need and connecting with possible mentors and role models.

---

9   Matthys, W., Van Goozen, S. H., Snoek, H. & Van Engeland, H. (2004) Response perseveration and sensitivity to reward and punishment in boys with oppositional defiant disorder. *European Child & Adolescent Psychiatry*, 13(6), 362–364.

10 Pardini, D. A., Lochman, J. E. & Frick, P. J. (2003) Callous/unemotional traits and social-cognitive processes in adjudicated youths. *Journal of the American Academy of Child & Adolescent Psychiatry*, 42(3), 364–371.

- Keep the lines of communication open and help your child to express a full range of emotions, so that if he or she is having difficulty meeting social expectations, you can be his or her ally and offer support.

- Look for ways your child can safely enjoy some independence and self-direction. A strict set of rules and a tightly supervised environment may limit your child's opportunities for rule-breaking in the short term, but this restrictive approach will not help to meet his or her need for belonging and independence.

- Keep looking for the good in your child[11] and don't withdraw your affection in response to his or her difficult behavior. Your unconditional love is a powerful protective factor, even as you set boundaries and teach limits.

Trauma

What does trauma have to do with Oppositional Defiant Disorder?

For years, people have struggled to understand the causes and results of trauma. While most people understand that trauma can affect a child's physical and emotional health as well as his or her behavior, too little is understood about how to recognize the signs of trauma and how to respond to it.

Even the roots of trauma can be unpredictable. When a frightening or life-altering event happens, some people seem to be affected deeply, while others appear to recover well. For instance, only about one in three children who have suffered severe trauma will develop the physical, emotional, and behavioral symptoms of Post-Traumatic Stress Disorder (PTSD).

Children suffering from PTSD may display many of the typical behaviors related to ODD, such as "refusing to comply with adult requests" and "easily losing his/her temper." A behavior may look the same, but the underlying cause and necessary treatments are very different.

What causes trauma?

Children can develop PTSD after experiencing a life event that is

11   Rolon-Arroyo, B., Arnold, D. H., Breaux, R. P. & Harvey E. A. (2018) Reciprocal relations between parenting behaviors and conduct disorder symptoms in preschool children. *Child Psychiatry & Human Development*, 49(5), 786–799.

extremely stressful, frightening, or distressing.[12] Children can develop PTSD following a physically violent episode, such as a criminal assault, domestic abuse, a vehicle collision, or a natural disaster. They may also suffer PTSD after witnessing others being hurt. Other common causes of PTSD include sexual assault, neglect, medical procedures, war and mass shootings, medical illness, or emotional abuse. The probability of trauma is not directly connected to the severity of the event. Trauma also depends on a child's subjective experience of an event, especially if the event is associated with feelings of helplessness, loss, isolation, and shock.

The symptoms of trauma can be hard to detect, especially when problems with mood, sleep, appetite, and behavior persist long after the traumatic event occurs. Common behavioral symptoms include:

- nightmares

- increased aggression

- memory problems

- lack of concentration

- repetitive, intrusive thoughts

- hypervigilance and exaggerated startle response

- persistent avoidance of memories and experiences associated with the traumatic event.

Trauma and motivation
After a traumatic event, you may notice a change in your child's ability to concentrate, which can affect behavior at school. Your child may also express a change in values and priorities after a traumatic event, whether that means spending more time with important people, focusing on short-term enjoyment, or helping others in need.

Trauma and distress
PTSD can affect your child's ability to regulate stress. Intense stress tends to prime children for a behavioral response of "fight, flight, or freeze." When in distress, a child with PTSD may "shut down" (refuse to speak or move, showing only a limited range of emotions) or become

---

12 Perrin, S., Smith, P. & Yule, W. (2000) Practitioner review: The assessment and treatment of post-traumatic stress disorder in children and adolescents. *The Journal of Child Psychology and Psychiatry and Allied Disciplines, 41*(3), 277–289.

"explosive" (threatening, pushing, kicking, biting, throwing objects, swearing). Trauma can also resurface in the form of play that re-enacts the traumatic event.

These behaviors are not designed to provoke you. They are not happening for the purpose of control, advantage, or gain. These behaviors are symptoms of intense distress, and they are likely outside of the child's control.

Why do I have to rule out the effects of trauma?

A traumatic experience can affect your child's ability to regulate emotions and react to everyday situations. When a person is struggling to regulate emotions and meet expectations, it is important to understand as much as possible about the underlying problem, and make sure that any support or intervention will actually help the person, rather than make the problem worse.

Just as your doctor should carefully assess your health before telling you to get more exercise, in the same way, behavior interventions should be carefully planned so to minimize the risk of harm and re-traumatization. Some types of behavior interventions can be ineffective and even dangerous when the effects of trauma interfere with the learning process.

What kind of help does a person need to be able to recover from a traumatic experience?

Research on recovery from trauma is still limited, but according to current best practices, traumatized children need time, secure attachment to safe caregivers, and support in the form of Cognitive Behavior Therapy.

With the right help, children can relearn how to manage their emotions, cope with distressing situations, and recover a sense of security and self-efficacy.

Of course, children who have suffered trauma will continue to learn and adapt to their environments. Some types of behavior start out as an expression of trauma but then persist because the child learns that the behavior "works," that is, the behavior gives him or her an advantage, a social connection, a sense of safety, or an opportunity to escape from a difficult situation.[13] If your child has been repeating trauma-related behavior, be careful not to jump to conclusions or

---

13 Cohen, J. A., Berliner, L. & Mannarino, A. (2010) Trauma focused CBT for children with co-occurring trauma and behavior problems. *Child Abuse & Neglect*, 34(4), 215–224.

assume that your child is manipulating you. He or she may still be in need of extra support.

Trauma and discipline

A trauma-informed approach to discipline can allow you to set limits with compassion. For example, you can learn to look out for environmental triggers that may bring back traumatic memories, with a focus on prevention and coping, instead of simply punishing a child for a disruptive outburst. For example, a child who is trying to avoid re-experiencing a traumatic event may have difficulty controlling the urge to run away or to fight back, and the usual behavior management techniques (e.g., rules, rewards, consequences) will have no effect on the severe emotional struggles faced by the child.

Safety, security, and support

You may choose to turn down the volume on your initial response to misbehavior. This approach can avoid further triggering your child's fight/flight/freeze response.

For example, a child who feels trapped in a room, threatened by a raised voice, or rejected by a caregiver may be in a state of intense stress and will not be able to participate in a rational conversation about consequences or ethical norms.

Noticing anxiety and patterns of avoidance

Not all trauma-related behavior is intensely disruptive or emotionally heated. You might notice the effects of trauma come to the surface when a child attempts to avoid a difficult situation or seeks a distraction from anxious thoughts. A trauma-informed approach to behavior does not rely on pressuring or ignoring a child who is in distress. Instead, parents and therapists can help children to build coping skills and handle anxious thoughts in a healthier way.

Replaying unhealthy power dynamics

If a child has been dominated or neglected, then behavior such as bullying or "acting out" in groups should be addressed from a trauma-informed perspective. This could mean looking for other opportunities for the child to experience a sense of power and control or teaching the child what a strong leader can do to help others.

CHAPTER 4

Is Oppositional Defiant Disorder Treatable?

Finding the right kind of help for your child

You already know that your child is struggling. You've heard the arguments, you've spoken to the teachers, and you've seen the ripped-up homework or holes punched in the wall. You may even understand *why* your child is struggling. You have watched your child's emotional roller-coaster racing out of control, and you have noticed the way your child sticks to his or her own rigid plan. You know that your child needs help.

The question is, what kind of help does your child need? You've heard all the recommendations, from elimination diets to tough love to horse therapy. You need answers.

Right now, research on how to treat ODD is limited. There are a few well-known treatments that are often helpful, but research on treatment effectiveness can only hint at how children respond *on average*. As discussed in Chapter 1, the diagnostic criteria for ODD includes three different dimensions (often referred to as *irritable, headstrong* and *vindictive*), but so far, very few studies have examined which treatment is best for a given dimension or comorbid condition.

If your child has an official diagnosis of ODD, your doctor or psychologist may have also tested your child for cognitive differences, emotional health, physical health, trauma history, genetic differences, and attentional issues, or you may simply have a report that says that your child's behavior is a clinical concern.

The more you know about the specific challenges your family is facing, the better off you will be. For example, a basic parenting course on setting limits and increasing cooperation may be an excellent choice for some families, but if there is ongoing tension in your marriage, or if your child is experiencing PTSD, then the right treatment for your family should also address those issues (or at the very least, avoid making them worse.)

The right treatment should also take into account any comorbid condition your child might be struggling with (e.g., anxiety, depression, or ADHD).

Where to start?

If you're not sure where to start, consult a qualified mental health professional who can assess your family's needs and recommend an appropriate treatment. Still, given that there are so many factors that can contribute to oppositional and defiant behavior, finding the right treatment option can be a maze for families.

Medication as a treatment for oppositional and defiant behavior

If your child has been diagnosed with ODD by a medical professional, the first line of treatment is likely to be a behavioral or psychotherapeutic form of therapy. However, if you have tried this kind of treatment, and you are not seeing a significant improvement, your doctor may suggest a course of medication[1] in addition to other interventions, such as counseling, parent training, or social skills training.

At the time of writing this book, there are no specially approved medications for the treatment of ODD, but your doctor may recommend medication to help your child's struggles in specific areas. The underlying struggles that cause oppositional defiant behavior are not simply physical. They also include behavior patterns and skills such as emotional self-regulation and problem-solving.

What does medication do?
Beneficial effect on impulse control, social learning, and emotional self-control

Some children who struggle with disruptive behavior may also have difficulty learning from social situations, paying attention to instructions, resisting temptation, or adapting to new information.

---

1   Gorman, D. A., Gardner, D. M., Murphy, A. L., Feldman, M. *et al.* (2015) Canadian guidelines on pharmacotherapy for disruptive and aggressive behaviour in children and adolescents with attention-deficit hyperactivity disorder, oppositional defiant disorder, or conduct disorder. *The Canadian Journal of Psychiatry, 60*(2), 62–76.

If your child's impulsivity and impaired executive functioning skills are contributing to frequent arguments, difficulty following routines, and poor problem-solving skills, then a stimulant medication may be helpful. Some studies show that stimulant medications[2] (e.g., methylphenidate) can help to improve social learning, focus, and self-control, especially for children who are also diagnosed with ADHD.

Reduced aggression and antisocial behavior

When typical behavioral intervention has not been successful in reducing high levels of aggressive or disruptive behavior, a psychiatrist may suggest using an atypical antipsychotic medication such as risperidone or a mood stabilizer. These types of medications may help to reduce the frequency of aggressive outbursts, but due to limited research on safety, they are not usually considered a long-term solution and are used only in very complex cases.

Treatment of comorbid conditions

If your child has any other medical or mental health problems that have not been fully addressed, your doctor may assess your child to see if a comorbid condition could be contributing to your child's disruptive behavior. Children diagnosed with ODD are commonly diagnosed with ADHD as well, and there is good research evidence to suggest that when a child has a diagnosis of ADHD, psychostimulant medications will often help to make behavioral interventions even more effective.[3]

Psychostimulant drugs may help children control *irritable* behavior related to emotional highs and lows, and it may also give children with *headstrong* behavior help to prioritize and focus when asked to complete everyday routines.

Other common mental health concerns include anxiety, depression, and PTSD, so your doctor may recommend a medication that is specific to these mental health challenges.

Risks of medication

Medication alone does not create positive learning opportunities; but using medication may help to stabilize mood swings and curb

---

2   Gadow, K. D., Arnold, L. E., Molina, B. S., Findling, R. L. *et al.* (2014) Risperidone added to parent training and stimulant medication: Effects on attention-deficit/hyperactivity disorder, oppositional defiant disorder, conduct disorder, and peer aggression. *Journal of the American Academy of Child & Adolescent Psychiatry, 53*(9), 948–959.

3   Masi, G., Milone, A., Manfredi, A., Brovedani, P., Pisano, S. & Muratori, P. (2016) Combined pharmacotherapy-multimodal psychotherapy in children with disruptive behavior disorders. *Psychiatry Research, 238*, 8–13.

impulses so your child can build the necessary life experiences to gain new skills. However, medication is not effective for every child. Some medications come with serious health risks, including weight loss, weight gain, tics, drowsiness, or difficulty sleeping, depending on the choice of medication, dosage, and how it interacts with your child's specific biology.

In cases of severe, hard-to-treat aggression or irritability, your doctor may recommend another class of drug, such as an atypical antipsychotic or a mood stabilizer, but the major side effects of these types of drugs tend to be more severe, and the research supporting their use is much more limited.

Is Oppositional Defiant Disorder brain-based or behavioral? Does it matter?

When you read about differences in the brains of children diagnosed with ODD, you may worry that your child is permanently disabled or incapable of coping with the demands of everyday life. Here are a few very important points to keep in mind as you read about brains, bodies, and behaviors.

Brain development and behavior are a two-way street

Remember that brains are plastic. No, not the kind of plastic you find in the soft drink aisle; scientists use the word "plasticity" to describe the ability to mould and shape something. Your child's brain will continue to grow and change until he or she is in his or her mid-twenties. Brain structures will change. Connections will change. Triggers and cues will change. Maturity and experience will re-landscape the brain, for better or for worse. Some connections will run deep and be hard to change.

When a brain makes a connection and the memory is infused with a strong emotional charge, that connection tends to be a durable one. However, it is always possible to build new connections, to draw new lines on the map, and connect ideas in new ways. Experiences will rewire the brain and bathe it in different kinds of hormones and neurotransmitters. Epi-genes will flip on and off, and blood flow will rush in and recede as you exercise. Everything you do helps to shape your brain.

The way your child is *now* is not a perfect representation of the way he or she will be later. Some functions will get much better, just because that's what brains usually do as they age. Practice and creativity can help to compensate for weakness.

No brain is a dead end

Does your child have real structural differences in how his or her brain works right now? Maybe. In most cases, you will not have the opportunity to see an electro-encephalogram or a magnetic resonance image of your child's brain in action. Therefore, be very cautious about jumping to any conclusions about what your child's prefrontal cortex or limbic system is *actually doing*. It is not possible to know for sure. Even if you could pinpoint a "defect" in one part of the brain, your child's brain is a work in progress. You can't reach inside and tweak that tangle of nerves but you still have the opportunity to influence your child's growth and learning in so many ways, every single day.

So, instead of "blaming the brain," find the right learning opportunities.

As you read, you can use what you learn about brains and behavior to lead you to new strategies and new perspectives. If your child does not behave the way you expect, then perhaps your child is experiencing the world in a different way. When you understand how people experience the world differently, it gets easier to find new ways of teaching skills and information. You can try to be flexible and creative, you can test out different expectations and strategies, and find out what works best.

The next part of this book will guide you through five different areas where children with oppositional and defiant behavior struggle the most. You can think of these as "maps," because they will help you get the lay of the land, predict some of the pitfalls, and find your way through. At the end of each section, you will find some questions for reflection, followed by a resource guide which includes practical ideas for self-help at home, and suggestions for identifying which professionals and interventions will be most suitable to meet your family's unique needs.

PART 2

ADDRESSING CHALLENGING BEHAVIOR FROM THE INSIDE OUT

CHAPTER 5

Strengthening Your Emotional Resilience

The importance of your emotional self-regulation

To the parent of a child with oppositional and defiant behavior, it can feel like other people are allowed to play in "easy" mode while you are stuck at "expert" difficulty level. There's certainly some truth to that. By the time your children are grown, you might actually be qualified to apply for a job conducting international diplomatic missions with hostile nuclear powers!

To raise this child and keep your sanity:

- You may have to navigate tough behavior situations, like a blindfolded downhill skier being chased by a bear.

- You may have to learn how to craft new tools and solve perplexing puzzles, patiently inventing new strategies for each new challenge.

- You may have to access a deeper, more forgiving and understanding source of love, capable of dissolving angry moods and emotional walls, like a powerful wave on the beach.

You will discover how to do all these things because that's what it will take just to make it through the day, being the kind of parent you want to be.

But first, you will need to do some work on your own emotional skill set:

- You will need to keep your own body calm when others around you are in the middle of a whirlwind.

- You will need a hopeful and resilient heart in order to withstand hurtful words and deep disappointments.

- You will have to learn to forgive yourself for past mistakes and put yourself back together again when old wounds ache.

Why is it so important to *work on* emotional resilience?

Your parenting style is more than just a list of rules or a set of techniques. Your parenting style is affected by how you manage your own emotions, how you perceive your child's behavior, and even how you see your own behaviour.[1] Your warmth, confidence, and sense of hope will carry you through some very difficult situations. Fear, frustration, and anger will cloud your judgment.

None of this is easy, but in the following chapters you will get acquainted with some of the tools you can use to build this steady emotional foundation.

Why your emotions matter

When parents let their negative emotions lead the way, it is often a combination of doing "what works" and an expression of intense stress

---

1   Slagt, M., Deković, M., de Haan, A. D., van den Akker, A. L. & Prinzie, P. (2012) Longitudinal associations between mothers' and fathers' sense of competence and children's externalizing problems: The mediating role of parenting. *Developmental Psychology*, 48(6), 1554.

and desperation. As explained in Chapter 1, parents of children with oppositional and defiant behavior are often more harsh and inconsistent than other parents.

This pattern might actually be shaped by your child's behavior. For example, if your child is struggling to follow instructions and meet expectations, you might try to push harder or you might back off entirely. If your child ignores or resists all your best efforts to be moderate and gentle, and only seems to cooperate after you have completely gone off at the deep end, then the cycle is likely to repeat itself in the future. However, too much parent reactivity is just not good for anyone. It is physically and emotionally harmful for the whole family.

Where does calm come from?

To respond calmly isn't just a question of willpower. Your ability to stay calm depends in part on regulating your body's physical response. Your thoughts and beliefs also help to drive your emotions. Together, physical and emotional responses help to drive your behavior. In this chapter, you will learn more about your body's emotional and physical responses and how to regulate them. As you gain more control over your emotional ups and downs, you will also be able to make different choices in the way you parent your child.

Note: As you look at your own emotional and physical reactions through this lens, you are also building an important foundation of knowledge that will help you later on. Remember these insights as you look for reasons why your child might overreact or struggle with self-control, and when you need to offer your child empathy and advice to help him or her learn to self-regulate.

What is emotional reactivity?

Reactivity is the way we respond to difficult situations. When unexpected and difficult moments pop up, our bodies respond. Our brains kick into gear. The nervous system pumps out instructions[2] to our organs, including eyes, muscles, digestive system, and skin. We find ourselves sweating and clenched, with our heart racing. This reaction

---

2   Porges, S. W., Doussard-Roosevelt, J. A. & Maiti, A. K. (1994) Vagal tone and the physiological regulation of emotion. *Monographs of the Society for Research in Child Development*, 59(2–3), 167–186.

is automatic. Without this response, we would be unable to find the strength we need to sprint away from danger or boldly confront it.

Certainly, it would make sense for you to have a reaction like this if you found a lion in your living room. You would need all your energy focused on survival in that moment. As your body directs oxygenated blood to the organs and parts of the brain needed for survival, there are fewer resources for other parts of the body (e.g., your body stops digesting food).

Even your ability to think changes. The parts of your brain needed to be creative, to crack a joke, or see someone else's point of view are not operating at full capacity. Your thoughts are primarily focused on finding a threat and dealing with it. In that moment, you are primed for action, ready to run, hide, or defend yourself.

What triggers emotional reactivity?

Unfortunately, this response sometimes kicks in when we don't need it. You may find yourself becoming "reactive" when you are:

- ill, hungry, tired, or in pain
- startled or irritated by noises or lights
- offended or emotionally hurt
- worried about the future
- coping with financial or relationship strain
- reminded of traumatic events in the past
- having thoughts about being helpless or out of control
- hearing others scream and yell
- expecting physical or emotional harm.

As you can see, reactivity can be triggered by other stress in your physical body, distressing events happening around you, and even your own thoughts about the past, present, or future. Some people find it very hard to cope with reactivity, especially when there is a personal history of ADHD, brain damage, chronic stress, depression, anxiety, history of drug use, abuse, or trauma.

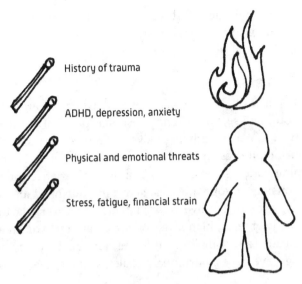

Figure 5.1: Increased risk of emotional reactivity

Being too reactive can make it challenging for you to respond to your family's needs in an appropriate way. With too much adrenaline pumping through your body, it's hard to use a gentle and encouraging tone of voice. When you feel panicked, you would much rather run out of the room and slam the door than help your child tie his or her shoe or resolve an argument with a sibling.

Your body in fight/flight/freeze mode

Speaking of overreacting, it's important to remember that your body's stress reaction is a survival mechanism. When your stress levels increase, you are primed for "fight or flight."

Stress can look different for different people:

- A "fight" response feels explosive and, as one parent described it, "It burns calories." You may notice your hands curling into fists, and you may start to pace, shout, stomp, or glare.

- A "flight" response gets you out of the situation as quickly as possible, sometimes by literally sprinting away.

- A "freeze" response can have you sitting very still, hiding in plain sight. Some people even experience intense sleepiness or simply feel "shut down" or numb.

Many people experience all three types of stress responses, in some order, as the intensity of stress changes.

Stress in excess

Not all stress is toxic. When you are excited, when you are in suspense, or when you exercise, you will notice similar physical changes in your body. However, persistently high levels of stress put a strain on your body. Your blood pressure and heart rate are elevated. Your appetite and sleeping patterns can change. You may experience the effects of stress as tension in your muscles, aches in your head and stomach, indigestion, insomnia, or even just a fatigue you can't shake off.

Over the long term, high levels of stress can hurt your mental and physical health, and can lead to depression, chronic anxiety, heart disease, digestive issues, hormonal problems, and sexual dysfunction.

Unhealthy behaviors associated with stress

Everyone develops their own coping strategies for managing stress levels, but a poor coping strategy can lead to unwanted side effects. Many people turn to overeating, substance abuse, or self-destructive behaviors to get short-term relief from physical and emotional suffering. Other common reactions to stress are avoidance and procrastination. Unfortunately, the time and energy you spend to avoid stress is time you cannot spend facing the challenges you most want to address. Lashing out at others can create a temporary sense of relief but it also perpetuates a cycle of more conflict and, ultimately, more stress.

Addressing stress on the inside and the outside

If you are trying to control the amount of stress you experience, you have a few options, but they are fairly limited. Many of your body's reactions are outside your control. The same goes for the people around you. Still, what you cannot control, you can learn to accept or reinterpret.

Reducing stressors in the environment

Your family and your job situations are not easily changed overnight. If you can add more calming activities to your schedule and avoid the kinds of activities that you find stressful (e.g., smoking, listening to the news, getting into another heated discussion in a particular Facebook group), then you will spare yourself some unnecessary bother. If there is a lifestyle change you have been meaning to make, go ahead and rearrange. Your body may thank you.

Building the body's ability to cope

When your body is depleted or in pain, you are more vulnerable to stress. If you can get a good night's sleep, eat healthy food, and drink plenty of water, your body will be much more resilient. You can even look for ways to release tension with exercise, art, relaxation, meditation, and pleasant sensory activities.

Changing your perspective

Stress is your body's natural reaction to the feeling of being threatened. Some events are objectively threatening. For instance, if your child is having a tantrum, you might have to react to an object being thrown at your head. Loud noises are naturally startling, and the sound of your child's cries will move you. Other types of threats are more subjective. Your physical reaction can actually change based on your perspective. As you learn about emotion processing, you will see that your thoughts can have a powerful impact on how your body reacts. In other words, your thoughts and feelings can alter the way you experience stress, even if your circumstances have not changed.

How can I manage emotional reactivity?

If you are ready to learn how to manage your stress levels and protect your mental and physical health, then it helps to understand the process of emotional self-regulation.

How the brain processes emotion

When the brain and the body work together to process emotions like fear, anger, or desire, there are several steps that help you choose how to respond. The process is extremely complicated, involving different parts of the brain, your hormones, and even other organs like your skin, muscles and eyes, but the abbreviated *step-by-step* version goes like this:

1. **Emotional reactivity:** This part of the brain works as a sort of "threat detection system." Something comes to your attention, such as a sound, a memory, a thought, or a physical sensation,

and your brain "flags" the signal as important. This signal can start a chain reaction that immediately affects your heart, your breathing, or your muscle movements.

2. **Emotional filtering**: Next, your brain re-evaluates. Is this worth the fight? What exactly are we dealing with? Was that a pitbull or a labradoodle? Was that a joke or an insult? With some additional information, you make a judgment: Do you switch off the alert system, or choose to deal with the threat?

3. **Effortful control**: Here's where you choose your words carefully, you put your hands in your pockets instead of throwing a punch, or you quickly turn and walk away. You put the brakes on your impulses and take action to deal with the problem.

4. **Emotional awareness**: Often, emotions happen before we even know what to call them. When you look at the whole situation, including your own body's reactions, you may come up with a label for what just happened to you, whether that was excitement, terror, unease or horror.

Let's now go through this process in some detail, looking for ways that you can set your body and brain up for success.

Emotional reactivity
Where does it come from?

Emotional signals, or "triggers" can come from anywhere. Everyone has their own unique set of triggers, but some are extremely common. A stress reaction can be triggered by anything that your body interprets as a "threat."

Some stress reactions are triggered by a single event, like a sudden noise, a painful jolt, or a hurtful word. Other stress reactions build up slowly over time, due to a noisy crowd, a decline in blood sugar, or an aching back.

Stress triggers can be found in the world around you, in your own physical sensations, or from your own thoughts. Throughout your day, you are managing upsetting headlines, surges in caffeine, and even uncomfortable memories or worries.

PARENTING IN THE TRENCHES

There are so many moments in a day that might feel like an attack. Whether it is a child yelling, a door slammed, or a book flying across the room, your body will naturally feel startled and wary when these things happen. Even verbal attacks such as name-calling, threats, or swearing can trigger a stressful response. Sometimes, the threat is very real and you actually find yourself being pushed, punched, or scratched.

IMPROVING YOUR EMOTIONAL SIGNALING: LIMITING TRIGGERS

Generally speaking, you can reduce your stress load somewhat by making certain changes to your circumstances. You may not be able to make any changes to the geopolitical situation where you are, but you can stop listening to the news in the morning if it upsets you. You can try to spend less time with rude people. You can wear noise-canceling headphones on the commute to work.

You might even be able to add some pleasant things to your environment to balance out the annoyances, like a great radio station, a pair of super-comfortable shoes, or a beautiful painting on your desk.

Still, there's only so much control we have over our environments. When you are a parent of a child with oppositional and defiant behavior, you face potential triggers every day while you are trying to go about your daily life and fulfill your responsibilities as a parent. You may not have much control over how many times you are shouted at, smacked, or insulted.

Fortunately, we can actually help our bodies to be less sensitive to those emotional signals in the first place. When you are taking care of your *basic needs*, you are less likely to overreact to potential threats.

Below are some simple preventative measures you can take to add some resilience to your emotional signaling system. Some of these suggestions may seem difficult, but without taking care of yourself, you will find it much harder to control your reactivity and be the kind of parent you want to be.

To support your *physical* health:

- Get enough sleep.

- Drink plenty of water.

- Move your body in a way that feels good every day.

- Eat healthy food and regulate your blood sugar throughout the day.

To support your *emotional* health:

- Spend time with people who make you feel safe, loved, and accepted.

- Take a few minutes to do something creative, so you can feel free and express yourself.

Emotional filtering
What does this mean?

A door slams late at night. You feel startled but then you think, "Is that someone I know? Am I expecting a visitor?" Even before you walk down the hall to see who it is, your brain is trying to filter this signal to decide whether or not it is a threat.

Your brain is asking a question here: What does this mean? The answer to this question is extremely important to the way you react emotionally.

Compare the following two situations:

1. You are walking through a pet store. You see a mouse in a cage.

2. You are standing in your kitchen. You see a mouse scurry around the corner.

(*Note:* Even though you're only looking at words on a page, your emotional signaling system might be going a bit wild right now, just thinking about having a mouse in the house. Of course, you probably didn't throw a book across the room, because your emotional filtering system reminded you that it's just a thought. There's no mouse here. See how it works?)

Now, back to the examples. Do you predict that your own emotional reaction would be different, depending on whether you were standing in a pet store or in your kitchen? If you are like most people, you would look at the mouse in the pet store, and tell yourself, "No need to worry, that mouse is in a cage and it's supposed to be there." Your emotional signaling would quickly switch off, and you would go on looking for whatever item you came in for.

However, if you saw that same mouse in your kitchen, you might be thinking, "Oh no! Those things carry disease! They're probably all over the house! How did they get in? This is going to cost a fortune to deal with." Your emotional filtering system has confirmed that THIS IS A THREAT! Your whole body gets in on the act, so you shudder, yelp loudly, hop up on a chair, and start googling "pest control."

Filtering your experiences at home

Your emotional reaction to your child's disruptive or difficult behavior depends very much on how your brain "filters" what you see, hear, and think. Perhaps you are probably so used to drawing conclusions and making judgments that you might not even see yourself doing it. You just react, because you "know" what it means. Still, there are some techniques you can try that will help shift your reaction from a despairing "Oh no, not again" to a more confident "Once more into the breach, my friends."

Improving your emotional filtering: Getting flexible

First, imagine that you've given your child an instruction, and he or she has started to stomp and loudly complain. Now stop and look: What are all the different ways you could filter this information? How might your emotional reaction change if you filtered your child's behavior differently? For example:

- the result of a late bedtime

- the effects of a difficult transition

- a sign that he or she might not be feeling well

- evidence of a possible misunderstanding.

Would you interpret the stomping and complaining as a threat? Would you feel an intense emotional reaction? Probably not.
Compare this with filtering your child's behavior as:

- evidence of a serious mental problem

- evidence that you are incompetent as a parent

- a sign that he or she will become a criminal or a drop-out

- proof that your child lacks manners and respect.

Would these filters influence your emotional reaction? It's the same behavior: Your child is complaining and stomping around. However, one set of filters doesn't make you feel like you are under threat, while the other feels more like the end of the world. Your physical reaction depends in part on the filters you choose.

Emotional filters that hurt

One of the biggest challenges of having a child with oppositional and defiant behavior is holding on to a positive and gentle attitude about yourself and your child. It hurts when your child is giving you zero-star reviews and ignoring your best attempts to guide him or her. It hurts when neighbors and teachers shake their heads and tell you to "control your child." It hurts when you have a picture of the kind of parent you want to be but you can't seem to live up to your own standards.

While it's true that your physical state will have an effect on how you think (the more stressed you are, the easier it is for you to notice the negatives, the threats, and the disappointments), the opposite is also true. Your thoughts can help you push back against the stress or take you deeper. The way you assess the situation, the way you judge yourself, and the options you weigh will help to determine whether your stress levels continue to increase or whether you start to cool down.

Changing your emotional filters doesn't happen overnight, but the first step is simply to notice them as they happen. Here are some unhelpful emotional filters to look out for. Do any of these sound familiar?

THE "HOPELESS" FILTER

"I can't." "This is impossible." "Everything is ruined."

All these thoughts describe a feeling of being stuck, trapped, with no way out. If you look around and see yourself as helpless and outmatched, your body's natural response is to send you an extra jolt of adrenaline to help you fight your way out, or to shut down and conserve energy until the crisis passes.

THE "SHAME" FILTER

"I'm a failure." "I keep screwing everything up." "I'm just not good enough."

In her book *I Thought It Was Just Me*, Dr. Brené Brown writes: "Shame is the intensely painful feeling or experience of believing we are flawed and therefore unworthy of acceptance and belonging."[3] Sometimes we act like our own worst enemies. When we can't see a way to solve a problem, we turn our disappointment and frustration on ourselves. These thoughts push us further into defeat.

THE "BLAME" FILTER

"Well, of course, because X should have..." "I can't fix this until X..." "This is all X's fault."

When we assign blame, the solution to the problem is outside our hands, and that feeling of helplessness and suffering can be overwhelming.

---

3   Brown, B (2008) *I Thought It Was Just Me (But It Isn't)*. New York, NY: Avery, p.30.

Emotional filters that help

To the extent that we are able to choose our thoughts, here are some "filters" that will help you look at the situation without so much reactivity. You don't have to particularly like what is going on and you don't have to ignore the problem, but if you can leave room for curiosity, kindness, and hope, then your emotions will certainly be more positive and your behavior will likely soon follow.

THE "EMPATHY" FILTER

"He/she's having a hard time." "He/she's really struggling." "He/she needs my help."

This filter was probably much easier to find when your child was a tiny infant or a chubby toddler. As kids get older, this mindset can certainly apply, but we sometimes stumble over other thoughts along the way, like "She should be past this by now" and "I'm sure I taught him better than that."

Some parents conjure up the empathy filter by repeating the mantra "He's having a hard time, not *giving me* a hard time." This mental leap from the role of "victim" to the role of "helper" can be a big one but it gets easier with practice.

THE "RESILIENCE" FILTER

"I am enough." "I have everything I need." "I can get through this."

One of the biggest barriers to using this filter is trying to solve too many problems at the same time. If your goal in that difficult moment is to "fix this behavior problem right now" or "make sure my child grows up with manners and respect for others," then it's hard to feel confident facing such a huge task. However, if you choose a goal that will carry you through the next minute with grace and love, the filter becomes much more manageable.

THE "OPTIMISM" FILTER

"I haven't figured this out YET." "All I need is my next step." "I can get help."

This filter includes the reminder that nothing has to get solved *right this minute*. The future is unknown, and full of possibilities. Instead of focusing on the mistakes of the past or the confusion of the present, it opens the door to hope. Believe it or not, optimism is actually a behavior that can be learned, and it is explored in detail later in this chapter.

What if I can't choose my filter at all?

If filters like shame, blame, or hopelessness just seem too overwhelming in the moment or you find you are often too reactive to "think straight," you may need to simply work on finding physical calm and take care of your basic needs until your body starts to self-regulate again. You can always come back to the problem later and try to look at it from a different point of view.

Effortful control
What do I do now?

The next step in the process of emotional processing involves taking action or actively resisting an urge. If you think of emotional reactivity as a sort of "automatic pilot," then effortful control would be the "manual override."

If your emotional signaling and emotional filtering lead you to believe that you're under intense attack, then you might completely let go of the controls and trust that your fight/flight/freeze response is the best option to get you out of there.

If you are feeling emotionally reactive but you can see that it's not safe or wise to express all of those thoughts in the moment, then you will focus your attention on "doing the right thing," while trying your best not to pay attention to any other triggers.

Inhibition

Inhibition is what stops you from slamming that door or squeezing a hand too hard. If your sympathetic nervous system is the engine, then your inhibition is the brakes. Inhibition is that quiet voice in your head that just says, "Stop. Don't do this. Not right now."

In some very specific situations, you might find you have an emotional "dampener" that limits your visible reactivity and helps you stay cool on the outside, even if you are boiling with anger on the inside. For example, you might be able to stay stoic and cheerful at work when you are interacting with clients and coworkers, but this mask slips off when you get to your car and you can express your true feelings. When you are driving by yourself, you might use some very colorful language to describe other people on the road, but when the children are in the car with you, that language gets heavily edited.

Emotional inhibition is usually limited to short periods of time or specific situations where you have essentially trained yourself to control your responses. Maybe you have learned to look at your child and visualize a reminder of how small they really are, or you choose to focus on how you felt when your own parent would start to stomp and yell. You flex your attention and tell yourself, "Not now, it's not worth it, just hold on."

It's still possible to feel all the emotions and sensations of "reactivity" when you are inhibiting your own behavior. It's not exactly the same as being calm. It's more like watching a house start to explode in a movie, then pressing the pause button. The flaming chunks of wood are frozen in the air mid-flight. Similarly, your muscles might feel locked into place while your heart continues to race.

Still, inhibition can be a very helpful reaction. It takes some effort and it is temporary, but when you say "no" to your own reactive impulses, you gain a moment to re-assess the situation.

Following the plan

When you are actively working against your own emotional reactivity, it becomes much harder to use a lot of your brain's "higher functions" (e.g., problem-solving, creativity, and humor). However, if you have a course of action that you are committed to, you can set yourself up for success by rehearsing this plan *before* the reactivity kicks in. The more planning and rehearsal you do, the less energy it takes to go ahead and follow the steps.

Emotional awareness
What just happened?

Emotional awareness is a step in the process of emotion processing but it doesn't always happen as soon as you first experience the emotion. Emotional awareness is, in a way, the story you tell yourself about how your body felt, what you thought, and what you did. Plenty of adults don't spend much time on emotional awareness, even if they have plenty of thoughts, feelings, and reactions going on.

Even if you find you can get by without this step, it's healthy to recognize your emotions as they come and go. You don't have to dwell on them or even act on them, but emotions do have such a strong effect on our thoughts and even our physical bodies, so it's probably wise to acknowledge them whenever possible.

Physical self-regulation: Coming back into balance

Of course, stress is not always in the eye of the beholder. It is still a process that is based in physiology.

Your body is regulated by two systems that work to balance each other out: the sympathetic nervous system and the parasympathetic nervous system. When the first symptoms of stress hit you, that's the sympathetic nervous system doing its job. Your muscles tense up. Your pupils dilate. Your heart races. Your stomach stops digesting food.

The job of the parasympathetic nervous system is to reverse the physical changes that happened in your body when you first became emotionally reactive. The parasympathetic nervous system promotes digestion and slows the heart rate. In this calmer state, some parts of your brain start to work better. For example, when you are calm, you generally find it easier to pay attention to social cues and respond to other people with empathy.

The parasympathetic nervous system can usually smooth out your emotional highs and lows, given enough time. After a few minutes or maybe a few hours after a stressful event, you will probably start to feel more like yourself again without even trying. However, if you spend your days trying to stay alert to danger, because of a difficult job or an unstable situation at home, then you might need to give your body some extra help.

To communicate to that nerve at the base of your brain that you are safe and all is well, here are some tools you can use. Remember those signals that told your brain to go on high alert? There are also signals that can help tell your brain that you are safe and okay. You can use these signals at every step as you process emotion.

Managing *emotional reactivity* for self-regulation

Some of the simplest and most effective strategies for managing emotional reactivity are *sensory* in nature. Sensory experiences are simply your body's reaction to a physical sensation. That sensation could involve texture, pressure, heat, cold, movement, sound, or smell. Everyone's sensory preferences are a little different, but here are some common examples of physical sensations that can be calming:

- being outside in nature

- listening to music

- getting a hug from someone you trust

- fidgeting with something

- walking

- snuggling up under a blanket

- squeezing something

- getting into a hot bath

- breathing in a favourite scent

- petting a friendly critter.

You probably have developed a few of these self-soothing strategies without even realizing it. Sensory strategies are essential because they can help you self-regulate when you are feeling too overwhelmed and reactive to use an emotional filter.

Helpful *emotional filters* for self-regulation

Emotional filtering happens when you take a closer look at a potential threat and add some information that helps you decide whether or not you are safe. Sometimes, it is effective just to remind yourself that you're okay and that this will pass, but you might find it helpful to look for a special phrase or mental picture of your own that helps you feel secure.

Making the most of *effortful control* for self-regulation

When you are feeling highly reactive, sometimes there's no way to escape the situation, and there's no apparent solution either. Used alone, effortful control is not enough to help you fully recover from stress. Even if you are successfully inhibiting your desire to throw a dish or start cursing, your body may stay in a heightened state unless you take action in a way that helps you self-regulate. For example, a controlled breathing exercise helps the parasympathetic nervous system to kick in. Mindfulness techniques can also be used in a moment like this, to shift focus away from thinking about the "threat" for long enough to let your body's self-calming system work. Calling a sympathetic friend can help to remind you that you are not alone.

Using *emotional awareness* for self-regulation

Emotional awareness for self-regulation can be as simple as noticing what you are doing, how your body is feeling, and what thoughts you are having. When you deliberately step back to assess yourself, you gain the benefit of perspective. This can help you decide whether you are already calm enough to handle the problem or whether it would be better to give yourself some more time to cool down.

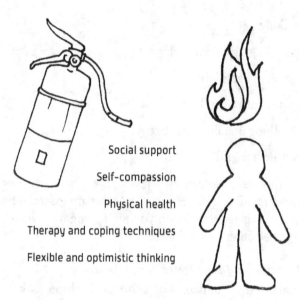

Social support

Self-compassion

Physical health

Therapy and coping techniques

Flexible and optimistic thinking

Figure 5.2: Support for emotional self-regulation

What does it mean to be an "optimistic parent"?

As you read earlier, optimism can be a helpful lens for emotional self-regulation. In fact, the effects of optimism can have a ripple effect that affects the whole family.

Of course, it would be helpful to know exactly what optimism is. Some people assume that optimism is just a positive attitude, or even just the unshakeable belief that "something will turn up" or "things will somehow get better." Fortunately, optimism is more than just a cheerful demeanor.

Psychologist Dr. Martin Seligman described optimism and pessimism as two different habits of thought with distinct patterns.[4] How do you explain bad events to yourself?

- Do you place blame on yourself, or *look for reasons that contributed to the problem*?

- Are you stuck with this problem forever, or *is the cause something that comes and goes*?

- Is this a symptom of a much larger issue, or something *specific*?

---

4   Seligman, M. E. (2006) *Learned Optimism: How to Change Your Mind and Your Life*. New York, NY: Vintage.

- See how this works? If you are a more "pessimistic" parent, you might explain your child's difficult behavior by:

  - blaming yourself or your child

  - responding to it as something that "always" happens

  - treating the problem as too big to handle.

- If you are a more "optimistic" parent, you react to difficult behavior by reminding yourself that:

  - your child might be struggling with a specific feeling or a missing skill

  - most problems are temporary

  - you can handle this one piece at a time.

The pros and cons of optimism and pessimism

Dr. Seligman acknowledged that a pessimistic outlook does have its advantages.[5] For example, when you are cautious, you can clearly see the problems around you and the possible risks. You can clearly see what might go wrong and prepare for it. You can also "pick your battles" in a healthy way; some risks are not worth taking, and some causes are indeed lost.

However, pessimistic thoughts can also make it harder for you to stay calm, and they can increase your sense of helplessness and frustration.

Do any of these thoughts sound familiar to you?

- "Why can't I just have a normal morning? I don't know where I went wrong."

- "I'm always going to be stuck cleaning up his messes."

- "My child always manages to get his own way in the end."

- "She lies constantly."

- "If it weren't for the Oppositional Defiant Disorder, we could have a happy family."

Can you spot what makes these thoughts *pessimistic* versus *optimistic*? Remember the three tell-tale signs: It's probably a pessimistic statement

---

5   Forgeard, M. J. C. and Seligman, M. E. P. (2012) Seeing the glass half full: A review of the causes and consequences of optimism. *Pratiques Psychologiques, 18*(2), 107–120.

if it involves blaming others or "the world," if the thought makes the problem look huge, or if it describes the problem as permanent.

If you find yourself getting stuck in these kinds of statements, you're not alone. Still, there might be a way to describe your problems that actually gets you closer to solving them.

Here are the same problems again, but without the pessimism:

- "This morning was rough, but there were a few good moments. I wonder how I can make tomorrow better."

- "I guess I could clean up this mess today, but I need a plan to get him cleaning more often."

- "That didn't end the way I wanted."

- "It seems like she is lying when I ask her about chores. I wonder how often that happens."

- "My wish is for us to have a happy family. I wonder what I could work on that would get us closer."

If this kind of thinking sounds difficult, well, it is. Fortunately, you don't have to do this on your own. There's actually research to show that optimism is a skill that can be trained and learned.

Choosing optimistic thoughts

Dr. Mark Durand researched the question of how to help parents become more optimistic.[6] Using techniques drawn from Cognitive Behavior Therapy, he taught parents to be more positive in the way they talked to themselves and then he measured the results. He found that parents who learned how to focus on more optimistic thoughts were more likely to benefit when they took a course on how to help their children; not only that, but the children of those parents had a noticeably bigger improvement in their behavior, compared with the children of parents who received the parent training but not the optimism training.

Thoughts such as "This is happening out of the blue" or "He's incapable of behaving" were replaced by more optimistic thoughts such as "There are patterns to this behavior" and "If I am consistent, I will see success."

---

6   Durand, V. M., Hieneman, M., Clarke, S. & Zona, M. (2009) *Optimistic Parenting: Hope and Help for Parents with Challenging Children*. Boston, MA: Springer.

Here is a quick overview of the process of "learned optimism" used in Cognitive Behavior Therapy, as described by Mark Durand:

- Situation (What happened?)
- Beliefs (What did you think or feel? What was your "self-talk" like?)
- Consequences (What happened as a result?)
- Disputation (Was that thought useful? Accurate?)
- Substitution/Affirmation (What is a more positive belief?)

If you have been struggling with pessimistic thought patterns for a long time, it will take some time to practice switching to a more optimistic explanation when you encounter difficult situations. Cognitive Behavior Therapy can help you through this process, and a skilled counselor, psychotherapist, or psychologist can do a world of good in this regard.

There's a world of difference between "My child can't stay calm" and "My child can't stay calm YET."

A strengths-based approach to your child

One of the most helpful tools in staying resilient is the ability to look at your child's behavior from a fresh point of view. It's usually easy to see the ways in which your child does not measure up to expectations at school or to count the number of times your child has broken the rules in a day. However, this is only a piece of the picture.

In the 1990s and 2000s, the social worker Bertha Reynolds advocated for what she called a "strengths-based approach," a practice that recognizes the skills and potential of the individual, not just the deficits.

Dr. Seligman (mentioned earlier in this chapter with regard to his work on optimism) promoted the strengths-based approach from his position as the president of the American Psychological Association, saying: "The most important thing we learned was that psychology was half-baked. We've baked the part about mental illness, about repair damage. The other side's unbaked, the side of strength, the side of what we're good at."[7]

Yes, your child has certain qualities that don't suit his or her current

---

7   Seligman, M. (1999) Speech given at the Lincoln Summit, September 1999. Cited in Buckingham, M. (2010) *Go Put Your Strengths to Work: 6 Powerful Steps to Achieve Outstanding Performance*. New York, NY: Simon and Schuster.

situation; after all, there is no line on your child's kindergarten report card that reads "Makes up his/her mind despite the best advice of others" and no place in your bedtime routine for "Venting emotions with maximum honesty," but that doesn't mean that your child doesn't have some amazing strengths.

A child with oppositional and defiant behavior may have some of the following strengths in abundance:

- creativity

- sensitivity

- honesty

- leadership

- mischievous sense of humour

- courage

- self-reliance

- individuality

- persistence

- curiosity.

In fact, some of these strengths can be hard to manage, as they have to be used with discretion, or in the right circumstances. Not every school lesson requires maximum creativity or courage. Not every conversation is improved by an extra helping of persistence and honesty.

Still, if you can look at your child and appreciate these qualities as strengths (even when they are being misapplied or exerted in a very inconvenient way), you can start to imagine a more positive future for your child.

Strengths as part of the solution

As you start to become more familiar with your child's abilities and understand them as strengths (not just excesses or liabilities) you will start to be able to see how a strengths-based approach can solve problems.

For example, a strengths-based approach can help you build up your child's awareness of his or her talents, and how to properly channel them. Once you understand how to work with your child's strengths (rather than working against them), you and your child will learn to use those strengths to meet challenges together. Knowing your child's strengths can also create opportunities for your child to excel, so you can both enjoy less friction and more celebration.

Here are some common struggles for children diagnosed with ODD, through the lens of a strengths-based approach:

Complaint: Doesn't accept feedback from others. Always wants to be in charge.

Strength: Leadership potential, self-reliant, motivated to follow own path, doesn't need approval from others to pursue goals.

Complaint: Ignores instructions, argues when asked to follow expectations and routines. Never does something the same way twice.

Strength: Creative, a true original, strong desire to try new things, courageous and curious.

Complaint: Rude, confrontational, defiant, not respectful to authority figures.

Strength: Brave, willing to stand up for what he or she believes, persistent, mischievous sense of humour.

Complaint: Easily upset, often cries and. shouts at others, refuses to calm down when asked.

Strength: Sensitive, expressive, wears his or her heart on sleeve, feels things deeply, passionate.

Strengthening your emotional resilience: Self-assessment
QUESTIONS FOR REFLECTION

– What kind of situations make you feel reactive (e.g., nervous, upset, jumpy, overwhelmed, or furious)?

– What kind of strategies do you have for soothing yourself and improving physical self-regulation?

– What rituals or routines help you de-escalate when you feel yourself getting reactive? Are these healthy strategies?

– How would you describe your child's strengths and positive potential?

ESSENTIAL SKILLS

- I notice when my mood starts to change.

- I'm aware of my triggers and the ways I usually respond to stress.

- I take care of my basic physical health needs.

- I have a social circle I can reach out to when I need support.

- I have strategies to help myself recover and stay calm.

- I can see my child's challenging behavior as part of what makes him or her strong and unique.

- I'm willing to get extra help in areas that are hard for me, such as depression, anxiety, marriage problems, attentional and learning difficulties.

PRIORITY QUIZ

Is strengthening emotional resilience a priority for your family? If you agree with three or more of the following statements, then strengthening your emotional resilience is likely to result in some powerful changes to your family dynamic.

- I often find myself feeling hopeless and embarrassed about my family's situation.

- When I start to get upset, I quickly feel my emotions spiralling out of control.

- My ability to stay calm mostly depends on what is happening around me.

- When things go wrong, I feel flooded with negative thoughts.

- My body goes into overdrive during family conflicts and it's hard to focus on anything but the physical symptoms of stress (pain, headache, racing heart, muscle tension, stomach ache).

Where can I find help with emotional resilience?

Some days, you may feel that you've reached the end of your patience and your mental resources. Dealing with challenging behavior can be a physical, mental, and financial strain. It definitely hurts to hear angry words from your child, to see your partner feeling defeated, or to see your other family members suffering as a result of another explosive outburst. Sometimes, you will reach out for support, but neighbors, teachers, or even friends will let you down.

In those moments, you can reach for the tools that you have in your emotional self-regulation toolbox:

- Take care of own your body, mind, and soul.

- Find safety and belonging.

- Indulge in some creativity and self-expression.

- Find something sensory that is soothing.

When you feel strong enough, you can start building up your resilience again and cultivating optimism. Even if you haven't seen much success yet, optimism can help you look at a tough situation with fresh eyes and renewed energy. The key to finding new possibilities, solutions, and perspectives is to stay *flexible*.

If you need some extra help or some strategies to build up your "emotional filtering" and stay flexible, try these exercises on your own or with a friend:

STRATEGIES TO TRY AT HOME

Exercise #1
Journaling

One way to be mentally flexible is to describe the situation in a new way. Memory can be selective, and when you tell the story of what happened, you always have choices about what details to include. As you write, notice how you start to recall new details that you had forgotten. Even if they are strange or painful, don't edit them out. Try to see the whole picture. Notice how some parts of your memory seem to be blank. Remember that memory is not perfect, so there is always room to tell another version of the story.

Exercise #2
Find the good

Instead of focusing on the ways you have been hurt or disappointed, review the situation with a fresh intention. To find the good in a hard struggle, ask yourself:

- "Did I have any moments of improvement or success along the way?"

- "Did I learn anything that will help me next time?"

- "Is my child demonstrating a strength in an inconvenient way?"

- "Is my child expressing a need that I didn't know about before?"

Exercise #3
Eat the elephant: One bite at a time

Avoid describing the problem in terms that are permanent or too huge to change. An overwhelming problem can often be broken down into small, manageable pieces. Try to describe the problem in terms that you can see and measure. For example, "My child refuses to do anything by himself" could become "When I ask my child to get dressed in the morning, I usually have to give reminders and physical help in order to get it done within 15 minutes, in time for us to leave." The more specific you are, the more possibilities for gradual change you will start to see.

Exercise #4
Set goals for your own behavior

Even though it is tempting to measure your success based on what your child did that day, remember that you can only control your own behavior. Set your intention, and give yourself some credit for following through, even if it doesn't always work out the way you had hoped. In other words, disconnect the outcome from the effort. Any time you make the effort to manage your own behavior and act like the kind of parent you want to be (e.g., you took the time to self-regulate, you helped problem-solve, you thought of some preventative strategies and tried them out), you deserve to be congratulated. Give yourself credit for handling the situation calmly, whether it helps or not.

Exercise #5
Add some reminders

If you find that the "best-laid plans often go astray," then you might need to add some reminders around the house. For example, what would help you remember to set up positive moments with your child? Do you need to remind yourself to set aside time for recovery, self-care, and relaxation? Don't forget to review your successes—write them down, or even add a notification in your phone.

Exercise #6
Take it one minute at a time

Remember that your control is limited and your child's reaction is temporary. Soon it will pass. Very soon, you will have an opportunity to reconnect, to see your child's "good side," and you can pick up the pieces together (perhaps literally) and get back to the important work of building your relationship and guiding your child along the way. One way to remember this is to set a timer on your phone. If you can make it through one minute with patience and grace, then you can probably make it through the next minute, too. Remember that people do grow and change, so leave room for it. For example, when you hear yourself saying "My child refuses to do anything by himself," you can try to remember that this is a temporary situation and describe the situation in a different way, such as "My child wants a lot of help from me right now."

Exercise #7
Try out a new, more optimistic emotional filter

When you are already feeling stressed out, emotional, and reactive, you might find it hard to remember how to look at the situation with a different perspective. Set yourself up for success by writing out the filter you want to use and keeping it handy. This can be a simple little doodle on a piece of paper, or even a picture that you save on the background of your phone, as a daily reminder.

Exercise #8
Just breathe

When you can't think of anything helpful to say, you might just need to breathe. Take a deep breath and let it out slowly. Not only does this give you a little extra oxygen and a boost to your self-regulation, it also sets a positive example for your child, who is still learning how to self-regulate.

Exercise #9
Zoom out...waaaaay out

All moments of stress do pass, and most problems can be solved or managed eventually. You might feel stuck and hopeless right now, but remember all the other times where you stumbled and recovered, and all the surprisingly good things that have happened to you. Although you cannot control what has happened to you, and you have limited control over what is happening now, as author John Maxwell says, "This doesn't have to be your story."[8]

Professional support for emotional resilience

If you are looking for more support, or you want to progress more quickly and easily toward your goals, here are some key terms to look for:

- **Trained professionals** who help with emotional resilience include: psychologists, psychotherapists, counselors, clinical social workers, trauma specialists, addiction counselors.

- **Interventions and treatments** that help with emotional resilience include: mindfulness training, Cognitive Behavior Therapy, Acceptance and Commitment Therapy. If you are interested in exploring optimistic parenting, you can read the aforementioned book by Dr. Mark Durand: *Optimistic Parenting: Hope and Help for You and Your Challenging Child.*

---

8   Maxwell, J. C. (2015) *Intentional Living: Choosing a Life That Matters.* New York, NY: Center Street.

CHAPTER 6

Supporting Your Child's Emotional Self-Regulation Skills

The importance of relationships and emotional self-regulation

As you know, oppositional and defiant behavior can be heartbreaking. It can be discouraging, offensive, and bewildering. It can interrupt a tender moment or shatter a peaceful day. Sometimes, it may feel like there is a vast distance between you and your child. You are probably struggling to understand each other, never mind connect on an emotional level.

This parent–child relationship might be hard for many different reasons. You might be feeling emotionally bruised or struggling with your own thoughts and worries. Your child may need help to reset dysfunctional relationship patterns. Your child might struggle mightily with emotional self-regulation. Your child might need to build problem-solving skills or manage his or her motivation. However, all of these supports rest on one essential foundation: your relationship with your child.

Without a warm, trusting relationship between parent and child, the work of teaching expectations, developing emotional self-regulation, and boosting motivation becomes much, much harder.

In this chapter, we will explore how to rebuild that foundation of trust, and create a warm and responsive environment that will help you in everything else that you do, including:

- setting the stage
- opening lines of communication
- problem-solving and discussion
- emotion coaching.

What sort of parent am I supposed to be?

Your idea of a "good parent" probably depends on the home you grew up in and the community that surrounded you. You were brought up with a set of values, and you might be trying your best to follow the same set of values, choosing a select few, or deliberately doing the opposite of what you were raised with.

There is simply no single definition of what constitutes a "good parent," or one proven way to raise a child who is obedient and happy. Every culture has its own expectations, and studies have shown that the same parenting style in one culture might actually have a different effect on a child who is raised in a different culture.

Many parents worry that they are either too "hard" or too "soft" with their children, either not "in control" or not affectionate enough.

What is "warm and responsive" parenting?

It can definitely be challenging to set firm boundaries with your child while building a positive relationship at the same time. When your child's attitude is prickly and rude, you might not feel like even being in the same room, let alone spending quality time together. When your child is ignoring your instructions or throwing your belongings around the house, you would probably much rather yell than offer a hug.

If your child would just be more cooperative, it would be easier to have a positive relationship, right? Still, here you are, and if you can change the dynamic a little bit, you might see some very positive changes. After all, research shows that:

- Children who are raised in a harsh and inconsistent family environment tend to have more challenging and disruptive behavior.

- Children who have warm and responsive parents have fewer behavior problems and better academic and life outcomes, even if they face other challenges in life, such as poverty or stress.

How do you know when you've got it right?

It's hard to know exactly when you're being a really amazing parent. Children certainly don't give you the most helpful or reliable feedback. They may not cheer your efforts to set boundaries, or express appreciation when you are patient. They may not even notice how hard you are working to stay calm, to provide opportunities for positive interaction, and to problem-solve with them.

Still, you often know when you're not meeting the mark. You can sense when something is a little off, but it's so hard to adjust your approach mid-stride. When you hear your tone becoming harsh or you start giving abrupt orders and making critical comments, you probably wish you could just tap out and start over.

The bedrock of a parent–child relationship

Every day has a thousand opportunities to connect with your child and it's impossible to nail every single one, but if you can remember to communicate the following messages, roughly in this order, you are probably on the right track:

- "I love you."

- "I'll try to understand what you need and to help you get it."

- "I will help you stop when you are hurting yourself and others."

- "I will help you learn what you need to know."

Keep reading to learn more about how to communicate with kindness and gentleness, how to create opportunities for your child to share his or her heart with you, and how to help your child express emotions in a healthy way.

Everyday preventative strategies for improving communication with your child

Research shows that having more positive interactions with your child can increase cooperation and decrease defiance.

Great! Easier said than done, right? If you notice that you are feeling tense and anxious before the conversation even begins, go back and review Chapter 5 on emotional resilience and the strengths-based approach. Your beliefs and attitudes will not always be easy to adjust, but it's much easier to start building this relationship from a position of hope and confidence (the rest of the time, you might need to "fake it until you make it").

Building connection through positive interactions
Positivity beyond praise

Most parents are told to praise frequently and to "catch 'em being good," and this is solid advice. You should certainly try to recognize your child's successes and celebrate his or her efforts even when they don't quite meet the mark. Let's assume you're already doing that, but the overwhelming tone in your home is still negative. Why is that?

Unfortunately, children who would qualify for a diagnosis of ODD will probably attract a lot of negative attention throughout the day. This is especially true when your child is impulsive or has been in the habit of refusing and complaining for a long time. Opportunities to "reward" positive behavior will be far outnumbered by moments when you have to correct your child, offer a reminder, ask him or her to stop, explain why not, refuse requests, and so on. The ratio of criticism to praise is heavily skewed, no matter how many small gestures of cooperation you try to acknowledge.

Given that you will probably have to give feedback that is not 100 percent congratulatory, you might need to dig a little deeper to find opportunities to add kindness, warmth, and patience into your communication style.

Noticing body language

When it comes to body language, people tend to mirror each other. When you see someone smiling, you tend to smile back. If someone folds his or her arms, you might fold your arms as well. From facial expressions to gestures, people imitate each other without even realizing it. (If you are not convinced, feel free to experiment with your own friends or just watch the people around you responding to each other.)

In order to change the mood in your home from hostile to hospitable, you can lead with your own nonverbal communication.[1] If you have spent most of your time in conflict with your child, you may have picked up some physical habits that reflect a defensive or frustrated mood, such as crossing your arms and sighing heavily when you turn away, walking with a heavy step, or towering over your child. This can send a powerful signal to other people in your family—specifically, "Watch out!"

As you prepare to turn over a new leaf and add more positive interaction to your relationship with your child, start with the message your body language might be sending. Try observing your own body language for a day. Notice where you are positioning yourself in the room, and what your posture is saying.

- When you speak, are you sitting beside your child, or standing behind?

- Are you keeping your back to the wall or hugging your body?

- Are you having conversations from way across the room or at a comfortable distance?

- Is your facial expression friendly or are you mumbling from behind a phone?

Communicate positive intentions with body language

Your ideal body language will depend on how old your child is and what kind of personal space he or she prefers. If you're not sure where to start, walk within arm's reach of your child and notice how he or she reacts. Do you see your child turning away or shuffling back a bit? Be sensitive, experiment together, and find a distance that is comfortable for both of you.

Your posture can also send a powerful signal. Notice how your

---

1   De Gelder, B. (2006) Towards the neurobiology of emotional body language. *Nature Reviews Neuroscience*, 7(3), 242.

child reacts when you sit down beside him or her. Try getting down to eye-level. Some children will prefer to sit side-by-side with you, while others might happily jump into your lap. Other families have their best conversations while doing another activity, walking together or chatting from the back seat of the car.

There is no one single style of nonverbal communication that is correct. The only thing that is important is that you are sending the message "I'm here for you. You're safe." Sometimes this first step, before you've even said a word, is a very important one in relationship-building.

It's not just what you say, it's how you say it
Where are you?

If you find yourself yelling on a regular basis, it might not be because you are frustrated. You might just be trying to communicate from one room to another as you go through your own routine. Unfortunately, it's hard for your child to tell the difference between "long-distance communication" and "being loud and frustrated," so you may need to adjust *where* you are when you speak to your child. If "calling" is a habit for you, but your child tends to ignore or refuse, then your next step could be to take a deep, calming breath, walk over to your child, and say, "I'm sorry, I'll try that again. It's time for..."

Be my echo: Mirroring with tone of voice

Remember, people tend to imitate each other. Instead of matching your child's irritated tone or insolent voice, you can use this phenomenon to your advantage when you speak. It might take some emotional self-regulation on your part, but a quiet voice can be surprisingly powerful. Using a gentle voice can help to tone down your child's emotional reactivity and it also sets an excellent example for how you would like to be spoken to.

Hang in there

It takes work to stay calm and to be kind, even when your child's behavior is not always appropriate or appreciative. It might seem completely unfair when your child ignores your attempts to lead with grace.

Remember the following points:

- The efforts you make today might not have an immediate

impact on your child but they are absolutely worthwhile. You are building a relationship to last, and that takes time.

- Don't be tempted to measure your success based on your child's reaction; you are only responsible for yourself.

- Set your own realistic goals for how you choose to communicate. Pat yourself on the back when you meet them.

- What you see on the surface of your child's behavior is not all there is, and the lessons you are teaching will take some time to learn.

- Every time you respond with grace and kindness, you are showing your child that he or she is loved, that you are ready and willing to rebuild a relationship, and you will not give up on that goal.

Opening lines of communication and creating more moments of connection

You've spent enough time arguing. You're ready to spend more time enjoying time with your child and building up positive memories. Where do you start?

The purpose of this step is not to make sure that every day is Disneyland in your home, or even to make your child happier overall. Your main priority at this stage is to send the message: "*I like you. I care about you. I'm interested in learning more about you.*"

Random acts of kindness

If your daily routines are spiraling into conflict and it feels too daunting right to try to plan some official "quality time" together, your first steps could include some deliberate, unexpectedly kind gestures (from a safe distance). For example:

- Buy an extra pack of gum to share.

- Cheerfully do a favor when your child asks, even if it's not in your job description.

- Give your child "the night off" from a chore.

- Assurances of love and affection, like "I'm glad you're my kid" or "I think you're adorable," can be offered in passing—no performance required. These positive messages can be passed along as written notes, too.

- Let your child hear how impressed you are with him or her (e.g., "I was telling my sister today what an amazing kid you are. I told her the story of...").

- Jokes are hard to think of in the moment, but you can quickly find age-appropriate (but probably cheesy) jokes with a quick search of your phone, or even buy a book to keep handy. Laughter can be an amazing way to reduce stress for you and your child and promotes a more positive tone in your interactions.

Making time to talk

Research shows that a little quality time can go a long way when it comes to cooperation.[2] More importantly, spending time together also gives you the opportunity to hear about what your child cares about the most. When you initiate more of these friendly, low-pressure conversations, you will find it easier to talk about the harder problems together when necessary.

- Keep it casual. Try to set up conversations where there's no right or wrong answer, like "Would you rather live near the ocean or in the city?" "Which do you think is the best: ice cream or cake?"

- Share memories. Many kids enjoy hearing stories about when they were very small, or looking at old pictures and asking questions.

- Research a topic that your child is interested in and invite your child to tell you more.

Getting personal and showing concern

Asking a direct question like "How was your day?" might result in shrugs or one-word answers. Still, it's important to let your child know that his or her life is important to you. Even if your child won't give you a summary of what his or her classes were like, you might be able to crack this nut by asking opinion questions, such as:

---

2   Kochanska, G. & Aksan, N. (1995) Mother–child mutually positive affect, the quality of child compliance to requests and prohibitions, and maternal control as correlates of early internalization. *Child Development*, 66(1), 236–254.

- "What do you think about...?"
- "Are you a fan of...? Why or why not?"
- "Do you think X will ever...?"
- "Who is the most...person you have ever met?"

Making time to do things together

While it's great to have positive interactions that are spontaneous and casual, a planned event sends an important message: "You are important to me. You are a priority." Your planned "quality time" doesn't have to be costly or time-consuming. It might simply be a chance for you to learn more about what your child enjoys doing. The resource guide at the end of this chapter contains a list of ideas if you are having trouble coming up with activities to do together.

Obstacles to finding connection time together

- When you suggest spending time together, your child may suggest his or her favorite activities (e.g., watching movies, playing video games). These kinds of passive activities may not feel like "spending time together" to you, but your willingness to spend this time together and to engage with your child's interests can be the start of an important connection.

- Your child may ask for an activity that is unhealthy or outside your budget. To stave off disappointment, you might want start by offering a menu of options and ask your child to choose, instead of leaving the field wide open.

- If you offer activities that are not familiar to your child, you may not get an enthusiastic response at first. If your child tends to be cautious about new activities, you can introduce the activity in an indirect way by watching a video of someone else doing it, or just demonstrating it yourself without inviting your child to join in.

- You may choose something really special to you or spend meaningful time and energy to provide a great experience, but the experience may not produce the hoped-for results. In cases like this, remember that you are both new to this process, and keep your expectations flexible. Give yourself credit for trying and remember that there will be other opportunities that follow.

- Your child may be so receptive to these opportunities that he or she will start to request them much more often, even when you are not available/busy/tired. Granted, this is a nice problem to have, but if you are dealing with more challenging behaviors or confusion about how often you should say yes, then you may find it helpful to plan a schedule with your child so you can agree on when these activities are available.

- You may be unsure of what to do at first, because your interests don't line up or your energy is limited. Fortunately, the opportunities are limitless; it's only a matter of experimenting and trying what works.

Maintaining your positive relationship during a conflict

Adding kindness and quality time is likely to help reduce the number of daily skirmishes you face at home, but you and your child will still sometimes find yourself at odds with each other.

- You might still be struggling to keep a lid on feelings of anger, disappointment, frustration and fear when your child's behavior falls short of your expectations.

- Your child might refuse to follow the family rules, in a way that is disrespectful or hostile.

- Your child might behave in a way that is inconsiderate of your feelings or even harmful to other family members.

When conflict happens, it's easy to fall back into a pattern of anger, criticism, complaining, or withdrawal. It's frustrating to find yourself debating whether something is "fair" or whether you are in fact a "mean and terrible" parent, when you would much rather have a peaceful and friendly home.

So, what do you do? This is probably the hardest moment. This book is not designed to give you a step-by-step playbook, because every child is so different, but here are some general guidelines that will help you prioritize and manage your own reactions.

Navigating conflict with kindness

First, *focus on your own emotional self-regulation*. Set a positive example for your children by choosing a helpful emotional filter and flexing your effortful control (see Chapter 5 for ideas). If you feel overwhelmed, it's okay to ask for some time to recover yourself, or to request help from another caregiver.

Next, check in to see what your child's emotional temperature is like. If you are seeing signs of intense distress and loss of emotional control, then your focus will be on keeping everyone safe and providing your child with enough support to self-regulate (more on the topic of your child's emotional self-regulation later in this chapter).

If you have never experienced this kind of support, it might be hard to imagine. Your own parents and teachers might have responded by dismissing, critiquing, mocking, punishing, or ignoring you when your behavior was considered out of line.

Parenting in a supportive role

When you are trying to react to rule-breaking or emotional outbursts, you might start by taking on a role similar to a police officer responding to the scene of a crime, or a judge handing down a ruling. This kind of condemnation, including attempts to "impound" privileges, might seem like an appropriate reaction from a disciplinary perspective, but it's very hard to communicate love and respect while treating your child like a suspect in a criminal case. Some parents respond as if they were a child's classroom teacher, restating the rules and doling out detention and extra homework. This is a little less stigmatizing but it's still missing an emotional component.

So, how do you offer emotional support to your child while still maintaining boundaries? Perhaps it would help to think back to a time when you were treated by a very capable and warmhearted nurse. If not, can you imagine how you wanted to be treated? How would a professional respond to a fragile but aggravated patient? If you are having trouble imagining, here's what it might look like: A nurse would not attempt to intimidate or shame a patient, but would calmly help the patient back to safety. Nurses are not personally offended and they don't cringe easily. They work on finding the underlying problem, and provide what is needed for the benefit of the patient (even while running a tight ship). It's not a perfect analogy, but in a conflict, you are probably better off emulating a nurse than a police officer, judge, or teacher.

This advice might run contrary to what you have been taught in the past. For example, parents are often advised to simply withdraw attention from the child in response to unwanted behavior. Some behavior experts advise parents to be "like robots" when responding to difficult behavior. This might be helpful to limit your own extreme reactions when you feel you are "losing it," but it doesn't address what psychologist Dr. John Gottman identified as the need for "warmth."[3]

Why is it so important to take your child's emotions into account during a conflict?

As you will see, your child's "emotional reactivity" is often associated with perception of a threat. The feeling of being "unsafe" can fuel all kinds of messy behavioral responses, because fear triggers an increase in stress hormones and a whole cascade of physiological changes. Since your child does not have a fully developed "emotional filtering" process, it will be hard for him or her to rationalize or understand your perspective, even if you are perfectly justified in being offended or furious. It will be also be difficult for your child to suppress the impulse to "attack" or escape the source of the threat.[4] Your anger, rejection, and physical intervention might feel like a "threat" to a child with still-developing emotional self-regulation skills, so it's wise to try to moderate your own behavior to help keep emotional reactivity to a minimum.

After all, a strong negative emotional reaction is not necessary for your child to be able to "learn a lesson." In fact, a strong wave of negative emotion can have the opposite effect, making it very difficult for your child to problem-solve or focus on the rational message you are trying to send.

Managing conflict without drama

If your child still has some capacity for effortful control, you can give feedback on where the boundary is, while still offering empathy. If you aren't sure what has prompted the emotional upset, it's a good idea to find out before drawing a hard line on the reaction. For example, if you hear your child yelling at a sibling, you might be tempted to give

---

3   Gottman, J. M., Katz, L. F. & Hooven, C. (1996) Parental meta-emotion philosophy and the emotional life of families: Theoretical models and preliminary data. *Journal of Family Psychology, 103*(3), 243.

4   Sebastian, C. L., McCrory, E. J., Cecil, C. A., Lockwood, P. L. *et al.* (2012) Neural responses to affective and cognitive theory of mind in children with conduct problems and varying levels of callous-unemotional traits. *Archives of General Psychiatry, 69*(8), 814–822.

immediate feedback on his or her exact choice of words. However, a more supportive approach would be to find out what the conflict is, validate both sides if possible, and then ask, "So, how can we talk about this in a way that's calm?"

How is my child going to learn to emotionally self-regulate?

"Never in the history of calming down has anyone calmed down by being told to calm down." (Unknown)

First of all, emotional self-regulation is not simply a rational decision to "calm down." Everyone understands what it feels like to be overwhelmed by feelings of fear, panic, shock, anger, frustration, or despair. Everyone has found themselves apologizing for behavior that happened in the heat of the moment, because emotion won out over reason and caution. Children diagnosed with ODD seem to struggle with this more than most.[5]

So, what is emotional self-regulation? If you read the first chapter of this book, you already know that it is not one single skill or ability. Emotional self-regulation is the result of many different processes throughout the body, including both involuntary reactions and intentional behaviors.

Your child's difficulty with emotional self-regulation could come from many different sources. To offer support, it helps to know what part of the process seems to be causing the most difficulty; whether it's emotional reactivity, emotional filtering, effortful control, or emotional awareness. Here's a review of how your child processes emotions, and how this process is different from yours. The overall process follows the same basic steps: emotional reactivity, emotional filtering, effortful control, and emotional awareness.

Your child's emotional reactivity
Emotional reactivity in action

As you may recall from Chapter 5, an emotional reaction can be sparked by a physical experience or just a thought. Anything at all can be a

5   Dougherty, L. R., Smith, V. C., Bufferd, S. J., Kessel, E. M., Carlson, G. A. & Klein, D. N. (2016) Disruptive mood dysregulation disorder at the age of 6 years and clinical and functional outcomes 3 years later. *Psychological Medicine, 46*(5), 1103–1114.

cue for an emotional reaction: the smell of oatmeal cookies, the sound of a car approaching, a favorite song, or an angry voice. This input gets flagged[6] by your child's brain: *Pay attention! This is important!* The input can be sorted as something pleasurable, such as safety, reward, connection, curiosity, and desire, or it may be labeled as something unpleasant, such as fear, threat, and loss.[7]

The human brain seems to be beautifully wired to sort out all kinds of experiences into different categories. This ability is sometimes referred to as "threat detection."

The body springs into action immediately. Your child may feel his or her pulse quicken, or the prickle of goosebumps. The first stage of emotional reactivity is a very physical one, and it happens with very little "thought" at all.

Getting stuck on "high alert"

A child's reactivity can be set on high alert when he or she is already in distress, feeling unsafe, in pain, stressed, or worried. A child's basic emotional reactivity varies naturally between individuals, but here are some factors that can stoke your child's emotional reactivity:

- sleep deprivation

- past trauma

- sensory overwhelm

- illness

- chronic pain

- hunger or problems regulating blood sugar levels.

Threat detection: Understanding your child's "oversensitive" behavior

If a child overreacts to new experiences, refuses to go near unfamiliar places, and breaks down into tears when a game doesn't go as expected, then the threat detection system is working overtime and creating extra stress for both parents and children. When your child's emotional filtering is not screening out threats effectively, you might see him or her

---

6   Cunningham, W. A. & Brosch, T. (2012) Motivational salience: Amygdala tuning from traits, needs, values, and goals. *Current Directions in Psychological Science, 21*(1), 54–59.

7   Parasuraman, R. & Galster, S. (2013) Sensing, assessing, and augmenting threat detection: Behavioral, neuroimaging, and brain stimulation evidence for the critical role of attention. *Frontiers in Human Neuroscience, 7*, 273.

having a very sincere overreaction to numerous little disappointments or frustrations throughout the day.

Ignoring the danger signs: Understanding your child's "undersensitive" behavior

On the other end of the emotional spectrum, insensitivity to "threat" can also cause trouble for a child. If a child fails to pick up on cues that alert him or her to danger or unpleasant consequences (e.g., ignoring a frowning friend or lunging toward a nervous dog), then the threat detection system cannot do its work to help the child avoid natural consequences such as a broken friendship or a nasty bite. Both of these extremes can lead to challenging, defiant, and oppositional behavior.

Before you try to address your child's emotional self-regulation by teaching social skills or setting up a system of rewards and punishments, it's important to rule out physical and cognitive factors like these that might be creating additional stress and reactivity.[8]

Emotional filtering: On second thought

When the brain processes a change that could potentially be dangerous, one system passes along the information to the next to assess the information and upgrades the alert to full-on panic or downgrades the threat to "minor annoyance" or "false alarm."

Emotional filtering is the way your child sorts out an accidental poke from a malicious jab or decides whether a missing toy is a momentary annoyance or a national emergency. In other words, your child re-assesses the alert known as "emotional reactivity," and then decides whether it is a threat or an acceptable challenge.

For example, when you read the story of "Little Miss Muffet" together, your child's threat detection system certainly took note of the outline of a spider on the page. The parts of the brain dedicated to threat detection leapt into action, but the system almost instantly determined that the spider was not moving and perfectly flat. Your child's brain determined that the spider was a harmless illustration and no further action was required. These systems are always running "in the background," filtering out information so effectively that your child may not have even noticed the possibility of a threat in the first place.

---

8   Schoorl, J., van Rijn, S., de Wied, M., van Goozen, S. & Swaab, H. (2018) Boys with oppositional defiant disorder/conduct disorder show impaired adaptation during stress: An executive functioning study. *Child Psychiatry & Human Development*, 49(2), 298–307.

However, cognitive challenges or life experiences can get in the way of your child's ability to tell a threat from an inconvenience. For example:

- difficulty with problem-solving

- rigid thinking patterns

- traumatic events

- unreasonable expectations and beliefs

- missing social skills and perspective-taking skills.

New faces, new foods on the dinner plate, and new places can certainly be flagged and treated as "threatening" to a child. A stern word from the teacher, or a silly gesture from a sibling can be misinterpreted and labeled as a "threat," too. Life provides endless opportunities to learn from trial-and-error, and over time, most children learn to manage their fears in a healthy way. Finding the balance between courage and caution is a complex process, and these types of mistakes are hard to change overnight.

Effortful control: Do not pass "Go"

Effortful control helps your child to stop, slow down, and put on the brakes when an emotional impulse doesn't match the situation at hand. Effortful control also helps your child to redirect his or her attention and choose a course of action that can help the body simmer down (e.g., counting to ten or taking some deep breaths). Here are some common problems that may prevent your child from deploying effortful control when it is needed:

- lack of practice

- limited range of self-calming skills or tools

- mistaken blame and missing social skills

- neurological weakness in inhibition (e.g., ADHD).

A very high level of emotional reactivity can sometimes overwhelm your child's still-developing inhibition and effortful control. Some children will have a fear response that freezes them in place and they will find it very hard to override that impulse. Some children have a fear response that is more reactive and aggressive and they may not be able to "catch themselves" in time to prevent that swinging elbow or flying fist.

Emotional awareness

It may come as a surprise to you to hear that your child's ability to regulate emotions does not depend on his or her ability to label those emotions. In fact, labeling an emotion sometimes happens well after an emotion has been triggered and processed. It is certainly helpful to be able to say "I'm upset" or "I'm worried," but as you have probably noticed, it is a step that even some adults struggle with.

If your child can recognize emotions in pictures and label emotions in other people but is not able to label her or her own emotions in the moment, try a more specific approach. Your child may first have to learn what emotions are associated with specific situations and physical sensations, on a case-by-case basis, but in the meantime you can still work on other steps such as managing emotional reactivity, building up helpful emotional filters, and practicing effortful control.

As you can see, a child's ability to regulate his or her own emotions requires a well-functioning nervous system, an adequate repertoire of calming behaviors, and the ability to look at a problem from a different angle. If your child is sensitive to stress, has trouble finding activities that work to calm him or her, or gets very stuck on a single point of view when he or she runs into a conflict, the result is likely to be an emotional outburst.

What can I do to help my child with emotional self-regulation?

It might seem like a contradiction to ask how you can help your child with emotional self-regulation. After all, it's *self*-regulation, right? It seems logical to assume that this is a skill that must be learned independently.

Some parents jump to this conclusion very early on and take a "less is more" approach to responding to their child's emotions. This practice varies between cultures, so there are cultures where a hands-off approach is quite common and other cultures where more nurturing is the norm.

However, the current consensus in the psychological research says that parents can help their children learn emotional self-regulation, first by modeling it and then by coaching a child through the process, using a "warm and responsive" approach.

Emotion coaching versus emotion dismissing

When Dr. Gottman interviewed and observed families, he saw a variety of attitudes toward emotions. Some parents had difficulty naming their own emotions or didn't really notice little changes in mood and attitude in their children. In these families, emotional expression was not welcomed. Dr. Gottman described this category as "emotion dismissing." When children cried, frowned, or yelled, some parents responded by teasing or mocking. Other parents reacted angrily or tried to ignore the unwanted reactions. Some of the "emotional dismissing" parents also tried to control their child's emotional expression, either by "taking over" or reacting harshly.

So, what did the other families do? Researchers[9] found that parents who provided "emotion coaching" supported their children through their emotional highs and lows by:

- accepting individual developmental and temperamental differences

- talking openly about emotions

- noticing small changes in emotions (both their own and their child's emotions)

- looking at their child's emotional experience as an opportunity for closeness or teaching

- providing encouragement and support in times of distress

- validating their child's emotion

- helping their child label the emotion

- problem-solving with their child

- setting behavioral limits

- discussing goals and strategies for dealing with the situation.

Dr. Gottman also measured what happened to these children over a period of time, to try to see the impact of different approaches to teaching and emotions. He tested a group of families to see how well the children could regulate their own behavior, and then tested them again three years later. Other researchers, inspired by this study, investigated different groups of families and found the same thing: Warm and responsive parenting helps children regulate their own behavior.

9   Lunkenheimer, E. S., Shields, A. M. & Cortina, K. S. (2007) Parental emotion coaching and dismissing in family interaction. *Social Development*, 16(2), 232–248.

Specifically, these children were better able to calm themselves when facing a challenge and stay focused on problem-solving. Dr. Gottman also tested to see what happened when a parent dismissed a child's emotional experiences and found that children in those families tended to have more behavior problems.[10]

For more details on how to carry out this emotion coaching process, check the resource guide at the end of this chapter. In the meantime, let's look at the process of emotional self-regulation again, and look for ways that you can help at each step.

How can I help my child with *emotional reactivity*?

If your child seems to be on edge, easily frustrated, and overreacting, as described in the *irritable* subtype of the diagnostic criteria for ODD, then your child's emotional reactivity, or "threat detection system," might be working overtime.

The more proactive you can be, the better. Assuming that you have ruled out medical causes such as pain and illness, here are some ways you can prevent or mitigate problems that can leave your child extra-vulnerable to emotional reactivity:

- Review medications, sleep patterns and basic nutritional needs, so your child's physical development is as optimal as possible.

- Look out for mood changes associated with low blood sugar, and make sure your child's meals and snacks are planned accordingly.

- Include as much physical exercise as possible into your child's daily routine. Cardiovascular exertion has been shown to improve executive functioning skills and reduce incidents of disruptive behavior in classrooms, and play activities like lifting, pushing, rolling, and swinging are considered calming activities by occupational therapists.

- Sensory activities, such as exploring texture, scent, noise, music, pressure, and movement (e.g., playing with water, sand, or ribbons), can help to keep your child feeling "just right," that is, neither under-stimulated nor over-stimulated.

- Look out for sensory experiences that can feel overwhelming or

---

10   Gottman, J. M., Katz, L. F. & Hooven, C. (1996) Parental meta-emotion philosophy and the emotional life of families: Theoretical models and preliminary data. *Journal of Family Psychology, 10*(3), 243.

uncomfortable for your child. This can include tags on clothing, bright lights, noisy crowds, or even strong smells.

- Look for ways to communicate a sense of safety and security to your child. This might include providing tents and cozy hiding spots around the house or offering plenty of hugs.

- Talk to your child about situations that might be triggering big reactions or big emotions, and plan accordingly. This might mean packing some "ear defenders" to help protect your child from uncomfortably loud noises, or you could create a special ritual together to prepare your child for being apart from you at school.

- Keep providing opportunities for connection and kindness throughout the day.

You may not be able to prevent every instance of emotional reactivity but if you can help your child identify early signs of that stress build-up, it will be easier to direct your child toward a calming activity and prevent an outburst. For example, you can watch your child carefully for little physical cues that precede an emotional outburst. Does your child's posture change? Do you see an increase in hyperactive activity? Have you noticed that your child uses particular phrases that signal that a bigger outburst might be imminent?

How can I help my child with *emotional filtering*?

Your child's "emotional filters" help him or her to sort out the real emergencies from the minor distractions... At least, that's what they are meant to do. Sometimes, your child will interpret a situation as a genuine threat and react accordingly, even when your rational adult brain is saying, "What's the big deal?"

Your child may need proactive help to prevent misunderstandings and mistaken beliefs. For example, your child might benefit from help with social skills and perspective-taking, especially if he or she is accusing others of being spiteful or intentionally cruel. Many children find it hard to make mistakes or to "fail," so a treatment program might help your child to tolerate mistakes or look at them in a more positive light.

If you and your child have noticed a pattern of misunderstanding or overreaction, you can also prepare a filter beforehand. For example, you can rehearse what your child might do in response to a disappointing result or a confusing situation. You can also watch other people dealing with challenging situations, and comment on the different filters and beliefs that might be guiding their reactions. Your child might not realize yet that there is a difference between his or her perception and reality, but you can point out examples as you read stories together or watch movies: "Oh, I see! He thinks there's a dragon behind that door, so he's very scared. Do you remember what's actually behind the door?"

Supporting your child's emotional filtering in real-time

When you are helping your child to emotionally self-regulate in the moment, you can work through this process by first validating the response. Validating an emotion simply means acknowledging it without judgment. For example, you might say, "It looks like you are really worried about..." Resist the urge to immediately correct or dismiss your child's belief. In the heat of the moment, this particular filter *feels* true to your child, so you can offer your sympathy and support. Simply offering your presence, your acceptance, and your love might be all that is needed at this stage.

In fact, your child might actively resist any alternative suggestions you offer, even if you are simply pointing out reality (e.g., "She'll be back tomorrow.").

Fortunately, the emotion or the belief itself is not a problem to be solved right away. You can clarify misunderstandings later or offer more information when your child is ready to hear it. As long as your child is expressing emotion in a way that doesn't hurt in any way, no argument is needed.

How can I help my child with *effortful control*?

If you grew up in a community where corporal punishment was common, then you might have concluded that a healthy fear was necessary to make sure children knew their place. Certainly, some children learned to control their behavior to avoid the wooden spoon or the switch; but for other children, no amount of fear or punishment was enough to guarantee an improvement in behavior.

In fact, you may have noticed that for some children a threat or a harsh response can have the opposite of the intended effect; a perceived "threat" increases stress levels and makes effortful control even less likely.

So, how can parents teach children to master their impulses and keep a lid on inappropriate behavior? One of the most effective teachers of effortful control is *practice, practice, practice*. If your child can build up a strong repertoire of appropriate responses ahead of time, he or she won't need to improvise or spend valuable mental resources trying to weigh the situation.

This kind of practice can act as an emergency back-up when your child has trouble accessing executive functioning skills, including problem-solving and inhibition (you will explore these in more detail in Chapter 8).

Appropriate responses that require effortful control include:

- taking a deep breath
- walking away
- using a fidget or a calming tool to reduce emotional reactivity
- asking for help.

Before your child faces another challenge where expectations and consequences have not worked out well, try creating a game plan together. Anticipate possible problems, and get creative with your ideas to prepare your child, with questions like "What can we do if...?"

Setting boundaries on aggression and rule-breaking

If your child is already so emotionally escalated that he or she is a danger to himself/herself or others, then you will need to put in place a plan that keeps everyone safe. It's wise to map this out beforehand, because your own emotional reactivity might be very hard to control otherwise. You can even practice it with your children when they are calm.

At this point, you might be tempted to give long explanations or make threats in the hopes that rationality or judgment might win the day, but you probably already know that this is wishful thinking. A safe, gentle place for everyone to weather the storm should be your first choice.

How can I help my child with *emotional awareness*?

As you may have read earlier in this book, emotional awareness does not always happen during an emotional event. Your child might feel a sense of unease or frustration but have difficulty narrowing it down to a specific emotion, such as "I'm nervous," or "I'm discouraged." (As it happens, plenty of adults feel that way too.) It might also be hard for other people to look at the way your child is behaving and correctly guess what is happening underneath.

This confusion can create a real barrier for children who struggle with emotional self-regulation, because when they express big emotions, it's often happening in such a distracting and disruptive way that no one thinks to ask, "Are you okay? I'm not sure what's going on with you, but I'm here to listen."

Still, parents who want to help children with emotional awareness can help in a few important ways. Parents can also offer guesses or even suggest choices to help children label their own emotions by asking, "Did you feel worried when...?" or "What did you think when he said...?" Some phrases that might open up a conversation include: "Oh, I wonder if you were feeling disappointed!" or "Hmm, it kind of looks like you felt lonely. Is that true?"

Parents can also help by articulating their own emotions when appropriate. These kinds of comments can help to illustrate emotional self-awareness in real-time, and this is a far better teaching tool than simply looking at flashcards depicting "emotions" (which are often posed and more symbolic than realistic).

A note of caution: a parental display of negative emotion can sometimes trigger feelings of worry or shame in children, who may assume it is his or her fault, or wonder whether it's possible that his or her parents still care for them. Try this technique with minor frustrations and check in to see if your child understands before attempting to narrate more intense emotions.

Weathering the storm

The process of emotion coaching might sound like excellent advice, but how do you provide loving guidance to a child who is yelling "SHUT UP!" How do you validate a child's emotion when he or she is hissing "I wish you would just die"? This is where the value of your resilient heart is priceless.

Emotional reactivity and emotion coaching are just not compatible with each other. You can't do both at the same time. If you take your child's hurtful words at face value and focus your attention on the sting of the insult, or your own frustration and disappointment, then it will be very difficult to respond in a sensitive, kind, or loving way.

In the same way, it's very hard to "manage" your child's behavior and mete out justice and discipline when you are trying to provide emotion coaching. If you take your child's hurtful words as a challenge to be overcome, and go looking for the threat or reaction that will stop him or her in his tracks, then you will find it hard to look at this experience as an opportunity for closeness or teaching.

Finding your emotional X-ray vision

To be a warm and responsive parent means responding sensitively to your child's emotions, but as you know, not all children will simply cry, ask to be reassured, or tell you what they are worried about. In fact, some children will express a whole range of emotions as one note, over and over: frustration, anxiety, sadness, disappointment, jealousy... It all comes out as anger, defiance, or even contempt.

Instead of saying, "I need help," your child might say, "Why don't you ever help me?"

Instead of saying, "I'm cold," your child might might say, "This is terrible, and we should go home IMMEDIATELY."

Instead of saying, "I'm ashamed," your child might throw a homework project against the wall.

Instead of saying, "I'm scared," your child might bite or spit.

Instead of saying, "I'm worried," your child might complain loudly about an unrelated problem.

When your child's behavior is oppositional and defiant, you may be so busy dealing with what the behavior looks like on the surface, that you don't have a chance to even ask yourself what emotion might have prompted it.

Overcoming emotional misdirection

Emotion coaching for a child with oppositional and defiant behavior is probably one of the single most difficult jobs you will face as a parent, and if you need help with this step, do not hesitate to reach out for support. A trained professional might be able to help you interpret some of your child's complicated signals and find the words to help him or her express the emotion that is bubbling beneath the surface in the moment.

You may already have your hands full dealing with your own emotional reactions or ensuring the physical safety of your family, so if you don't immediately see what emotion is being expressed by your child, you can always circle back, check in, and try to talk it through when the dust settles.

Oppositional Defiant Disorder and social skills

Emotional self-regulation is also a key skill that supports social relationships. If a child is diagnosed with ODD, it's probably fair to say that child has a hard time "getting along with others," at least some of the time. Without the ability to stay calm, communicate needs, or take another child's emotional perspective, your child will find it hard to do the hard work of social interaction, including:

- staying calm in a disagreement

- understanding the motives of others

- waiting and sharing

- suggesting a compromise

- accepting feedback or objections from others

- communicating needs in a socially acceptable way.

Why do children diagnosed with Oppositional Defiant Disorder struggle with social skills?

If your child is struggling socially, he or she needs more than just a list of social rules to follow. Without a strong set of emotional and cognitive skills, your child will not be able to put these rules into practice or experience the natural rewards that comes with social success.

Irritability as a social liability

If your child struggles to calm down or is easily irritated, it follows logically that your child will spend less time in positive social engagement with others.[11] After all, it's much harder to notice friendly cues and subtle conversational shifts when you are feeling defensive or vigilant. When your child pays less attention to others, then opportunities for social learning pass him or her by. When researchers measured the brain activity of a group of children and compared those with and without disruptive behavior disorders, they noticed that the brains of some of the children were extra-sensitive in reacting to sad, angry, and even neutral faces.[12]

Unfortunately, this cycle continues when other children react negatively to your child's irritability.[13] Some children may avoid teaming

11   Porges, S. W. & Furman, S. A. (2011) The early development of the autonomic nervous system provides a neural platform for social behaviour: A polyvagal perspective. *Infant and Child Development*, 20(1), 106–118.

12   Sebastian, C. L., McCrory, E. J., Cecil, C. A., Lockwood, P. L. *et al.* (2012) Neural responses to affective and cognitive theory of mind in children with conduct problems and varying levels of callous-unemotional traits. *Archives of General Psychiatry*, 69(8), 814–822.

13   Dunsmore, J. C., Booker, J. A. & Ollendick, T. H. (2013) Parental emotion coaching and child emotion regulation as protective factors for children with oppositional defiant disorder. *Social Development*, 22(3), 444–466.

up with your child if disagreements tend to lead to angry confrontations, while others may intentionally provoke an outburst or goad your child into a physical confrontation.

Headstrong behavior and social struggles

Not all children diagnosed with ODD are emotionally volatile in social situations, but children with *headstrong* tendencies can find themselves at odds with others too.

Headstrong children are highly motivated to reach their goals, and they can be very persistent in getting what they want. If a child's attention is focused on finding the fastest or most reliable way to get to that reward, he or she may fail to notice important social cues from others and spend less time thinking of what other people want. Children who are highly motivated to reach their own goals may even rationalize antisocial behavior such as aggression,[14] if others are "in the way."

This overreaction to the possibility of reward might be connected to other cognitive struggles, such as difficulty with shifting attention, flexibility, or planning. Executive functioning abilities are explored in more detail in Chapter 8.

Emotional insensitivity and disruptive behavior

In one study of teenagers with disruptive behavior disorders, researchers noticed that the brain scans of these young people showed less activity when they were shown pictures of people with sad or fearful facial expressions.[15]

It's hard to say whether these young people were struggling to understand social cues throughout their lives or whether this lack of brain activity was primarily shaped by their life experience. After all, by the time they reached adolescence and had been diagnosed with severe behavior problems, they would have had many, many opportunities to receive negative social feedback and gradually learn to ignore it. There is some evidence[16] to suggest that people who struggle to recognize sad

14   Coy, K., Speltz, M. L., DeKlyen, M. & Jones, K. (2001) Social-cognitive processes in preschool boys with and without oppositional defiant disorder. *Journal of Abnormal Child Psychology, 29*(2), 107–119.

15   Huebner, T., Vloet, T. D., Marx, I. V. O., Konrad, K. *et al.* (2008) Morphometric brain abnormalities in boys with conduct disorder. *Journal of the American Academy of Child & Adolescent Psychiatry, 47*(5), 540–547.

16   Neumann, D., Westerhof-Evers, H. J., Visser-Keizer, A. C., Fasotti, L. *et al.* (2017) Effectiveness of a treatment for impairments in social cognition and emotion regulation (T-ScEmo) after traumatic brain injury: A randomized controlled trial. *Journal of Head Trauma Rehabilitation, 32*(5), 296–307.

or angry facial expressions (such as those with a traumatic brain injury) can be taught to pick up on those cues, and by doing so, they improve their empathetic responses and social interactions.

How do I help my child learn empathy?

Empathy is at the heart of most pro-social behavior. If your child can sympathize with others, share experiences, and build alliances, then he or she will be less inclined to use coercion, argue, or attack others. Social connections can provide emotional support and positive models for behavior, too.

As a parent, you can help your child by explaining social consequences and showing an interest in the experiences of other people, but the most important work you will do to build your child's empathy is much more personal. Building up your own emotional self-regulation will help you cope with depression or other mental health problems, which prepares you to tune into your child's emotional needs.[17] As you go through the emotion coaching process together,[18] your child's emotional self-regulation skills will be strengthened, which sets the stage for him or her to start noticing and responding to the emotional needs of others.[19]

The message you send to your child in the emotion coaching process is the message he or she will be able to share with others:

- "I care about you."

- "I'll try to understand what you need, and to help you get it."

- "I will help you stop when you are hurting yourself and others."

- "I will help you learn what you need to know."

17   Levy, J., Goldstein, A. & Feldman, R. (2019) The neural development of empathy is sensitive to caregiving and early trauma. *Nature Communications, 10*(1905), doi:10.1038/s41467-019-09927-y.

18   Katz, L. F. & Windecker-Nelson, B. (2004). Parental meta-emotion philosophy in families with conduct-problem children: Links with peer relations. *Journal of Abnormal Child Psychology, 32*(4), 385–398.

19   Gerdes, K. E., Segal, E. A. & Harmon, J. K. (2014) Your Brain on Empathy: Implications for Social Work Practice. In H. C. Matto, J. Strolin-Goltzman & M. S. Ballan (Eds.) *Neuroscience for Social Work: Current Research and Practice.* New York, NY: Springer Publishing Co.

Supporting your child's emotional self-regulation: Self-assessment

QUESTIONS FOR REFLECTION

- Can you find more opportunities each day to relax and connect with your child?

- Do you notice small changes in your child's emotional state?

- When your child gets upset, are you able to offer empathy?

- Can you think of a "challenging behavior" that might be connected to a struggle to communicate or regulate emotions? What is the message your child's behavior might be trying to tell you?

ESSENTIAL SKILLS

- I can keep the mood fairly positive and encouraging in our home.

- I pay attention and celebrate "wins" (both mine and other family members').

- I don't take it personally when my child has emotional ups and downs.

- I make sure to help my child share thoughts and feelings on a regular basis.

- I can look beyond the noise and rule-breaking and understand my child's real needs, worries, and struggles.

- I can help my child understand what other people might be thinking or feeling.

- I help my child express difficult emotions while respecting the needs of others.

PRIORITY QUIZ

Is relationship and emotional support a priority for your family? If you agree with three or more of the following statements, then learning how to offer emotional support and build relationship will help you support your child's emotional self-regulation skills.

- It's hard to remember the last time we had some pleasant quality time together.

- I get so frustrated that I find it hard to be empathetic.

- My child refuses to share feelings and thoughts with me, so it's hard to be supportive.

- I'd like to be supportive but I'm not sure what to say, and nothing seems to help.

- My child seems to have a very hard time offering empathy to other people, or seeing their point of view.

Where can I find help with building relationships and emotional self-regulation?

STRATEGIES TO TRY AT HOME

Exercise #1

"Porky Pies" conversation game

If everyday conversation is a struggle, this simple game can turn the dreaded "How was your day?" into a fascinating guessing game between family members. The name of the game comes from the rhyming slang "Porky Pies," meaning "lies." To play, ask your child to tell you the story of what happened today...with a twist. Your child must include one fib. Your challenge is to listen to the whole story, then guess where the lie might be hiding. Of course, you can play too. You might find that your child has never listened so intently to your daily routine. This game creates the opportunity to listen without judging or interrupting, and you may hear important true stories that would never have come out otherwise.

Exercise #2

Compliment battle

When behavior is a constant battle, it's hard to find a positive moment. This game will focus all your attention on saying kind, positive, silly, and encouraging words. It's also perfect for children who thrive on non-comformity and doing the unexpected. All your child has to do is listen to your barrage of sugary words without smiling. Can he or she listen to your pleasant and encouraging words without cracking a smile? The longer he or she resists, the better the opportunity for sharing every positive thought you can muster! Your child may also try the challenge, saying kind and encouraging things to you while you try to keep a straight face. You can be silly and over-the-top, but always keep a note of sincerity as you pile on the praise.

Exercise #3
Time well spent

To add more memorable, fun, and positive experiences to your family life, you don't have to spend a lot of money. You might be in a rut, with family members glued to electronic devices or running back and forth to lessons. Still, try to expand your repertoire a little once a week with activities that are simply fun and a bit novel. Here are some ideas to get your imagination going: open-ended sensory activities (e.g., playdough or magic sand); exploring the outdoors; building (or smashing!); looking through old photos and videos; movement-based activities (e.g., yoga or dance); science experiments; music; dressing-up board games; puzzles; decorating projects.

Professional support for communication and expectations

If you are looking for more support, or you want to progress more quickly and easily toward your goals, here are some key terms to look for.

- **Trained professionals** who help with building relationships and emotional self-regulation include: family therapists, art therapists, occupational therapists, certified Parent-Child Interaction Therapy (PCIT) therapists.

- **Interventions and treatments** that help with relationship building and emotional self-regulation: Emotion coaching is the term used by Dr. John Gottman to describe how parents can provide a "warm and responsive" environment that helps children to regulate their own emotions. His book *Raising an Emotionally Intelligent Child*,[20] is evidence-based and written to be understood and used by parents. In addition, Mona Delehooke's book *Beyond Behaviors: Using Brain Science to Understand and Solve Children's Behavioral Challenges* offers parents an in-depth look at how emotion can drive behavior, with practical suggestions to help parents become more attuned to a child's emotional state, building connection and calm.[21]

---

20 Gottman, J. (2011) *Raising an Emotionally Intelligent Child*. New York, NY: Simon and Schuster.
21 Delehooke, M. (2020) *Beyond Behaviours: Using Brain Science and Compassion to Understand and Solve Children's Behavioural Challenges*. London: John Murray Press.

CHAPTER 7

Communicating Your Boundaries and Expectations

The importance of boundaries and expectations

Boundaries and expectations are an essential part of parenting. They keep your family safe, they create a sense of security and belonging, and they help your child learn skills such as problem-solving and self-control.

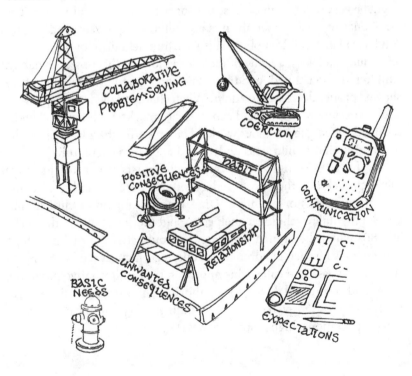

If your boundaries and expectations have been eroded by family conflict, or if you have difficulty keeping track of the family rules from one day to the next, you can use this chapter to orient yourself and to decide where to set your intentions.

If you are not sure which boundaries are worth battling over, or how to respectfully "put your foot down," this chapter will explore how to communicate your expectations and gain more cooperation from your child, without resorting to yelling or harsh punishments.

For children diagnosed with ODD, coping with boundaries and expectations can often be the most obvious struggle. Clear communication and consistent feedback can help to anchor your family as you build skills in other areas.

Where do your expectations come from?

What's your idea of the perfect family? How would you like to make decisions as a family?

Depending on where you were raised, your ideals and aspirations might be very different than those of your parents and grandparents. The traditional approach to family in many cultures is quite straightforward: Adults lead and children obey. This structure held firm for generations, and adults had a wide array of tools for enforcing this power dynamic. Children demonstrated "good breeding" and "good morals" when they showed proper deference to adults. When children failed to comply with adult expectations, they could expect to be smacked, whipped, shamed, secluded, or assigned arduous work. In other words, the adage "Spare the rod, and spoil the child" was understood to be the general rule.

As the 20th century wore on, psychologists began to challenge this approach and they proposed a more cooperative and democratic parenting style. For example, Dr. Diana Baumrind, a clinical and developmental psychologist, helped to shift the status quo in the 1970s and 80s when she argued that parents should strive to maintain high expectations for their children, while offering a high level of warmth and responsiveness.[1] She called this approach the "authoritative parenting style" and contrasted it with the "authoritarian" approach (high expectations, low responsiveness) and the "indulgent" (permissive) approach (low expectations, high responsiveness).

---

1   Darling, N. & Steinberg, L. (1993) Parenting style as context: An integrative model. *Psychological Bulletin*, 113(3), 487.

Authoritarian
Low responsiveness, high expectations

Permissive
High responsiveness, low expectations

Authoritative
High responsiveness, high expectations

Figure 7.1: Parenting styles

Meanwhile, Dr. B. F. Skinner's work on behavior inspired a generation of parents and teachers to look at how to change behavior systematically. Clinicians, teachers, and parents explored "behavior management" techniques, using careful applications of rewards and punishments to shape the behavior of children. Parents were reminded of the importance of the "carrot" (positive behavior management techniques, including praise, tokens, and tangible rewards) and were advised to use the "stick" as sparingly as possible (in milder forms than corporal punishment, such as withdrawing attention and time-outs).

In the space of only a generation or two, the prevailing wisdom went from "seen and not heard" to "catch 'em being good," and parenting methods quickly followed suit.

Meanwhile, another revolution was happening in the field of psychology. Sigmund Freud's theories of psychoanalysis, such as the study of dreams or the importance of the ego, id, and super-ego, started to give way to new perspectives on the "why" of behavior. Other scientific fields added their contribution to the study of child development, and what we now know about childhood behavior has been influenced by fields including (but not limited to) genetics, psychiatry, biochemistry, neurology, occupational therapy, psychotherapy, sociology, and applied behavior analysis.

The result is a cacophony of competing theories and a tangle of cultural norms. Parents in the 21st century now have access to more information than ever, but certainly feel less "wise" than previous generations. Even in the last 20 years alone, theories of attachment, communication, and mental health have changed dramatically.

Collaboration, not compliance

In this chapter, you will get an overview of some techniques that can help you when you are maintaining the "high expectations" of the authoritarian parent. Before you learn how to get "compliance," however, here are some important things to remember.

The goal of parenting is not to gain 100 percent compliance. Your expectations for your children are very personal, and will be shaped by your own preferences, culture, community, abilities, and history. They will also be influenced by your child's gender, age, lifestyle, school, surroundings, culture, abilities, and preferences.

If you are at an impasse with your child regarding a specific expectation, this is a good opportunity to re-evaluate your expectations and consider whether this is a non-negotiable issue or a question that can be approached in a collaborative way.

Questions might include:

- Is my child developmentally ready to meet my expectation?

- Does my child need more help to learn this?

- Is this essential for my child's safety?

- How much of this expectation comes from my own preferences and values?

- Is there a risk of harm if my child does not meet this expectation?

- How much freedom can my child safely handle?

- What responsibilities does my child need to take on?

The question of "What should I expect my child to do?" could fill a whole other book, but ultimately the answer will be up to you and your family to decide together.

In the meantime, you probably have a list of expectations that are important for your child and your family, so this chapter is designed to help you set those expectations and boundaries, with as little drama and struggle as possible. This is not a comprehensive list of techniques and topics for managing behavior but it's a good place to start.

Cooperation, compliance, and expectations

This section contains some general advice for giving instructions and managing your household in a calm and reasonable way. If you follow this advice, your communication will be more effective and you will be able to avoid some common pitfalls.

Clear and respectful communication will take you a long way, but not all of the way, all of the time. If you are able to follow these guidelines and you still find that your child is behaving in an explosive, defiant, or indifferent way, keep reading as other chapters in this book contain advice that addresses some of these issues. Your child may need support in areas such as emotional self-regulation, problem-solving, or motivation. Meanwhile, these behavior basics will build a consistent and calm foundation for you to build on as you learn more about your child.

Back to basics
Your communication style

One of the most important steps in gaining cooperation from your child is simple: Let them know what you want them to do. However, this task can be surprisingly tricky. The words you choose can make all the difference, so here are some proven tips for giving instructions that your child will actually follow:

- **Keep it positive**: Say what you want (not just what you *don't* want). Instead of saying, "Don't sit on the table," try "Sit on your chair, please."

- **Avoid asking**: If you are truly offering a choice, it's fine to ask, "Do you want to...?" However, it's important to make sure your child can clearly hear the difference between an instruction and a request.

- **Keep it gentle**: A harsh tone of voice can invite your child into "fight mode." You can even sweeten it up with an affectionate phrase, like "Hey, pumpkin, it's time to put on your pyjamas." For everyday, non-emergency requests, stay relaxed and friendly.

- **Keep it short**: If you are having trouble gaining your child's cooperation, try shortening your phrases (many parents use so many words that their child's attention has wandered by the time the key words are spoken) or even shortening the task (a brief task will get more cooperation than a long list of things to do).

- **Get up close**: Try to make sure you are in the same room, even within arm's distance, instead of shouting up the stairs. If possible, get down to your child's eye level to give important instructions.

- **Give yourself a runway**: Instead of interrupting a favourite activity by giving an instruction, try to connect with your child first. Show a friendly interest, make a curious comment, and get a sense of what your child is doing at that moment. This will help you figure out a reasonable transition together.

Replace your "stop that" with a "positive opposite"

Dr. Alan Kazdin, a psychologist who worked with families for decades at the Yale Parenting Center, recommends that for every challenging or difficult behavior, parents should describe a "positive opposite."[2]

For example, if you are frustrated because your child yells when asked to wash hands before dinner, then the positive opposite would be: Says "okay" and walks to the sink to wash hands.

You might have some specific parameters in mind (e.g., "with soap" and "dry your hands on the towel") or you might simply be happy when your child walks in the direction of the bathroom without yelling.

If you are having a hard time when your child refuses to clean his or her bedroom, you might define the "positive opposite" with some specific expectations, such as "will clean bedroom at least once a week" or "cleans bedroom when asked." Of course, your definition of a *clean* room might be different from that of your child, so you can try to describe a "clean floor" or "folded clothes" or even just take a photo of the room in its ideal state.

---

2   Kazdin, A. E. (2009) *The Kazdin Method for Parenting the Defiant Child.* New York, NY: Houghton Mifflin.

As you can see, it is important to define the positive opposite for two reasons:

- You'll be able to explain exactly what you are looking for.
- You'll be able to react in an encouraging way when it happens.

What's in it for me?

Very often, a power struggle is the result of a conflict in priorities. You and your child want something different in that moment. Understanding your child's motivation is extremely important. Motivation is covered in more detail in Chapter 9, but for now, we will talk about motivation in general terms. So, what do you do when you're asking your child to do something and they just don't *feel like it*?

Willing compliance versus forced compliance

In the best-case scenario, your child will follow instructions without any overt pressure. Perhaps your child will cooperate because he or she agrees that your expectations are reasonable and necessary. Sometimes your child may agree to go along with your wishes to be considerate to others. This type of "internally motivated" behavior can also be described as "willing compliance." Of course, this kind of reasoning requires the ability to understand long-term consequences and to engage in emotional perspective-taking, so not every child will be ready to operate from this kind of motivation in every case.

If you ask your child to follow a rule on the basis of logic and altruism, and he or she is not able to see your point of view, you may find yourself using tactics that appeal to your child's more immediate concerns. If your child is cooperating in order to gain an immediate reward or avoid a punishment, he or she is responding to external pressure, which could also be described as "forced compliance."

Obviously, your child's "buy-in" is priceless, because willing compliance is more sustainable and requires less pressure and conflict. To build your child's willing compliance, you can prioritize two important factors: *habit* and *relationship*. Still, your child's view of the world will differ from yours, and his or her understanding of health, relationships, safety, and courtesy has a long way to go. As much as you would like your child to be guided by values, morals, and common sense, he or she may be more persuaded by *positive short-term consequences* and *unwanted short-term consequences*, so you will find it advantageous to arrange those consequences in your favor.

However, artificial systems that rely on "forced compliance" should be approached with caution, because they don't always work long-term, and they are only as effective as the consequences that maintain them. At the end of this chapter, you will find a list of resources to help you set up consequences in a way that is healthy and respectful.

How to build "willing compliance"
Provide the "why" of your request

It's usually a good idea to offer a reason, if asked, for the request you are making. If your child agrees with your logic, then you have gained willing compliance and perhaps even cooperation. The most effective rationale is usually one that appeals to your child's short-term interests, or helps your child avoid unpleasant outcomes (e.g., "Please put on a sweater; it's cold outside," or "Use both hands! The device will break if you drop it."). Longer-term goals like "preventing cavities" and "going to a good college" tend to be less persuasive. Even if your child doesn't want to go along with your request, you have still shared some information that might turn out to be useful.

Some children thrive on logic and will happily go along with anything that makes sense. However, these same children may resist cooperating with a request that doesn't seem to have a purely logical basis (e.g., "Why should I say please?" or "How come I have to say thank you if I don't like the present?").

Family habits and routines

Family routines are built on the foundation of a rationale: This is how we all get our needs met. Family routines should be a collaborative effort. Instead of just making a to-do list and posting it on the wall, ask your family members how they prefer to tackle daily tasks, and invite them to come up with ideas to solve common problems. For example, you can ask questions such as: "What kind of activity would you like to do after dinner?" "What shall we do after we get our pyjamas on?" "What can we do on days that you're not feeling hungry?" As you discuss these routines, you can help your children understand the rationale behind them, and invite your children to think about why the rules are the way they are (and what would happen if they were different).

Of course, parents can veto suggestions that are not realistic; but when you invite your family to offer suggestions, you are building "buy-in" and also providing an important opportunity to practice problem-solving skills. Create a poster or a visual to remind everyone that this is what we agreed on. Once you have made a proactive plan, your family is more likely to follow it independently than if you were handing out a new set of expectations each day.

Routines are also helpful because you and your child can plan a chain of events that includes both responsibilities and preferred activities. Skills such as "deferred gratification" and independence are much easier to support when they are embedded in a daily routine.

Relationship-driven cooperation

A warm, affectionate and respectful relationship can make all the difference. When you think of great teachers and employers in your past, do you remember how you felt when they asked you for something? Even if it was hard, you would hop to it, because their approval meant so much. Can you think of a time when your work suffered because of a hostile or indifferent boss? Resentment and frustration in a relationship can also get in the way of cooperation.

A warm, responsive relationship can help to build your child's willing compliance, because when you ask them to follow an instruction, they are more likely to assume that you are setting that requirement because it's necessary or even beneficial for them, and they may eagerly look forward to see how pleased you are.

Consequences that are based on "forced compliance"

When consequences are deliberately arranged to increase compliance, regardless of whether the child agrees, the result is "forced compliance." For some families, "forced compliance" is just considered part of "good parenting." Some adults are taught that the role of parents is to know what is best and to give instructions, and children are expected to comply, no matter what. Some children will tolerate this fairly well and are considered to be "well-behaved." However, there will always be those children who fearlessly throw down the gauntlet to fight for their own goals and priorities. In that case, you have a number of options to try to influence what happens next.

Planned incentives

Planned incentives include rewards, if–then statements, and compensation for tasks completed. Most adults have jobs where payment depends on a defined set of behaviors. Planned incentives can be a reasonable part of your family economy but they do have some limitations. Planned incentives can go wrong if the parent and the child disagree about the definition of success. If the child stops wanting the proposed incentive or finds other ways of getting the incentive, then motivation collapses. Planned incentives can sometimes create additional conflict if the task is not completed but the child is frustrated when the incentive is withheld.

Planned compensation can also be confused with plain old bribery. The key lies in the sequence of events. If you have given your child an instruction, and he or she refuses to cooperate, this is NOT the time to offer compensation or conjure up an appealing offer. This can spiral quickly into a complex bribe negotiation, with parents "upping the ante" every time the child refuses, or children trying to "set terms" in exchange for their cooperation. If there is something to be gained in exchange for cooperation, whether the reward is natural or contrived, be sure to let your child know about it *before* they have a chance to say "no" (e.g., payment for chores).

Punishments and penalties

In previous generations, parents had quite a wide repertoire of consequences on hand to prop up their authority, including belts, switches, spoons, and temporary starvation! Psychological pressure was also common, including shaming, exclusion, and terrifying stories of mythical avengers that would enact punishment upon "naughty" children. These days, parents have a much more limited set of options. Contemporary penalties include "time-outs," planned ignoring, revoked privileges, or loss of tokens or points.

In any case, if your child places a higher value on personal freedom and autonomy than on the privileges you can control, then your attempts at forced compliance are not likely to be very successful. Your child does not need to be sad or fearful in order to learn from an experience. In fact, if your child is agitated or distressed, he or she may completely miss the important lesson you are trying to teach.

Even though mild punishments have been shown to be effective in improving compliance in the short-term, deliberate punishment can also complicate your relationship with your child and even change his or her behavior in unhealthy ways (e.g., children may learn to tolerate punishments or simply get better at not getting caught). Punishment as a means of control often fails for the following reasons:

- When a mild punishment is ineffective, parents may resort to harsher and more damaging forms of punishment.

- To avoid punishment, children may become more skilled at

hiding their lack of compliance or getting access to off-limits items.

- A warm, trusting parent–child relationship may be compromised when parents use tactics that are painful or emotionally cold.

- Punishment alone does not teach new skills.

- Children may resist punishment with increased aggression, self-harm, or escalated forms of rule-breaking.

- Children may attempt to use "forced compliance" with others (resulting in a coercive cycle, which is explored more fully in the following section).

- Children may find it rewarding to be able to provoke you to go through the punishment routine, as a means of capturing your full attention, having an intense and explosive interaction, or even predicting and controlling your behavior.

Some studies show that mild punishment techniques such as "time-outs" are effective in reducing disobedience. However, these tactics can have unwanted short-term side effects, and researchers admit that their long-term impact has not been well understood. Any kind of consequence should be weighed against your child's need for safety and trust. Any kind of punishment should be weighed against the importance of a loving, warm relationship with you.

Habits that support cooperation and willingness
Offering help and support
Your child's motivation is also sensitive to the perceived difficulty of the task. On some days, you may see that your child is tired, easily distracted, or anxious to get on with another activity. Instead of relying on reasoning, rewards, or penalties, you can simply offer a helping hand to gain a quick boost in willingness.

Choice and self-determination
Research shows that people are calmer during painful experiences if they are given some degree of control. If your child has to complete a frustrating task, you may not be able to make the task itself optional but you can offer choices about when, where, and how the task gets completed.

Simplifying

Sometimes your child doesn't have a strong objection to the task itself, but there are just so many other interesting things to do first. Many children diagnosed with ODD also have a diagnosis of ADHD and need help with getting started and getting organized. Pay attention to when you are expecting the task to be completed. Are there plenty of distractions happening around that time? Can you set up the physical space in a way that is less cluttered and confusing?

Meeting important needs

What if you have tried appealing to your child's common sense, altruism, and even the potential of an immediate pay-off or punishment, and you are still completely at odds? In this case, it's important to consider whether all your child's essential needs have been met. When *important needs* (e.g., hunger, sleep, safety, comfort, relief from pain, thirst, etc.) are not satisfied, children are not likely to be wise, patient, flexible, or even reasonable. You may get a different answer if you ask after snack time, so pay close attention to these patterns and try not to ask for cooperation when you know your child's willingness is wearing thin.

Consequences that are not effective

Some attempts at forced compliance fall apart because they are not realistic or even likely. For example, if:

- You make a threat that is virtually impossible to enforce (e.g., "If I catch you kicking the dog again, we're going to give it to another family.").

- You make a threat that no one wants to enforce (e.g., "If you don't go to bed right now, then no television for a week!").

- You make a threat that is in the distant future (e.g., "If you keep teasing your sister, I'm canceling your birthday party.").

- You make additional threats when the first threat is not effective (e.g., "If you don't go to your room like I asked, then I'm taking all your toys.").

- You offer incentives or make threats when children are extremely distressed, angry, or aggressive. Consequences are more likely to be ignored or even be counter productive when children are in a reactive state.

Most of this these mistakes happen when parents are trying to improvise in the moment, when emotions are high. If you find yourself making these kinds of spontaneous threats, you are better off waiting until you are all calm, and talking as a family to come up with reasonable and feasible consequences.

Mild annoyance

Nagging, reminding, hovering, nudging... This type of pressure isn't aggressive or punitive, but it is one way of prompting your child to take action. Simply put, if your annoying behavior stops when your child starts to cooperate, then your child's sense of relief acts as a kind of reward.

However, this tactic can also become an unwelcome burden for you. If your child does not exert him or herself independently and relies on you for constant harassment, you won't have time to do much else. In fact, you may have inadvertently rewarded your child's inaction by providing frequent and lively interactions for as long as he or she refuses to cooperate. Gentle encouragement is going to be necessary at times, but be sure that you are not setting up the expectation that your voice will provide constant background noise.

How to reduce your reliance on "forced compliance"

If your child's "willing compliance" is very limited these days, then you may find yourself relying on "forced compliance" the majority of the time. However, if you are using rewards and punishments just to get your child to go through daily routines such as coming to the table, then wash his or her hands, then put his or her bowl in the sink, your relationship is in danger of becoming overwhelmed by the constant power struggles. Your relationship will grow tense and negative, and you will both start avoiding each other.

If "forced compliance" has become the norm in your household, now would be a good time to review your expectations and make sure your child's basic physical and emotional needs are being met. Are any of your expectations negotiable? Which ones are not strictly necessary? Which expectations could possibly be good candidates for "willing compliance" if your child were given more input, choice, or accommodation?

Strategic responding

There is one more form of consequence that can help to shape your child's behavior, and it does not require a reprimand or a rationale. If you can understand what is driving the behavior or what is rewarding it, you can help your child find a better way to get that "pay-off." It's not always easy to understand what might be motivating the behavior (more on this in Chapter 9), but if you can observe your child's behavior and what seems to be driving it, you can help your child meet that need in a healthier way.

Instead of simply reacting to the "non-compliance" and delivering a penalty, you can look for ways to:

- pre-emptively meet your child's needs

- proactively teach and rehearse replacement behaviors

- limit your reaction to the challenging behavior or limit the potential pay-off.

For example, if you can anticipate that your child might be needing extra comfort and relaxation before starting homework, because he or she usually insists on lying on the couch for 45 minutes after you've asked him or her to get started, you can plan an evening routine that includes some downtime first.

If you can help your child make requests politely (*before* he or she starts yelling or throwing things), then you will be able to respond to your child's legitimate needs before your attention is diverted by colorful language and flying objects.

If you can hear your child's complaints and accusations without arguing or correcting, you can avoid the counterproductive arguments that follow.

An ounce of prevention is worth a pound of cure

When you discuss difficult moments with your family under calmer circumstances, you are less likely to make unreasonable threats or react in a highly emotional way. Even better, you are also giving your child a chance to moderate his or her own behavior and problem-solve ahead of time. When life is calm, you can talk it through without blaming or shaming.

- You can discuss when it is happening, and why (e.g., "It seems like there's been a lot of arguing right after dinner. I wonder what that's about?").

- You can introduce perspective-taking and empathy (e.g., "I bet it felt...for you. How do you think...felt?").

- You can talk about alternatives (e.g., "What would you like me to do instead?" or "It's important for you to get clean, but I see you don't want to take a bath. I wonder if there's another way you could get that dirt off?").

- You can even try to arrange a preventative solution (e.g., "What would happen if you gave a reminder/sat somewhere else/ brought extra...?").

- Plan ahead (e.g., "What are we going to do if our plan doesn't work, and this problem happens again?").

What if the answer is "no"?

If your child's answer to your instruction is "no," it might be helpful to think about how you communicated, and if your expectations and your timing set you both up for success. If you review your approach and you find that you asked the question when your child was very distracted or in the middle of an argument with you, then you may want to attempt a do-over.

Still, there's only so much you can do. When you have built up the relationship, explained the rationale, provided context, and communicated respectfully, your child may still reply with a flat refusal or an "absolutely not." You might not even get a spoken answer at all— just an eye roll or an eerie silence.

Every child is different, so the reason for this refusal will vary. It would be a mistake to classify this response as mere "defiance" and treat it as a symptom to be overcome. After all, you sometimes say "no" to your children or even to your friends and colleagues. You might turn down a request if you are feeling tired, if you're sick, if you're busy, if it's extremely uncomfortable for you, or if it just doesn't seem feasible. Your child's refusal might have a basis in a real concern, so it's worth leaving some room to consider what might be behind it.

Of course, when you turn people down, you have probably learned to say "no" or deflect with tact, and to provide a socially acceptable answer (even when the real answer is "That sounds terrible and I would hate it.").

The talkative "NO"

Your child's refusal might not be so tactful, but you can choose to set that aside if there are other issues to dig into. If your child is willing and able to answer questions at that point, you can open up a conversation, with questions and statements such as:

- "I see. What's going on?"
- "Sounds like you really don't want to. How come?"
- "Can you tell me more about that?"

At this point, your child might provide a clue that he or she is struggling with anxiety, overwhelm, or anger. He or she might also be focused on another goal, or having trouble understanding why your request is important.

The quiet "NO"

If your child is not very talkative but still calm, you can invite a reaction with speculation, offering choices, or even drawing pictures. For instance, instead of repeating the request, offering more reasons, cautioning, persuading, or complaining about the lack of cooperation, you can try saying:

- "I wonder if you are feeling..."
- "Could it be that you don't want to...because...?"

Your guesses don't even have to be correct. If you are wrong, your child may pipe up to correct you. Sometimes it's worth being so wrong that your reluctant child can't resist jumping into the conversation to tell you just how ridiculous you are (and hopefully this will be followed by the correct answer to your question).

The heated "NO"

If your child's refusal is heated, possibly emotionally reactive, or even aggressive, you may need to be patient. You can pause and you can offer empathy but be careful to avoid immediately withdrawing the request or suggesting accommodations as soon as your child shows a sign of emotional upset. This may help to avoid conflict in the short term but it doesn't give your child a chance to learn how to communicate calmly and advocate for himself or herself. Work through the emotional reactivity first, then address the objection afterwards.

Choosing how to respond to refusal

When your child refuses to go along with your plans, you have options: You can insist, you can back off, or you can try to work out a compromise.

As Dr. Diana Baumrind put it, the "authoritarian" parenting style insists and leans upon "forced compliance" most of the time. The "permissive" parenting style avoids conflict, generally speaking. The "authoritative" or "warm and responsive" parenting style is sensitive to the child's needs but comes with high expectations. This approach requires some skilled problem-solving and negotiation, but the result is usually an increase in "willing compliance."

Dr. Ross Greene describes all three options as very valid choices for parents, depending on the situation, in his book *The Explosive Child*.[3] For instance, there will be instructions that are not negotiable. Any rules that relate to safety are rigid for a good reason. Parents must insist that children get some form of schooling and respect others according to the law. On the other end of the spectrum, there are some rules that are meant to be broken. In an effort to pick your battles, you may decide to turn a blind eye to a late bedtime, a snack eaten in the living room, or a carelessly dropped article of clothing. In the centre of this continuum is a gray area, where parents and children do their best to meet in the middle.

Finding a compromise

Navigating these conversations is not easy, especially for parents who tend to rely on forced compliance or avoidance. Dr. Greene's advice is worth reading in its entirety, but before you purchase that book or investigate his website (www.livesinthebalance.org), here is a concise outline of the steps he suggests:

1. **Empathy and listening**: Learn more about what might be standing in the way of your child's willing compliance.

2. **Defining the problem**: Reflect your child's concerns and share your own. This includes setting boundaries and working around real-life limits.

3. **Inviting your child to problem-solve with you**: Listen to your child's suggestions, discuss pros and cons.

---

3   Greene, R. W. (1999) *The Explosive Child: A New Approach for Understanding and Parenting Easily Frustrated, Chronically Inflexible Children*. New York, NY: HarperCollins.

Meeting important needs

If cooperation and communication is a major struggle in your home, the consequences are impossible to ignore. Your child's protests are probably loud, disruptive, and difficult. However, a very noisy behavior can distract you from noticing the quiet but important need hiding behind it. Despite the fact that our children are often very talkative, they sometimes struggle to tell us what they need most.

If you first met your child as a newborn, your first and most important job was to try to interpret those snuffles and cries, and to figure out what your baby needed most. When he or she was tired, it was hard for him or her to eat. When your baby was hungry, it was hard for him or her to sleep. Anticipating those needs became your full-time job, and life was better when you learned to interpret your baby's signals well before he or she was in distress.

As children grow, they learn to express their preferences more clearly. Still, there are times when nothing has changed at all and children need their parent's help to interpret those cries and to provide all the same old things: food, comfort, relief, some fresh air, movement, attention, and love. If your child is still having difficulty anticipating or communicating his or her own needs, then you will need to do some work on this together before working on "compliance" as a goal.

Anticipating and planning for these needs can be a part of your routine-building. Your child's input into this process can be essential, as you provide the time and space for him or her to ask, "What do I really need, and what would be the best way to get it?"

When you find that your child is especially resistant to an instruction, check to see if some of those basic needs are all being met.

- Is your child tired or "hangry" (grumpy due to hunger)?

- Is your child uncomfortable, ill, or in need of movement?

- Does your child feel safe, secure, and loved?

Give yourself time to experiment and observe. If your child is especially resistant to following instructions at a particular time of day, look for what needs you can meet. If you are struggling, give yourself some time to look at the big picture and analyze the situation. For example, if you are often struggling in the hour after school ends, plan some relaxation and snack time before you start giving instructions, and check to see if that helps. It is more important to change an overall *pattern* of behavior than to make sure you "win" every single confrontation.

In fact, the need to "win" every confrontation can develop into a harsh and dangerous pattern known as "coercion." Keep reading to learn more about what happens when parents (or children!) try to use unwanted consequences to force the other person into submission.

Reacting to challenging behavior

When your family is in conflict and your child's behavior is headed off the rails, you might feel compelled to "do something" that will "fix the problem."

For instance, when your child is breaking an important family rule, whether that is trying to get access to an off-limits item, expressing emotions in a rude and hostile way, or doing something that is annoying and offensive, what is your first priority?

- I make sure my child stops as soon as possible.

- I help my child to understand why the important rule is in place.

- I try to let my child know how I'm feeling when that rule is broken.

- I ensure that everyone is safe.

- I need to repair the damage that was done and restore fairness and order.

- I want to make sure my child does not do it again.

- I try to understand why my child broke the rule in the first place.

If you found it hard to pick just one, you are not alone! Each of these priorities seems valid and urgent in that moment, but it's simply impossible to handle them all at once.

So, which one do you choose? If you don't understand why the behavior is happening, it may be hard to prevent it from happening again. If your child doesn't understand the reason for the rule, he or she might not see why you are asking for the behavior to stop. Other people may have been affected or hurt by the behavior, so they might need help too. You obviously care about the safety of your children, and you might feel the need to have someone understand your point of view and how the whole thing makes you feel. Often, a parent's first response is a jumble of all of the above.

Even worse, parents might not even be clear what they are trying to achieve; they simply know they *have to* react.

Rethinking the "consequence"

You may have been told that how you respond in that moment will be the difference between failure and success. You have probably wondered how to avoid rewarding the wrong behavior, how to make the most of learning opportunities, and how to be the kind of smart, disciplined parent that your child needs.

Before you keep reading in search of the "correct" reaction to that challenging behavior, pause for a moment. Remember that when challenging behavior happens, it's just not possible to get your response "right" every time. You might not have all the important information yet. You might not be mentally prepared in that moment. You might be distracted or dealing with your own difficult issues when it happens. This might be an old problem that has been entrenched for a long time, or a brand-new problem you have never seen before. You are not a detective or a psychologist or a psychic. You are an adult who loves your child, and that is enough right now.

Furthermore, even when you do the very best that you can, your response in that moment might not "fix" the problem. Even if you can see exactly what your child needs and how to solve the problem, and you share this information in the sweetest and calmest way, your child may not be ready to hear it. It may take some time for your child to understand what you are saying. The "right" response doesn't always end with a hug and a "thank you" from a humbled child. Even if it takes hours, days, months, or even years to solve a particular problem, that doesn't mean you were not handling it well.

Choosing your priorities

If you do not have a clear goal in mind when you react to challenging behavior, how will you know if you are successful? It's impossible to react, support, educate, repair, analyze, correct, and mete out justice all in the same moment, so here are some suggestions for setting your priorities:

Priority #1: Is everyone safe?

Of course, if someone has been injured or is about to be hurt, you will leap into action and take the appropriate steps, such as providing first-aid or de-escalating the aggression. However, the question of safety can extend a little further if there is no immediate danger.

Your own sense of safety is important. You can check in with yourself, take a breath, and find a measure of calm and confidence before interceding further.

It's also important for your child to feel safe in this moment. Perhaps your child was feeling unsafe before the challenging behavior began, and he or she was reacting in a defensive or unsettled way. Your reassurance and calm presence might help to lower the tension.

Finally, it's vital to consider whether your child will feel safe interacting with you. If your first reaction is to shout, use sharp words, or to become dominating in your body language, your child may have a strong emotional reaction that undermines your other intentions. Without a sense of safety, your child will struggle to listen and learn the lesson you most want to teach. If you see that your child is in fight/flight/freeze mode, some of your other goals (e.g., education, repair, and justice) will not be feasible in that moment, but you can return to them later when the dust settles.

Priority #2: Warmth

"Warm and responsive" parenting in the midst of a conflict can be a very difficult habit to learn. When you are concerned, frustrated, and confused, you might naturally express yourself in a heated or even an icy way. It might take time to learn how to relax your face, lower your tone of voice, and re-train your body to settle into a more supportive posture instead of pacing around the room. The signals you send can make all the difference to a child who is especially emotionally sensitive or "*irritable*." Watch out for words and actions that send a message of rejection, disdain, or hostility. You may have some excellent insights, important lessons, key strategies, and solutions to share, but all of this great stuff will be wasted if your child forgets that you are on his or her team. Remind your child that you are on his or her team in any way you can. Even as you are setting limits and reminding your child of the rules, use kind words. Approach calmly and stay at a comfortable distance for both of you. Dig up some empathy. Remember that this is temporary and you will all come through it together.

Priority #3: How can we all get our needs met?

There's one more thing that might be standing in the way of gaining your child's cooperation or offering a valuable life lesson: Your child's challenging behavior might be expressing a need. The behavior might be a misguided attempt to meet the need, or it could just be a source of stress that is contributing to your child's *irritable* or disruptive behavior. If your child is struggling with an unmet need, he or she probably won't be receptive to much sage advice; but once you do understand what that need is, you can work together to find a more appropriate way to meet that need. Ideally, you will want to figure out what that need is before trying to give guidance.

How do you know if your child needs something in that moment? Sometimes you can find out by listening. Perhaps your child is expressing a need clearly but in an inappropriate way. If your child is not aware of being hungry, tired, thirsty, lonely, anxious, needing the bathroom, or just restless after sitting still for too long, he or she may not be able to ask. In that case, you may have to inquire or observe and put together the pieces yourself.

In the meantime, everyone else in the family has needs, too. You may need to get to work in that moment or keep things quiet so other people in the family can sleep. You all need to be able to eat, rest, feel safe, play, and live. Your reaction will have to take into account all of that, too. As your child gets older and more mature, he or she will be able to participate in that kind of discussion and help to figure out how everyone can get their needs met. In other words: "What do we all need to be doing right now?" In the meantime, you will be modeling that question and problem-solving as best you can.

Priority #4: What about next time?

Is it possible for you to respond in a way that helps things turn out better next time? Of course, you will naturally look around for the logical consequence that "teaches a lesson." For some children, an unpleasant outcome or a logical consequence can become a learning experience. They will remember and try to "do better" next time in order to avoid that situation again. However, research shows that children diagnosed with ODD often struggle to change their behavior in response to unpleasant consequences, or to adjust based on past experiences.[4] Instead, they continue to struggle. They repeat the same mistake again and again, and they suffer the same painful outcomes.

As a parent, of course you want to do something to make life better and easier in the future. You want to be able to worry less, trust more, and move on. When it comes to changing behavior for the next time, your immediate reaction is important but it's not the whole story. Keeping everyone safe, staying emotionally "warm," and meeting

---

4   Humphreys, K. L., & Lee, S. S. (2011) 'Risk taking and sensitivity to punishment in children with ADHD, ODD, ADHD+ ODD, and controls.' *Journal of Psychopathology and Behavioral Assessment, 33*(3), 299–307.

everyone's needs will help set the stage for the three keys to proactive behavior change. Remember, not all of this must be done immediately. When everyone is calm again, you can work on setting your child up for success by:

1. **Finding the positive opposite**: Does your child know what could have prevented or replaced the mistake? What would you have liked your child to do instead? What preparations or situations would make that more likely? What kind of practice would be helpful? Is there more work to do in understanding your child's needs and how to meet them?

2. **Information and education**: Can you help your child understand why a particular behavior needs to change? Can you understand the situation from your child's point of view? Is it possible for your child to advocate for himself or herself and communicate with other people to prevent a similar problem in the future?

3. **Clearly communicating consequences**: A mild, predictable consequence can't do all the heavy lifting, and it is no substitute for the hard work of relationship-building and skill-development; but if your child is able to remember the rule and put on the brakes in time, a planned consequence can have a helpful preventative influence. After all, sports referees rely on their yellow and red cards to discourage players from breaking the rules, but this type of penalizing must be used sparingly and only when the infraction is an obvious departure from the agreed-upon regulations.

Note: If you find that you have been consistent in giving those reminders, then carrying out those consequences as agreed, but your child continues to make the same mistake, it's time to re-evaluate. Some children do not learn well from consequences, because they haven't yet learned how to stop themselves from making the mistake, or the consequences don't factor into their decision-making at all. In fact, these struggles are a major part of why some children are considered "oppositional" and "defiant." If they *could* learn the hard way, they probably would have done so already. Consequences are a natural part of life, but over-punishing your child can hurt your relationship with your child; and if it's not effective in changing behavior, it's certainly not worthwhile.

You will find more information on proactive behavior change

strategies in Chapter 8. Meanwhile, although this section cannot possibly offer a suitable reaction to every type of challenging behavior, here is one final battle-tested piece of advice:

Get more by doing less

There will be times where your child's minor misbehavior is getting on your nerves. He or she might be complaining, criticizing you, wasting time, or flouting the rules in creative ways.

Even worse, your attempts to correct that behavior might be counterproductive. When you say, "Please don't do that," or "How could you say that?", the behavior only escalates. The longer you stand there and argue, defend yourself, correct your child's attitude, or explain why you don't deserve such treatment, the further into the quicksand you sink.

You may be reasonable, and you may be correct, but sometimes the wisest course of action is to say very little. Bickering doesn't serve your purpose. Perhaps your child is in a bad mood, has been having nightmares, is struggling with a headache, or is being bullied at school. Maybe the argument is part of your child's attempt to create a distraction, provoke a parental meltdown, or just drag out a conversation long enough to avoid (or delay) an unwanted task.

If you recognize this pattern and you see yourself getting embroiled in pointless verbal battles, commit to *saying less*. Stay on topic. Be polite but be brief. Learn the subtle art of humorous deflection. Change the subject. Save the rhetoric and debate practice for a worthy topic; just smile instead.

The coercive cycle

Contrary to popular belief, ODD is not "caused" by lazy parenting.

In fact, the relationship between parenting style and child behavior is complicated, but researchers have found that harsh and controlling parents are more likely to have children who display oppositional and defiant behavior at a young age.[5]

Of course, the relationship between harsh parenting and oppositional behavior goes both ways; as you can imagine, parents may respond to children who are hard to manage by becoming more harsh and

---

5   Smith, J. D., Dishion, T. J., Shaw, D. S., Wilson, M. N., Winter, C. C. & Patterson, G. R. (2014) Coercive family process and early-onset conduct problems from age 2 to school entry. *Development and Psychopathology, 26*(4pt1), 917–932.

controlling. However, the role of parents seems to be key in influencing the level of disruptive behavior, and much depends on how they solve conflict at home.

When family conflict is routinely handled in a harsh, negative, and unpredictable way, a cycle can start to build, and this relationship between the parent and child behavior is known as "Coercion Theory."

Coercion theory (Patterson, 1982) describes a process of mutual reinforcement during which caregivers inadvertently reinforce children's difficult behaviors, which in turn elicits caregiver negativity, and so on, until the interaction is discontinued when one of the participants "wins."[6]

What is coercion?

Coercion[7] is defined as "the simple use of aversive behavior to win a conflict."[8] "Aversive behavior" just means something you find unpleasant. In some cases, your child's behaviour might fit the definition of "coercive." If you are a parent, you will easily be able to list the kinds of behavior you would rather avoid: glaring, talking back, slamming doors, stealing, lying, cheating, throwing things, running away, hitting, pinching, name-calling, self-injury, ignoring...and some behavior you never even imagined until it happened in front of you, in your own living room.

Coercive behavior can be as mild as whining and pestering, or it can be dangerous and harmful. The type of behavior in this pattern is not as important as *how it is used*.

"To win a conflict" is also quite easy to for parents to define. Children and their parents come into conflict many times each day. Sometimes these conflicts begin when the alarm clock goes off and the child refuses to get out of bed. Battles can be waged over whether or not to eat candy for breakfast, what to wear (and when to get dressed), how to speak to other family members, how to treat the family pet, when to leave for school, who will carry the backpack, who will pick

---

6   Smith, J. D., Dishion, T. J., Shaw, D. S., Wilson, M. N., Winter, C. C. & Patterson, G. R. (2014) Coercive family process and early-onset conduct problems from age 2 to school entry. *Development and Psychopathology, 26*(4pt1), 917–932.

7   Dishion, T. J., Patterson, G. R. & Kavanagh, K. A. (1992) An Experimental Test of the Coercion Model: Linking Theory, Measurement, and Intervention. In J. McCord & R. Tremblay (Eds.) *Preventing Antisocial Behavior: Interventions from Birth through Adolescence.* New York, NY: Guilford Press.

8   Patterson. G. R. (2016) Coercion Theory: The Study of Change. In T. J. Dishion & J. Synder (Eds.) *The Oxford Handbook of Coercive Relationship Dynamics.* Oxford: Oxford University Press.

that towel up off the floor or put the cereal away...and that's just the first few hours of the day.

When a child discovers that a parent backs off from his or her demand to complete an annoying task when he or she screams and kicks, or when the biggest bribes are offered when he or she refuses to cooperate and covers his or her ears, then coercion starts to become the easiest and fastest method for a child to get his or her "own way."

What is the purpose of coercion?

Coercion is usually used to:

- avoid an unwanted task
- escape an uncomfortable situation
- gain access to a preferred object
- enforce a position of control over others.

Essentially, coercion is a one-sided way of problem-solving. Threats, intimidation, and harassment are all coercive ways for a person to get his or her own way. In a nutshell: "Do it my way OR ELSE." "I'm going to keep hassling you until you OBEY."

How children learn the habit of coercion

Coercion usually starts with a power struggle. A parent says, "Do it," and a child says, "I won't." A child says, "Give it to me," and a parent says, "Not right now." It ends when the child's behavior is so unpleasant that the parent backs off and says, "Never mind. Have it your way. Here you go."

Why does this happen? Good parenting seems simple in theory, right? Parents are told to be consistent and to follow through with their demands. At the same time, parents are told not to be physically forceful. So, how do you compel a child to clean up the milk he or she has spilled? How do you prevent a child from swearing at his or her father? Can you really make a child put on a pair of shoes when he or she is refusing with all his or her might? You can make threats or remove privileges but what do you do when a child simply says, "I don't care. Go ahead."

Parents also have responsibilities for so many other parts of life, such as keeping the house quiet so that the baby can sleep, avoiding too much noise from the living room so the landlord doesn't complain, or just getting to school on time. There are always pressures that limit the amount of time and energy that can be spent on "winning" a conflict.

It's inevitable that sometimes parents just say, "Fine, have it your way," because in that moment, they may have no other choice. There isn't enough time, there's no practical way, or there are other people who just want the situation to be over and done with. This is a natural part of life, but when it comes a habit, then the cycle of coercion starts to set in.

Why do parents give in?
It's just not a "fair fight"

Although parents seem to have plenty of advantages when it comes to size, experience, money, and physical strength, children do have some leverage. In addition to simple refusal, children have no *legal reason* why they should not hit, scream, tear up papers, throw toys, or swing objects against the walls. They can, technically, bite, bury your wallet in the back yard, or hold your grandmother's vase out the window.

They also have all the time in the world. Children may not mind if you are late for work, if it's long past bedtime, or if it's been 45 minutes of non-stop yelling. They don't have to wash the dishes or get up early tomorrow. They can hold out for as long as they can stand it.

Emotional and physical pressures

Conflict is stressful, generally speaking. Parents also cope with a lot of stress in other areas, including work, marriage, physical health, and mental health, so when they are extra-motivated to avoid yet another struggle, then it is very hard for them to maintain a strong disciplinary position.

Emotional stress can also put extra pressure on an adult in the middle of a power struggle. The sound of a child crying can be very upsetting, and naturally parents (and grandparents or other caregivers) simply love their children and want to avoid seeing them unhappy. The words "You don't care about me!" can send them running. When parents have strong cultural beliefs about the importance of a child's happiness, or difficult childhood memories of their own start to surface, they may scramble to stop their child's protests. Parents who were raised in an overly strict or deprived environment can find it hard to say "no" to their own children, in response to the suffering they experienced in their own childhoods.

Parents may also experience fear and panic as a conflict escalates. This is especially true for parents who have a history of abuse or trauma. Even a small child can inflict pain on an adult, and as children get older, they may become physically strong enough to dominate or menace their parents.

Parents who are ill or physically disabled are also at a disadvantage in a power struggle with their children, because they may find it exhausting or impossible to "put up a fight."

The growth of a coercive pattern

When parents try to set boundaries but then fold and retreat because of fear, exhaustion, or emotional distress, kids learn that power struggles can be "won" by being the loudest or the scariest person in the room. Of course, parents will push back against this type of behavior whenever possible and look for safe, legal ways to encourage cooperation and enforce boundaries. When this push-back is successful, the child's pressure tactics don't work and they fall into disuse. That's the ideal scenario.

However, reality can be more complicated. Sometimes, difficult behaviors pop up again after a while (behavior analysts call this "spontaneous recovery"). These moments can catch you off-guard and set you right back at the starting line (or worse), depending on how you handle them.

Here's an example. Suppose your child has been asking to watch television before dinner, and you have stood your ground, night after night. You dodged the arguments, and tuned out the grumbling, whining, and moaning. Then one night, dinner is late. Everyone is tired and fed up, and your child comes to you with a request: "Please can I watch a show before dinner?"

At first, you say "no." You stick to the plan. However, your child is very tired, very hungry, and apparently very optimistic, so he stands there, repeating the request. You continue to refuse. He gets louder. He gets angrier. Then he shouts, "I'm NOT eating dinner! I'm NEVER eating anything you make! You're THE WORST!"

Then you hear your partner call from the living room: "Just give him the show."

Defeated, you sigh and mumble, "Okay, just go." The drama subsides. Your child scurries out of the room, and switches on the television.

In the short term, you've been given some relief from the hassle, and you can focus your attention on getting dinner on the table. Your partner no longer has to listen to the whinging and carrying-on. In a sense, you've been "rewarded" by agreeing to the demand after the conflict escalated. Of course, your child might conclude that he has achieved his goal as well.

Now take a look at this story and notice exactly which behaviors were rewarded, and which ones were not rewarded. This pattern will give you a glimpse of the kind of behavior you can expect next time.

- Your child's first and second polite requests were not rewarded (*no TV was given*).

- Your refusal was not rewarded (*the pestering continued*).

- Your child's loud threats were rewarded (*the TV was finally given*).

- Your partner's reversal was rewarded (*the escalation stopped, you felt relieved*).

When a parent tries to resist but then gives in to the child's demands just at the moment that the behavior is getting more intense, the child learns that more drama yields better results, and he or she is more likely to use that tactic next time.

This is a mild example of coercion, but take a look at the pattern and consider how this could get worse over time. If your partner learned to ignore the yelling, your child might try making a more serious threat, or throw a plate across the room. This type of frightening display would certainly cross your mind the next time your child asks for television, so you would understandably agree to the first polite request "to avoid a fight."

As a general rule of purposeful behavior, people tend to do what "works" and they don't waste time doing pointless things. If your child's polite requests proved ineffective, he or she might skip directly to the yelling next time. Similarly, if your attempts to refuse didn't work, you might be inclined to just give up and save yourself the drama.

How coercion escalates, and keeps escalating

But what if you didn't give in? Unfortunately, this isn't the end of the story. When a particular behavior "works" for your child, you're likely to see it again. That is what behavior scientists call the "principle of reinforcement." What happens when the behavior stops working?

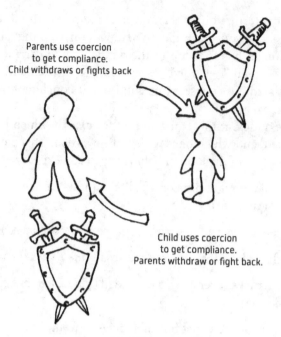

Parents use coercion
to get compliance.
Child withdraws or fights back

Child uses coercion
to get compliance.
Parents withdraw or fight back.

Figure 7.2: The coercive cycle

To understand the behavior pattern that comes next, think about how you might interact with an object that stops working. For example, imagine a well-used drawer in your kitchen. When you pull on it, it usually opens. Suppose, one day, you pull on this drawer, and it sticks. It won't open. What do you do? If you are like most people, you pull harder. If that doesn't work, you slam it shut and then pull harder still. You put your fingers in the gap and push items around, then try again. You persist. This escalation is what behavior scientists call an "extinction burst." When your first attempt didn't work, you tried harder.

Now let's go back to the example of your child and the television show. When asking politely didn't work, your child asked *harder*. Next time, if you ignore the yelling and threatening, your child may find a more intense way of getting the message across (e.g., knocking a chair over). Once a behavior "works," it is hard to get rid of, and it may get worse before it gets better.

Why coercion persists

There are two important reasons why your child may attempt to use coercive patterns with you.

The first is simple: People keep doing what works, and they do less of what doesn't work. Behavior patterns change. So, the next time you pull on that sticky drawer, you might pull much harder than usual, just in case. The next time your child asks you for something, he or she might spend less time politely pleading and more time yelling, assuming that's what has worked in the past. People in general are just efficient that way. When the parent tries to stand firm, the child pushes harder. When the parent backs off, the child learns that this strategy can be successful, and will try just as hard next time. Over time, an unpredictable mix of standing firm and backing off can actually shape a child's behavior into a more persistent, more aggressive coercive pattern.

There is a second possible reason for persistent coercive behavior and it goes beyond simple power struggles. If your child's attempts at coercion have not been very successful, but you are still seeing threats and aggression, it may be that your child still has not found a way to meet an important need, or has not learned how to ask for your help in a clear and appropriate way.

Not all conflict is coercion

It's important for parents to understand how coercion works and to see when this pattern might be starting to develop. Consistent boundaries and rules can help to prevent or stop coercive behavior from happening. However, it's also important to notice that not all conflict is about coercion. Many parents mistakenly assume that all disruptive, aggressive, or persistent behavior is an attempt to use "aversive behavior to win a conflict."

If you have been successful in maintaining a very predictable boundary, and the answer has always been "I meant what I said," then your child may still have a big emotional reaction when he or she hears the words "No, that's not available." Contrary to what you may be told by a well-meaning neighbor or teacher, being a consistent parent does not guarantee that your child will cope well or follow the rules you have set in place.

What if parents are consistent but kids are still explosive and disruptive when told "no"?

For children diagnosed with ODD, the word "no" can be the trigger for behavior that is exasperating at best, and explosive at worst. Why do some children accept being told "no" and other children melt down on the spot? Hearing the word "no" can present a number of different challenges.

Coping with disappointment

Dealing with disappointment requires emotional coping skills, such as inhibition (putting the brakes on an impulsive first reaction), perspective-taking (considering whether the problem could be solved in another way, analyzing the benefits and costs of pushing the matter any further), and self-talk (reminding himself or herself that it's okay, saying comforting statements like "maybe later").

Lack of perspective-taking, low trust

If your child is already feeling *irritable* or struggling with difficult emotional challenges related to low self-esteem or insecure attachment, hearing the word "no" can spark a conflict that extends far beyond the simple disagreement. If you have heard a child exclaim, "You don't care about me," or "I NEVER get to do anything!", then this simple request denied may be triggering some insecurity about a much bigger struggle.

Disruption and confusion

When a child has a plan or a dream, the word "no" could mean having to scrap the plan and start over. Thinking up a new plan requires problem-solving skills. If your child has a hard time switching from one idea to another, or being flexible, then this kind of cognitive stress may lead to a big emotional reaction. What seems to be a minor setback to you can feel like the end of the world to a child who doesn't know how to come up with a better plan or how to stay calm long enough to think it through.

If you have set up firm rules or boundaries, and your child is regularly pushing against them, throwing tantrums or having meltdowns, then he or she might be struggling with:

- attention-switching—looking at a situation from a new perspective

- problem-solving, or finding an acceptable alternative

- planning, managing time, and understanding sequences

- emotional self-regulation and coping with frustration and disappointment.

You will find more information on these skills and abilities throughout the book, especially in the Chapters 6 and 8. In the meantime, hang on for another moment and learn about the rest of the coercive cycle...

How parents learn the habit of coercion

Coercion is rarely a one-way street. It is a cycle that repeats across generations, in classrooms, in courtrooms, and in workplaces. Many parents experience coercion from their own parents as they grow up, and they acquire a set of expectations about what it means to be an adult:

- Adults have authority, which gives them the right to decide what's best for children.

- Adults can expect to be respected and obeyed by the younger generation.

- Adults have a responsibility to control the behavior of the younger generation.

These expectations may be a little "old-fashioned" in some cultures, but more traditional communities still place a high value on the role of the parent as an infallible leader within the home, for better or for worse. For some families, this structure works well, especially when children and parents have strong positive relationships, and when children can adapt to the expectations placed upon them.

Meanwhile, outside the home, the cultural norms of how children are expected to behave have shifted away from simply obedience and compliance. In books and entertainment media, children are depicted as independent and unique. In schools, children are asked to share their opinions and make choices about what they would like to do. The rebel is celebrated, and the self-advocate is heard.

When parents and children confront this cultural divide, both sides are convinced of their own values, and both sides go to great lengths to "win."

Parents and power struggles

Here's some parental advice from a parent on an online forum, in response to a question about destructive and disrespectful behavior: "Take every last thing away from him. Make him earn stuff back. He must ask permission to do anything or eat any snacks or watch tv or anything. Prison-like setting."

Technically, this fits the definition of "coercion." Severe forms of coercion could also include spanking, threatening physical punishment, or physical intimidation. The message is simple: "OBEY, OR ELSE."

When parents and children are locked into a power struggle, both sides try all kinds of common strategies to "win." Some milder ways to get the upper hand include yelling, criticizing, threatening to remove privileges, or even an extended silent treatment.

Parent communication and the Jekyll-and-Hyde effect

Often, these coercive tactics, whether mild or severe, are not planned in advance. Many parents start out each day with the best of intentions and the sweetest of voices.

At first, they make a polite request. A friendly reminder. "It's time to go, sweetie." The child carries on, apparently ignoring or unaware. The parent tries calling out with a little more volume and urgency. "Hey, this is important. I need you to turn that off and get your shoes on." Still no response. Finally, the parent slams a door, stomps into the middle of the room, and bellows, "IT'S TIME TO GO! GET YOUR SHOES ON OR I'M TAKING AWAY YOUR BIKE FOR A WEEK!"

This kind of reaction is partly an expression of frustration but also an attempt to find some kind of leverage. Nothing else "worked," so the conflict escalated. This pattern, when repeated over and over, can steadily shape a parent's behavior, so eventually there is no attempt to be gentle or polite at all. When the most intense pressure on the child is the only thing that "works," then parents will find it easier to default to more and more intense and intrusive strategies.

Eventually, parents say things like "I tried asking nicely, but she only listens when I yell!" or "He just ignores me until I threaten to take away his X-Box," and they are accurately describing a learned pattern of behavior.

The coercive cycle: How parents and children teach each other

When parents are struggling to understand and respond to a challenging or defiant child, they may resort to what they learned from their own parents as they grew up. For adults who grew up in authoritarian or highly coercive homes, that means laying down the law and being prepared to defend it by any means necessary. If one type of enforcement doesn't get a result, parents may reach for more and more intense forms of control and punishment, in the hope that a bigger reaction will yield a bigger result.

Research shows that some families are at increased risk of coercive cycles if parents have:

- learned patterns of behavior (raised in an abusive household)
- a history of criminality, drug and alcohol abuse
- a brain difference associated with lack of inhibition (e.g., ADHD)
- limited self-regulation skills—a tendency to be reactive and easily upset
- a lack of interpersonal skills (e.g., expectation of 100% obedience).

Parents often justify this escalation because they cannot see an effective alternative, and they fear that if they do not act, there will be even worse consequences. For example, a parent may use more and more intense forms of punishment or pressure because they hold beliefs such as:

- I can't allow him/her to grow up to be an abuser.
- I can't allow myself to be abused.
- I need to get this child under control.
- He/she needs to learn that he/she can't get away with this.
- Give 'em an inch and they'll take a mile.
- Kids need to learn to respect their elders.

Risk factors in the development of coercive cycles

Researchers studying families with oppositional and defiant behavior have pointed out three key factors that work together to foster a pattern of conflict and stress:

1. Parents' reactivity versus self-regulation.
2. Child's reactivity versus self-regulation.
3. Learned behavior where aggression, refusal or withdrawing gets desired results.

The more *irritable* or rigid your child is, the more likely it is that you will be stressed and snappish, and the higher the probability that conflict will end in frustration and yelling.

The more stressed and reactive you are, the more likely it is that your child will be *irritable* and uncooperative, and the conflict could easily end in you giving in or giving up.

The longer you live in this pattern, the more stressed you are, and the more stressed your child will become, and the cycle begins all over again.

This book touches on all of these three factors. If your own emotional self-regulation is a major struggle for you, please see Chapter 5 to find resources and coping strategies. If your child's emotional self-regulation is the most urgent need, you will learn how to build those skills in Chapter 6.

How punishment backfires

Unfortunately, research has shown that when the intensity of punishment grows, it does not become more effective in influencing behavior. In fact, punishment and other coercive tactics backfire in some very important ways:

- Children learn to ignore or adapt to the unpleasant consequence.

- Frequent punishment interferes with positive relationships and damages them over time.

- Children observe and learn to use the same techniques on their parents or on other children.

Risks of using coercive parenting tactics

When both parents and children are using coercion as a tool to control the other, the pressure to "win" a conflict can create a dangerous cycle of escalation. If a parent "wins" by yelling, threatening, pressuring, physically menacing, or causing pain to the child, then the parent is likely to continue this pattern of behavior in the future, because it was "successful."

If a child "wins" the conflict by resisting parental control, by engaging in "aversive" behavior such as spitting, kicking, screaming, running away, ignoring, lying, or simply refusing, then the child is likely to continue this pattern of behavior, because it was "successful."

Most families will interact this way occasionally, but there is a cost to using coercion; research has shown that over time, coercive parenting styles do have a negative impact on children's physical, emotional, and social development, and their relationship to their caregivers.

If children cannot avoid unwanted consequences by improving their own behavior, they may learn to resist or avoid their parents' coercive control. At this point, the interactions between parents and children are especially toxic. Children may insist that they are immune to their parents' disapproval, and smile when parents frown. They ignore warnings, and shrug when parents take away privileges. They shout, "I don't care!" and "Go ahead!" They crave freedom, even if it comes at the cost of harsh punishments and troubled family relationships.

As the cycle continues to perpetuate, children also learn to imitate the types of pressure and coercion they see in the home. They begin to issue their own warnings and deal out their own "punishments." The phrase "That's what you get when you don't listen" gets applied equally to parents as it was with children.

Unfortunately, in the cycle of coercion, there is a logic to this behavior. Children resist and protest, and parents who do not yield may shift from mild to more severe punishments, each side working to find the most effective form of pressure. In turn, children look for ways to escape the cycle, even as they act out the same coercive attempts to control with their friends, teachers, and siblings.

Breaking the cycle of coercion

Fortunately, there are alternatives for both parents and children. Parents do not need to subscribe to a policy of either "compliance at any cost" or "anything goes" in order to maintain an orderly household. Children do not need to be perfectly pliant or wise beyond their years to get along peacefully in a family dynamic.

Important skills that support non-coercive problem-solving

In order to handle conflict without resorting to coercion, both parents and children need a strong set of self-regulatory skills. Problem-solving calls for self-control, emotional self-regulation, and communication.

Joint problem-solving also requires adults to lead by example and to demonstrate significant emotional coping skills and cognitive flexibility. Children who have long relied on emotional outbursts to convince others to comply can be taught to plan ahead and work out a preventative solution when they are best able to think calmly and logically.

Emotional coping skills and cognitive flexibility can be hard work, but the positive results that follow are undeniably worthwhile. While coercion erodes trust, problem-solving builds empathy. When parents commit to undoing their own coercive training and setting a better example for their children, they set their children on a healthier path to becoming considerate adults, loving partners, and supportive parents.

How do families escape a coercive cycle?

If parents experience feelings of guilt or shame after using these heavy-handed techniques, if the relationship between parents and children becomes strained, or if friends and community members report concern and disapproval, then parents will be more likely to look for training and support to avoid repeating the pattern.

Unfortunately, children who use aversive behavior to "win" may not find it as easy to change their patterns of behavior. If they have learned that coercion "works" some of the time, and they have witnessed coercive behavior modeled by parents, teachers, or peers, then this pattern is hard to "unlearn." In addition to the pattern of learned behavior over thousands of interactions, children simply have a harder time coming up with another approach. Children have more difficulty using the cognitive strategies, self-regulation, logic, perspective-taking, and empathy required to work through interpersonal conflicts. Meanwhile, this type of behavior is also likely to result in more unwanted reactions and rejections from parents, teachers, siblings, and friends.

Attitudinal barriers to cooperation

By the time a child has been given a diagnosis of ODD, it is likely that this child has had many, many opportunities to "disobey." There may have been some missing skills or disrupted relationships that contributed to those transgressions in the first place, but when a child experiences a long history of ineffective disciplinary effects, he or she can develop a real philosophical resistance to the very idea of "obedience."

You're not the boss of me

As children grow, they must inevitably seek out opportunities for independence and choice. It's how they learn, and it's how they will develop the skills to take care of themselves one day in the future. As children mature, they negotiate more freedom for themselves, and parents must gradually concede their control. In the meantime, however, parental leadership in the home is necessary, and most children will accept it or even appreciate it as a condition of being safe and cared for.

When children refuse to accept adults as leaders, they may be holding some misconceptions about what it means to be led, missing the link between leadership and sacrifice, or lacking a positive history with accepting authority.

Loss of trust in authority

Sometimes a child's belief system reflects a lack of trust in adult leadership. If a child sincerely believes that "parents are bossy," "parents are selfish," or "parents don't keep promises," then of course there is no incentive to cooperate or recognize adult boundaries and expectations.

If a child cannot understand the rationale for a boundary and does not assume that parents have his or her best intentions at heart, then any cooperation provides "material comfort to the enemy" and should be avoided.

If you have heard your child express these attitudes, you might be understandably hurt and offended. Children cannot possibly understand the sacrifices you make on their behalf every day, so their gratitude cannot be expected. Instead, take the time to listen and find out more. Ask for examples and make apologies if necessary.

You may find that trust regrows as you rebuild a positive relationship, set a gentle example, and spend more time calmly discussing the rationale for the boundaries you set. Proactively inviting your child to help set the rules can also give your child a sense of ownership, and an appreciation for how difficult it can be to set boundaries that work for the whole family.

Rigid understanding of freedom

If your child has developed an inflexible idea of what it means to be free, then you may see him or her refusing to make concessions or to follow rules, simply on principle. Guiding your tiny libertarian can be challenging, as long as he or she believes:

- Any compromise is a defeat.

- Obedience means losing power.

- Defiance is self-determination.

- Rebellion offers opportunity.

Children are naturally self-centred and shortsighted in their judgments, so this kind of attitude may take time before it evolves into a philosophy that recognizes the good of all, the importance of compromise, or the joy of teamwork. Children who struggle with social perspective-taking are especially vulnerable to this kind of individualism, because they simply cannot put themselves in your shoes.

Your child may always be independent at heart, but your work in the meantime is to help your child experience the benefits of belonging to a team, and altruistically helping the community.

Communicating boundaries and expectations: Self-assessment

QUESTIONS FOR REFLECTION

- How often do you rely on forced compliance?

- What kind of strategies do you use to try to get compliance and cooperation?

- When you react to challenging behavior, are you following a consistent plan or are you improvising?

- Have you ever tried to use punishment and seen it backfire unexpectedly?

ESSENTIAL SKILLS

- I can give instructions simply and gently.

- I review my expectations to make sure they match my child's needs and abilities.

- I make sure to get my child's attention before giving an instruction.

- Our daily routines ensure that my child's basic needs are met (rest, food, water, safety, sleep, movement, belonging).

- I can stay consistent with rules and consequences, even if my child is persistent or highly emotional.

- I can maintain expectations and get cooperation without harsh punishments, constant negotiation, or bribery.

PRIORITY QUIZ

Is communicating boundaries and expectations a priority for your family? If you agree with three or more of the following statements, then learning how to clearly communicate boundaries and expectations will help you avoid some unhealthy patterns.

- When my child starts to argue or threaten others, I give up. It's not worth the fight.

- My child doesn't really listen unless I get in his or her face.

- Our family doesn't have much of a routine. I have to nag and threaten to get anything done.

- I think my child actually enjoys provoking me.

- I avoid asking my child to do anything, because it leads to so many arguments.

Where can I find help with communicating boundaries and expectations?

STRATEGIES TO TRY AT HOME

Exercise #1

The law of the land

Every family has its own values and norms, including lists of "Thou shalts" and "Thou shalt nots." When you are trying to communicate expectations in the heat of the moment, it can be hard to express them calmly. If you create a poster or similar visual reminder, every member of the family can access a proactive and positive reminder of what kind of behavior is expected.

To set rules, choose your top three priorities as a family. If you can express these rules in a positive way, and in a way that everyone can follow, then you are giving everyone a clear, fair goal to reach for. For example, "We make sure everyone is safe" is a general rule that is phrased in a positive way, and the rule can be followed by every family member. "No screaming" is not a good example, because it doesn't illustrate what family members should do instead. "Don't be bossy" is not a good example, because it wouldn't be easy for parents to follow. Once you have articulated these goals, design a colourful poster to put on the wall.

Exercise #2

The "Bug Book"

Children diagnosed with ODD are often angry, frustrated, and not very cooperative. When this happens many times a day, it can be very hard for parents to think back and remember exactly what happened, how they responded, and what could be improved next time.

The "Bug Book" technique can help parents to track outbursts, react with patience and kindness, and look for patterns. After all, if you are busy asking questions and writing down your observations, you are less likely to jump to conclusions or get carried away by emotion.

To create your own "Bug Book," use a notebook or even a writing app, and title it "What's Bugging You?" Whenever you notice a frustrating moment, write down what might be "bugging" your child. For example, it could be a conflict with a sibling, or an unexpected noise. Was the "bug" small, medium, or large? Then, as you try to help your child recover, make a note of what worked and what didn't.

At the end of the day, you can look back and get a good sense of where you were successful, and try the same tactics again tomorrow. You can check to see if certain problems are coming up over and over again, and focus your efforts on solving that particular puzzle. Memory is unreliable, so just looking at the information with fresh eyes can be extremely helpful.

Exercise #3:
Family routines and rituals

A routine doesn't have to be a boring to-do list. It can be a familiar, comforting way of meeting everyone's needs. What routines are most important and enjoyable in your family? Collect your family's ideas, decide on the winning choices, and write the tasks down as a short, simple list. Try to limit the length of your routines to just three or four tasks at first. Give yourself time to try out the routine and learn it by heart together before adding a new one. Create a poster or a visual to remind everyone: "This is what we agreed on."

A routine takes the guesswork and improvisation out of that section of your day, but more importantly, it reduces the risk of unhappy surprises and disappointments. An unpredictable schedule can set your child up for hopes and expectations that you didn't plan for, so if the possibility of those favourite activities can be counted upon (or is out of the question) you will save yourself some serious drama (most of the time).

Professional support for communication and expectations

If you are looking for more support, or you want to progress more quickly and easily toward your goals, here are some professionals and treatments that can offer support with setting boundaries and communicating effectively.

- **Trained professionals** who help with boundary-setting include: Board Certified Behavior Analysts, psychologists, and licenced clinical social workers.

- **Interventions and treatments** that have been proven to help with boundary setting include: structured classes such as Parent Management Training (PMT), Parent–Child Interaction Training (PCIT), Incredible Years Parenting Program, and Positive Parenting Program, also known as "Triple P." When parents receive guidance about how to respond to challenging behavior, they are less likely to use harsh punishments and more likely to maintain healthy limits with their children. Studies have shown that communities with access to Triple P classes have lower rates of child abuse, fewer foster care placements, and fewer injuries related to child abuse.

    Dr. Ross Greene's aforementioned book *The Explosive Child: A New Approach for Understanding and Parenting Easily Frustrated, Chronically Inflexible Children* has also been very successful in helping parents to set limits and problem-solve with children to find a reasonable compromise when necessary.

    Daniel J. Siegel and Tina Payne Bryson's book *No-Drama Discipline: The Whole-Brain Way to Calm the Chaos and Nurture Your Child's Developing Mind* contains some helpful descriptions and illustrations of how to offer warm and responsive parenting when you are responding in a conflict.[9]

---

9   Siegel, D. J. & Bryson, T. P. (2016) *No-Drama Discipline. The Whole-Brain Way to Calm the Chaos and Nurture Your Child's Developing Mind.* New York, NY: Bantam.

— CHAPTER 8 —

Building Your Child's Executive Functioning Skills

The importance of executive functioning skills

When your child is struggling to meet expectations, it may not be due to a problem with your family dynamic, an emotional barrier, or a lack of motivation. Your child's behavior struggles might just be telling you *"I don't understand. I can't solve this. I'm stuck."*

It might be hard at first to understand how a child's planning, logic, and problem-solving skills might be related to their ability to meet expectations. After all, we do our best to give clear instructions and set up simple routines. What's so hard to understand?

In this chapter, we will explore some of the pitfalls that children encounter when their thinking skills falter in the face of adult expectations.

Exploring the relationship between behavior and executive functioning skills

Your child's ability to plan and problem-solve is based on a set of abilities called "executive functioning skills." These cognitive skills help your child to navigate the past and the future, think flexibly, wait patiently, and solve problems creatively.

Your child's executive functioning skills will continue to develop and mature until early adulthood, and in the meantime you might notice him or her becoming upset and defiant during transitions, because he or she struggles to see what is coming next or how to make strategic decisions. He or she may have trouble accepting parental instructions that don't align with his or her individual plans and desires. This kind of cognitive gap can lead to a sense of anxiety and overwhelm, so if your child also has difficulty with emotional expression, then you will find yourself facing a perfect storm of frustration.

As you gain insight into your child's executive functioning skills, you will be better equipped to notice if your child is struggling with any of the following:

- planning and understanding time management

- setting priorities and resisting impulses

- managing transitions from one activity to another

- adapting when plans change suddenly

- using logic and creativity to solve problems

- understanding the perspective and emotions of others.

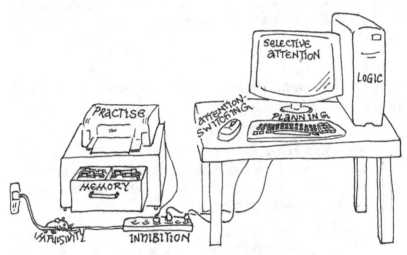

Figure 8.1: Building executive functioning skills

What are executive functioning skills, exactly?

The words "executive functioning skills" describe the skills we use to make wise decisions and solve problems.

Specifically, executive functioning skills are the higher-level cognitive skills that help with self-control, memory, and problem-solving. Executive functioning has been the subject of intense study in the educational and psychological field, because it is connected to so many important skills and abilities. Your executive functioning skills (also known as "higher level thinking skills") are essential because they balance out so much of the more primitive, automatic responses of the brain.

Why do you need executive functioning skills?

Executive functioning skills are especially important when your first reaction is not the most helpful one. For example, when you see an obnoxious coworker and you have the sudden urge to run out of the room, your executive functioning skills can weigh out the costs and benefits and help you take some deep breaths. When you see an especially beautiful pair of shoes on sale, your executive functioning skills help you imagine what it might mean to spend those hundreds of dollars and list how many different events you might wear them to, versus the likelihood that they would collect dust in your closet.

You use executive functioning skills to think about the future, to plan ahead, to bite your tongue before saying something unwise, to plow through those annoying administrative tasks. Your executive functioning abilities are one of the wisest, most rational aspects of the mind.

Why do some people struggle with executive functioning?

In order for executive functioning skills to work really well, you need three things:

1. **Time and experience**: Your child's brain is not considered "mature" until he or she reaches the age of 25. Until then, it is a work in progress, shaped by physical development and plenty of positive learning experiences.

2. **Emotional self-regulation**: When you are experiencing high levels of stress, your brain works hard to help you survive. However, when you are in fight/flight/freeze mode, you will have fewer of the brain's resources to use on those higher-level thinking and problem-solving skills.[1] Staying calm can free you up to be creative and focused.

3. **Good mental and physical health**: Executive functioning skills are based in the frontal lobes of the brain. Healthy brain development can be compromised or slowed down by genetic differences, traumatic stress, environmental toxins before or after birth, nutritional deficiencies, or other types of deprivation.

---

1   Thayer, J. F., Hansen, A. L., Saus-Rose, E. & Johnsen, B. H. (2009) Heart rate variability, prefrontal neural function, and cognitive performance: The neurovisceral integration perspective on self-regulation, adaptation, and health. *Annals of Behavioral Medicine, 37*(2), 141–153.

There are very few medical tests available to families to determine a child's brain health, but if your child seems to have persistent difficulty with executive functioning skills such as switching attention, are some possible reasons are:

- damage to the brain, caused by injury, illness, long-term environmental toxins (e.g., water or air pollution), and long-term stress caused by physical or emotional neglect

- developmental delays caused by genetic differences, or disruption to prenatal development (e.g., maternal drug addiction, exposure to alcohol, trauma)

- temporary difficulty due to intense physiological states, including sensitivity to stress and fear, sensory overload, effects of post-traumatic stress.

What difference does executive functioning make to my child's behavior?

Understanding executive functioning skills can teach you so much about the *why* of your child's behavior. To become a focused, flexible problem-solver, your child needs a strong set of executive functioning skills. Without them, you are very likely to see frustration, refusal, meltdowns, and misery.

What do executive functioning skills help my child do? How do they work?

If you are interested in getting an in-depth look at your child's current executive functioning skills, you may seek out a psychoeducational assessment from a psychologist. This type of assessment gathers information through checklists and interviews, and also measures your child's performance on tasks that test memory, attention, and self-control. Here are some examples of what a psychoeducational assessment might test, and how these abilities can impact your child's behavior.

The ability to remember sequences

3-6-4-9-5-2-0... Your child might be asked to listen to a sequence of words or numbers, and then repeat it back a minute later. The tester might also ask your child to say the sequence backwards. As the test gets more challenging and pushes beyond the limits of simple recall, your child will need to manage and process the information somehow. These strategies are part of "working memory."

Your child's sequencing and memory skills in daily life

If your child has difficulty remembering lists or juggling information, this can lead to struggles in other areas, particularly when it comes to remembering instructions and following instructions. If your child's working memory is not able to handle some of the important tasks your child is given, this can lead to refusal or even emotional outbursts.

For example, when you ask your child to tidy up his or her bedroom, he or she must assess what is out of place, remember where it goes, and decide what to pick up first. If your child tries to place a crumpled paper in the garbage and finds that the garbage is full, then he or she has to create a new list of steps for emptying the garbage, which might be complicated by the fact that your child's hands are already carrying three library books and five old sweaters, so those have to be first placed on the floor or perhaps the table... When your child's working memory can no longer manage that much information, you may see your him or her either give up completely or become very emotional and frustrated.

The ability to ignore distractions and edit one's own responses

In a formal psychometric assessment, your child's ability to ignore distractions and resolve conflicts may be tested with a task like the Stroop task, which requires your child to read a list of words like "red," "green," or "black" that are printed in various colors that do not match the word. The challenge lies in the fact that the words are printed in different colors, so the child is reading the word "red" but seeing the word "green."

Children who have difficulty with impulse control often struggle with this task, because their first response might naturally be to say the color of the word they see, instead of reading the letters that are printed. Some children take longer to read the list, possibly because they are working harder to override the color-related information, and pay attention only to the printed words.

The importance of selective attention in daily life

If your child has difficulty with this task, he or she may also have difficulty paying selective attention to information. For example, your child may find it difficult to understand a spoken message while also paying attention to your tone of voice. Your child may find it very difficult to attend to the teacher saying "Don't touch this, just listen," while ignoring the presence of interesting gym equipment. Executive functioning skills help your child resolve the conflict between the immediate urge to try it out, and the verbal message to simply wait. In truth, any important decision requires the ability to prioritize important information and filter out the rest. The most common example of this tension is probably familiar to you if you've ever told your child "That's not available," and he or she passionately replies, "*But I want to.*" In that moment, your child is struggling to resolve the importance of those two pieces of information in a way that makes logical sense.

The ability to GO... Now stop!

"*Press the space bar when you see the arrow pointing up, but don't press it when you see the arrow pointing down.*" Your child's ability to stop is a key skill. The ability to stop, also known as "inhibition," plays a major role in behavioral self-control, as well as in emotional self-regulation. Psychologists sometimes measure this ability with a test called the Stop Signal Reaction Test. The test is presented as a game where participants must quickly press a left arrow when they see one symbol, and a right arrow when they see another symbol; but when a third symbol appears on the screen (e.g., a stop sign, or an arrow pointing up), the participant should try not to press anything at all.

Every child has difficulty with inhibition, but the ability to stop tends to improve with age. Other factors, such as lack of sleep, chronic stress, traumatic brain injury, or an ADHD diagnosis, are associated with more errors and delays when performing tasks that require inhibition.

The importance of inhibition in daily life

As you can probably confirm from your own experience, the ability to stop comes into play when it comes to resisting temptation, avoiding emotional outbursts, and completing challenging tasks. If your child has a very "short fuse" or tends to rush ahead with "no brakes," then a lack of inhibition could be part of the problem.

The link between Oppositional Defiant Disorder and executive functioning skills

Do all children diagnosed with ODD struggle with executive functioning skills? The answer is, according to the research: *yes and no.*

If your child also has a diagnosis of ADHD, then the answer is almost certainly "yes." ODD and ADHD are very commonly diagnosed together. Problems with executive functioning skills are a key symptom of ADHD, and probably contribute to your child's oppositional and defiant behaviors.

What about the children who don't have an ADHD diagnosis and perform perfectly well on those psychometric tests? Do they have difficulty controlling themselves, keeping track of different kinds of information or remembering sequences?

Here's where the research gets a little confusing. Some research studies would say that that children with an ODD diagnosis (but no ADHD diagnosis) have no trouble with executive functioning skills.[2] When tested under typical conditions, children with an ODD diagnosis performed just like their typical peers.[3] Good news, right?

Executive functioning skills under emotional stress

There may, however, still be important differences in how children behave when they are under emotional stress. What would happen if executive functioning skills were tested when the children were calm, and when they were upset? How would those two scores compare?

One recent study asked that very question, and when experimenters tested children diagnosed with ODD under typical conditions, they found the typical result: not much difference between the ODD-diagnosed children and their peers.[4]

However, the experiment was also set up to investigate how the children would react when faced with emotionally stressful situations. For example, the children were asked to play competitive games and were told that their opponent had a higher score, or they were asked to play a computer game that kept freezing up.

Both the ODD-diagnosed group and the typical group were given the frustrating tasks, and then asked to complete more tests of executive functioning. The test scores in both groups were lower, but researchers saw a much bigger drop in performance from the children who were

---

2   Oosterlaan, J., Scheres, A. & Sergeant, J. A. (2005) Which executive functioning deficits are associated with AD/HD, ODD/CD and comorbid AD/HD+ ODD/CD? *Journal of Abnormal Child Psychology*, 33(1), 69–85.

3   Van Goozen, S. H., Cohen-Kettenis, P. T., Snoek, H., Matthys, W., Swaab-Barneveld, H. & Van Engeland, H. (2004) Executive functioning in children: A comparison of hospitalised ODD and ODD/ADHD children and normal controls. *Journal of Child Psychology and Psychiatry*, 45(2), 284–292.

4   Schoorl, J., van Rijn, S., de Wied, M., Van Goozen, S. & Swaab, H. (2018) 'Boys with oppositional defiant disorder/conduct disorder show impaired adaptation during stress: An executive functioning study.' *Child Psychiatry & Human Development*, 49(2), 298–307.

diagnosed with ODD. They concluded that children who struggle with emotional-coping skills are less able to use executive functioning skills in stressful situations.

This is worth saying again: *Your child's problem-solving skills can really take a hit when life gets frustrating.* Without emotional coping skills, your child's ability to plan, remember, and switch attention may go straight down the drain.

Is your child having difficulty managing time and priorities?

- Does your child start shouting when you ask him or her to stop an activity and switch to something else?

- Does your child wait until the last minute and then suddenly ask for activities that you don't have time to set up?

- Does your child consistently ignore reminders to get ready?

The ability to plan, sequence, and manage time is an often overlooked skill, and an important piece of the skill set known as "executive functioning."

To an adult with years of experience estimating time or planning ahead, it may seem absolutely obvious. To a child who struggles with planning and understanding time, five minutes can seem like five hours. "Later" is a lifetime away, so if it doesn't happen now, it feels to your child like it will never happen at all. Without a good sense of time, life can be full of extremely frustrating challenges for both children and adults.

Why do children diagnosed with Oppositional Defiant Disorder have such a hard time following routines and cooperating with plans?

Depending on your child's unique set of strengths and needs, the reason might be different, but the result is often the same: arguments, yelling, refusal, drama, or even crisis. To follow a schedule, your child needs to be able to:

- imagine and remember a sequence of future events

- anticipate what might interrupt the schedule, and think of a plan to work around those barriers

- switch attention from one task to another, to monitor time, or move on when time runs out

- stay calm through emotional ups and downs along the way.

Time-related struggles and the *irritable* Oppositional Defiant Disorder subtype: A matter of TIME

If you notice that disagreements and meltdowns often happen during transitions from one activity to another, your child may have difficulty with executive functioning skills related to planning, sequencing, and time, in addition to a significant lack of emotional self-regulation skills.

Do any of the following scenarios seem familiar to you?

You remind your child of the agreed-upon schedule for the day, and you hear a scream of frustration. You realize that your child has created his own plan, but it doesn't fit with your priorities, leading to intense frustration and disappointment.

Right before leaving for a fun family event, you notice your child is ignoring instructions and snapping at you. Later, you ask her what the problem was, and you realize that she was anxious about missing out on other activities or feeling unprepared because she hadn't planned ahead.

A family health emergency requires your attention, so you have to reschedule a promised trip to the movies to the following week. Your child expresses anger at not being consulted and refuses to accept any delay in the trip.

It's time to leave to go on holiday. Your child has had plenty of notice, and she has been looking forward to the holiday. However, when you ask her to get ready to go, she starts angrily muttering and throwing objects around.

In these situations, your child is very upset and struggling to make plans for the future. A gap in the executive functioning skills needed for planning and sequencing future events, when combined with difficulty with emotional self-regulation, can be a recipe for absolute misery.

Frustration and anxiety as a result of transition

A lack of emotional self-regulation skills often overlaps with a lack of planning skills. In fact, one skill deficit *multiplies* the effect of the other. A lack of planning leads to frustration and anxiety, but when that emotional temperature starts to rise, it becomes even harder for your child to calmly problem-solve using those executive functioning skills.

Irritable children, that is, those who are easily overwhelmed by stress and have trouble with emotional self-regulation, will often have extra difficulty adjusting to changes in the schedule, or coping with transitions from one activity to another. Scheduling can be a frequent source of frustration and disappointment if your child cannot understand when you say "We just don't have time," because his or her priorities do not fit in the parameters of the day.

Helping *irritable* children through scheduling upsets

If you can foresee that planning is going to be an issue, and you can set up an opportunity to talk it through (using visuals to help with memory and focus), then you may be able to prevent the emotional meltdown.

However, if that vicious cycle has already begun, then your child will need help with emotional self-regulation before the more logical questions of time and planning can be addressed together.

Time-related struggles and the *headstrong* Oppositional Defiant Disorder subtype: No TIME like the present

Full speed ahead! Children who are diagnosed with ODD because of their *headstrong* behavior do not find it easy to just go with the flow, or think very far ahead.

Do any of these scenarios seem familiar to you?

You say, "It's time for music practice. You have a school concert coming up." Your child replies, "I just need ten more minutes to finish this video game level." Forty-five minutes later, you come back and you realize you are having exactly the same conversation all over again.

Your child avoids any task that seems "boring" whenever progress toward the long-term goals is slow or hard to see (e.g., brushing teeth, packing his/her backpack the night before, completing daily homework).

You ask your child to get dressed and have breakfast, and you give them 30 minutes to complete these tasks. Twenty-five minutes go by and nothing has been accomplished, but when you give a reminder, your child yells, "You should have told me!", then hands you a list of eight items they need for a school project which is due by noon.

Many children diagnosed with ODD have difficulty with planning,[5] organization and priorities, especially if they also have symptoms of ADHD.[6]

If your child is more *headstrong*, impulsive, and determined, then following a plan can be extremely difficult. If your child is extremely driven by the availability of rewards, and not very concerned about possible negative outcomes (especially when those consequences are not immediately obvious), then any delay in getting straight to "the good part" may cause a conflict.

For creative ideas about how to plan ahead with your child, see the resource guide at the end of this chapter.

Is your child "being difficult" or having difficulty switching attention?

"Why doesn't he just listen?"

"I think she's tuning me out."

"It's like he's in a world of his own."

As you read earlier in the chapter, psychologists sometimes test to find out whether your child has a hard time switching attention from one thing to another, or ignoring unnecessary information.

In real life, children don't have to read strangely colored words aloud but they do have to switch attention between important things. Anger and emotional outbursts often bubble up when children are caught between conflicting demands. To make the right choice, they must sort out what information to ignore and what they should pay attention to. If they pay attention to the wrong information, trouble ensues: They end up ignoring people, resist changing, or fail to notice important details.

Specifically, the left prefrontal cortex plays an important part in

---

5   Barkley, R. A., Edwards, G., Laneri, M., Fletcher, K. & Metevia, L. (2001) Executive functioning, temporal discounting, and sense of time in adolescents with attention deficit hyperactivity disorder (ADHD) and oppositional defiant disorder (ODD). *Journal of Abnormal Child Psychology, 29*(6), 541–556.

6   Smith, A., Taylor, E., Warner Rogers, J., Newman, S. & Rubia, K. (2002) Evidence for a pure time perception deficit in children with ADHD. *Journal of Child Psychology and Psychiatry, 43*(4), 529–542.

helping children sift through conflicting demands, and studies show that damage to this area of the brain leads to trouble changing demands and ignoring irrelevant information. When children struggle to switch attention, or seem overly fixated on unimportant details, they are often called "willful" or "disrespectful." However, parents and teachers must remember that paying attention is not simply a choice; it is a function of the brain, and for some children, this task is challenging.

Switching attention and the *irritable* subtype: It's not you, IT'S ME

Do any of these scenarios seem familiar to you?

> Your child has a big assignment to complete for school, due tomorrow. She asks, "Can we watch a movie tonight?" You reply, "Maybe, it depends if you've done your homework." Your child throws her pencil on the floor and pounds the table, grumbling, "This is stupid!"

> Your child is immersed in a video game. You come into the room to ask whether he would like to come and have dessert with the family. You repeat your question a few times, a little louder each time. Finally, he shouts, "FOR GOODNESS SAKE! CAN'T YOU SEE I'M BUSY!"

> Your child walks into the room and sees that a sibling is eating a bowl of ice cream. She narrows her eyes, balls her fists and shouts, "How come HE gets to have ice cream? I'll never trust you again!" before stomping out of the room. You try to point to the other bowl of ice cream on the table, waiting for her, and ask her to come back, but there is no reply.

If these types of situations make your blood boil with frustration, you are not alone. Plenty of parents would feel quite justified complaining:

> "Why can't you be more considerate? That doesn't even make sense."

> "Do you have to be so rude? You're not even giving me a chance to explain."

> "Why do you have to ignore me? That's completely disrespectful."

From your point of view, you may see a child who is avoiding schoolwork, disregarding your perfectly reasonable requests, and deliberately refusing to respond to the needs of others. There are plenty of other words that get thrown around when it comes to kids like these, including: "careless," "lazy," "stubborn," and "inconsiderate."

Irritable behavior and the struggle to switch focus

When your child seems to be overreacting, failing to grasp a logical argument, or refusing to switch from one activity to another, remember: What is obvious and sensible to you might be very hard for your child. Your child is not just "being difficult" in this moment. The anger, defiance and even the absurd declarations might be absolutely sincere, because your child just can't see the whole picture. If it helps, remember that the part of the brain responsible for switching attention isn't fully developed yet (the brain continues to grow and develop until it reaches full maturity across about 25 years).

Therefore, in the examples you read earlier, the child may be having an emotional outburst because he or she is still stuck on one piece of information.

> The child who asked for a movie might not be able to imagine both being able to finish the homework and watch the movie, and needing more time, so she hears only a refusal.

> The child who shouted at a parent when asked to shift attention away from a video game may be trying to pay attention to both the game and the parent, which leads to intense confusion and stress.

> The child who protested about a sibling getting ice cream was extremely focused on that one piece of information, and didn't stop to look around for more answers before concluding that the whole situation was extremely unfair and terrible.

Helping the *irritable* child switch focus without anger or overwhelm

If your child struggles with big emotions when asked to switch attention or pay attention to more than one kind of information at a time, and you've realized that this struggle explains some of the blow-outs you've been seeing, here are some tools you can use to resolve the situation with more calm and common sense:

- Think about how your child processes information. For example, if your child finds visual information very hard to ignore but is slower to respond to spoken words, think about how you can communicate in the way that works best for him or her. Can you send a note? Hold up a sign? Stand very close?

- Notice your own emotional wavelength, and if you are communicating with a sharp tone of voice or accusatory words, remember that your child can think best when in a calm environment. A soft voice and a kind tone can actually make it easier for your child to be logical.

Attention-related struggles and the *"headstrong"* subtype
Do any of these scenarios seem familiar to you?

It's almost time to leave for school, but your child picks up a magazine and starts to leaf through it. You gently remind her to go put on her shoes, because there are only a few minutes left. "Just a minute..." she murmurs.

Your child is attending a friend's birthday party, and the kids are passing around a cool collectible toy, each taking a turn to inspect it then handing it to the next child. Your child holds it and doesn't let go. A friend elbows him, and your child doesn't let go of the toy until the request is repeated four or five times.

Dinner will be ready in five minutes, and your child is circling the kitchen, asking for a snack. You've asked her to wait, but she continues to ask for snacks and complain. Finally, she walks off. By the time you have put dinner on the table, she has started reading a book and refuses to come and eat until she has finished the chapter.

For parents who want to raise children who are responsive, independent and considerate, this type of behavior can be extremely frustrating.

"Why can't you be responsible?"

"Do you have to be so rude?"

"Why do you have to ignore me? That's completely disrespectful."

Headstrong behavior and the struggle to switch focus
Another quality that is common among *headstrong* children is a tendency to get very focused on their own goals. When the *headstrong*

child is motivated to achieve something, he or she has trouble switching attention to accommodate other points of view or consider other important factors. On the flip side, when you are asking a *headstrong* child to get on board with your goals, he or she may find it very hard to stay focused.[7]

Unlike children who are *irritable* and have big emotional reactions when asked to switch attention, *headstrong* children can quite calmly appear to ignore your instructions and persevere toward their own goals even when all signs point to say "No, this is a terrible idea, you should really stop right away."

Switching attention: Not as easy as it looks

The next time you give your child an instruction and you don't get a response, pause before you assume your child is ignoring you. It's hard to tell at a glance if he or she is paying close attention to something and hasn't yet switched his or her attention to you.

The ability to switch attention back and forth is actually a skill that depends on a certain level of brain development. This skill tends to improve with age, so it's natural for younger children to find it much harder. If your child is struggling with this task, then it might be helpful to think of the problem in this area as a development delay.

You wouldn't blame a child who was hard of hearing for ignoring you, or a child with visual impairments for failing to respond to your hand gestures. Naturally, it's much harder to be sympathetic and supportive when your child's struggle is invisible, but if you can remember that your child may not be deliberately ignoring you or refusing to acknowledge conflicting information, you can handle the problem without being offended or exasperated.

Researchers have found that children with diagnosed attentional problems (e.g., ADHD) switch their attention back and forth between different tasks,[8] but if you ask them to switch between tasks that are similar, they are more likely to get confused and thrown off track.

---

7   Pearson, D. A., Lane, D. M. & Swanson, J. M. (1991) Auditory attention switching in hyperactive children. *Journal of Abnormal Child Psychology, 19*(4), 479–492.

8   Hanania, R. & Smith, L. B. (2010) Selective attention and attention switching: Towards a unified developmental approach. *Developmental Science, 13*(4), 622–635.

Helping the *headstrong* child switch focus without nagging or yelling

The next time you give your child an instruction and you don't get a response, pause before you assume he or she is ignoring you. It's hard to tell at a glance if your child is paying close attention to something and hasn't yet switched his or her attention to you.

It's also important to remember that what seems very important and motivating to your child may not be an example of what you would like him or her to prioritize. If at all possible, do not take it personally and do not despair. What you are seeing is a work in progress, and no amount of disapproval or lecturing is going to change this developmental stage.

Some researchers believe that children diagnosed with ODD have difficulty following social cues,[9] and so their behavior is not easily shaped by the same kinds of social messages that would get the attention of a typical child.

Use a gentle approach to capture and hold your child's attention (e.g., a gentle hand on his or her arm) and look for the opportunity to make eye contact, to practice socially appropriate cues while reducing distractions.

Is your child having difficulty with self-control?

- Does your child hit, kick, or swear when asked to wait, or when you tell him/her "no"?

- Does your child often break the rules when you are out of the room?

- Does your child shout or throw objects when very upset?

Every person has moments when they would like to shout, kick, or curse. In fact, if you have driven a car and been suddenly cut off by a careless neighbor, you probably feel quite justified in muttering some choice words, pounding the steering wheel or even honking your horn. However, you wouldn't grumble curse words or punch your desk in the presence of your boss, and you don't yell at cashiers who get your change wrong. You are a respectable grown-up, and you have a filter that helps you limit the expression of emotions that aren't socially

9   Matthys, W., Vanderschuren, L. J., Schutter, D. J. & Lochman, J. E. (2012) Impaired neurocognitive functions affect social learning processes in oppositional defiant disorder and conduct disorder: Implications for interventions. *Clinical Child and Family Psychology Review*, 15(3), 234–246.

acceptable (at least, most of the time). If this filter is working well, then you'll also be able to follow the rules even when you are by yourself, resisting tempting situations like shoplifting, avoiding inadvisable flirting, or stopping yourself from eating too many cookies.

Self-control is, like other executive functioning skills such as planning and switching attention, a skill that develops with both practice and maturity. When children are able to use self-control, it is not simply because they are "making good choices" or because they have been "well trained" by sensible parents; it is because they have the necessary physical maturity, and in that moment all other basic physical and emotional needs are probably met. In some cases, fear of punishment can help to inhibit behaviour, but as you have certainly noticed, the effects of punishments are often temporary and sometimes backfire dramatically.

Why do children diagnosed with Oppositional Defiant Disorder have such a hard time with self-control?

This is one of the most complicated and frustrating questions you will probably face as a parent, but as you start to understand it better, you will find it easier to stay calm even in the face of dramatic overreaction, impulsive rule-breaking, offensive language, and even aggression. When your child seems to be unable to put on the brakes, here are some things to remember:

- Everyone is a little bit impulsive and reactive sometimes.

- No one follows all the rules all of the time.

- Self-control is sometimes influenced by past consequences, so a consistent set of expectations can be helpful.

- People exert more or less self-control depending on what they expect from the situation, so a child who does not notice social cues may appear to be "too wild."

- Self-control tends to plummet in high-stress situations, so extreme emotions, physical pain, or traumatic memories can make self-control much more challenging.

- A noticeable lack of self-control can sometimes signal an unmet physical or emotional need.

- Good physical health and appropriate sensory input can support good self-control.

- Too little or too much sensory input sometimes triggers a stress response, which can make self-control more difficult.

Self-control and the *irritable* Oppositional Defiant Disorder subtype: No holds barred

Do any of these scenarios seem familiar to you?

> You call out to your child at the park, "It's time to go home!" There's no time for the usual negotiations, so you lay a firm hand on her shoulder and say, "Come on, we have to go, now." Before you know it, your child has wriggled away, and sprinted to the other side of the park, yelling insults and ultimatums.

> You hear your child's voice start to rise in frustration, as he argues with a sibling over who gets to go first. Before you have even walked into the next room, you hear a shriek. By the time you get there, fists have already flown, and the tearful sibling shows you a tender bruise on his upper arm.

Children who are described as "*irritable*" often struggle with emotional self-regulation, which does have a negative impact on self-control. When people experience intense stress, the desire to run away, fight back, or hide can be extremely strong. Even if your child seems to have the ability to resist temptation and weigh the pros and cons *most of the time*, an episode of intense anger can wash that self-control away like a powerful wave hitting a sandcastle.

However, when a child is experiencing these intense emotions, it is easy for bystanders to judge the reactions as manipulative, cruel, vicious, or simply weak. It's easy for parents to feel discouraged, personally attacked, and completely overwhelmed.

> "When are you going to learn to control yourself?"

> "Why do you want to wreck everything I give you?"

> "You're just cruel, and you have no respect for us."

Irritable behavior and the struggle for self-control

When your child's behavior seems to be way out of proportion, and all the rules and expectations have been tossed out the window (sometimes literally), remember what you have already learned about your child's brain and the four steps required for emotional self-regulation:

- **Emotional responding**: The brain receives a signal: Something might be wrong! What's up?

- **Emotional filtering**: Other parts of the brain weigh in: Is this really a problem? Are we OK?

- **Effortful control**: The rest of the body joins in: Should we walk away? Bite our tongues?

- **Emotional awareness**: The brain tells a story about what happened, such as "I felt scared/excited/happy."

Unfortunately, adults often expect children to be able to skip straight to effortful control or emotional awareness, even though a child's emotional responding and emotional filtering systems might still be busy flashing lights and sounding the alarm.

Remember the following:

- As you have certainly noticed, children are just physically quicker to "heat up" and respond to a possible threat in an emotional way. Different types of "emotional responding" are sometimes called "temperaments," and even newborn infants show a variation in the way they react.

- Similarly, some children struggle with "emotional filtering." Without sufficient perspective-taking, attention-switching, or logical reasoning, these children will interpret a harmless change as a possible threat. A confusing facial expression or an accidental nudge can be labeled as intentionally "mean."[10]

- The bigger the "threat," the more likely it is that your child's response will be a form of fight/flight/freeze, and the harder it will be for your child to demonstrate "effortful control" and bring his or her behavior into line with social expectations and rules.

- "Emotional awareness" is actually an advanced skill, because it requires the child to reflect on the situation and his or her own thoughts and feelings. If your child is extremely focused on the "threat" (i.e., still in fight/flight/freeze mode), it will be hard to shift focus and gain that perspective.

---

10 Van Goozen, S. H., Cohen-Kettenis, P. T., Snoek, H., Matthys, W., Swaab-Barneveld, H. & Van Engeland, H. (2004) Executive functioning in children: A comparison of hospitalised ODD and ODD/ADHD children and normal controls. *Journal of Child Psychology and Psychiatry, 45*(2), 284–292

For instance:

> Remember the child who ran away when a parent insisted it was time to go home? A firm voice and an unexpected hand on the shoulder might have prompted a fearful response. Without the ability to "filter" the information and use "effortful control" to follow a reasonable request, the child responded as if she was being chased by a werewolf (stuck on "emotional responding").

> Remember the child who argued with a sibling and then threw a punch? The "emotional responding" was probably anger, but better "emotional filtering" would help the child think through the possible consequences of punching a sibling (mixing the anger with caution), or the possibility of getting the toy back another way (mixing anger with the desire for another reward), which would result in "effortful control" (keeping hands from punching, asking a parent for help).

Helping the *irritable* child develop self-control without harsh punishment

As you have certainly discovered, it's impossible to "control" a child's emotions; but as your child learns to exercise emotional self-regulation, you may see a corresponding increase in self-control. The next best thing is to help your child go through the process of emotional self-regulation, with as much of your own self-control and empathy as you can muster.

Emotional responding

If you can recognize your child's fear, anger, and desire, without immediately trying to control or dismiss it, and without getting swept away by your own reaction, then you have taken a very positive first step. Some emotional responding is actually very hard to detect. Some children learn to "effortfully control" the expression of the emotion, without first learning how to filter it, so a very sad or frightened child might laugh or keep a neutral expression. Keep an open mind and don't jump to conclusions. Above all, don't take it personally. If you can see an emotional response in its earliest stages, you have the best chance of helping your child go through the process of emotional self-regulation, before it gets too "hot."

Emotional filtering

The ability to take perspective, look for alternative explanations, or investigate to find more information is a complex process, and sometimes this doesn't happen until the heat of the first emotional reaction has cooled a little. If your child seems to be "stuck" on one interpretation of the events (e.g., "You're so mean" or "It's all ruined"), then you might be tempted to give plenty of logical or helpful explanations, and you'll quickly be able to see whether your child is processing that information or not. If your child responds by saying, "Shut up," or "I hate you," then chances are that the emotional responding is still overriding the logic of "emotional filtering," and "effortful control" is not fully working either.

At this point, you may be struggling with your own emotional responding, or looking for ways to get leverage until your child demonstrates an acceptable amount of effortful control. Many parents were taught to use threats and punishment to change a child's "unacceptable behavior" and gain compliance. However, this is usually where a power struggle starts to escalate. Whereas some children will "freeze" or "flee" when a parent starts to threaten or dominate the situation with yelling or physical confrontation, children with the *irritable* response are more likely to fight fire with fire, and match a parent's threat with a threat of his or her own.

Fortunately, if logic or danger does not tamp down an angry display, the body has its own way to cool a hot temper. No one stays angry forever, thanks to the body's parasympathetic nervous system, which is always working to bring muscles and hormones back into balance.

To help this process along:

- Offer your child a safe, quiet place to be.

- Give him or her a few gentle words of support (yes, even when he or she seems to be vicious and hateful).

- Give your child time.

- Give your child access to a calming activity or tool.

- Let your child be at a safe distance from other people. (This will vary, and children sometimes don't express this clearly. Your child may need to know you are near to feel safe, even if he or she doesn't want you to look at him or her. Use your own observations and ask your child to let you know, if possible, to learn what distance makes him or her feel safe in those moments.)

When your child is cool enough (and you have had a chance to cool down, too), then you can go through the emotional filtering process in retrospect, offering more information and alternatives to consider.

Effortful control is a skill that works best when the response is rehearsed, so don't hesitate to practice! Role play together, script your responses, write or draw it out, and actually play through the situation so that the next time either of you needs a reminder, it's easy to remember.

Self-control and the *headstrong* Oppositional Defiant Disorder subtype: By any means necessary

Do any of these scenarios seem familiar to you?

> You are emptying your child's backpack after school, and you find coins, toys, and candy that wasn't there before. You ask your child where it came from, and she replies, "Oh, I don't know... I just found it there." Your heart sinks as you realize that the items are probably stolen.

> It's time for bed, but your child is sitting on the couch, reading a new comic book. You try another reminder: "Hey sweetie, did you hear me? It's time for bed." No movement. "Excuse me? Can you hear me?" You tap him on the shoulder. Finally, he replies, "I'm reading. I'll go to bed later." He goes on ignoring you.

> You're leaving the store but your child stops in her tracks beside the vending machine. She asks for a dollar. You refuse, saying, "It's not time for candy, and we really need to leave now." She stands glued to the spot, begging, whining, jumping up and down, arguing, complaining...anything but walking with you to the car as planned.

If your child isn't having emotional meltdowns but has great difficulty with impulsivity[11] and rule-following, then he or she might be having a particularly hard time with self-control in connection with what he or she wants.

This kind of behavior can make you dread every potential distraction or temptation. How do you get through a day without getting stuck in one of these sticky situations? A child who seems fixated on having

---

11 Menon, V., Adleman, N. E., White, C. D., Glover, G. H. & Reiss, A. L. (2001) Error-related brain activation during a Go/No Go response inhibition task. *Human Brain Mapping, 12*(3), 131–143.

his or her own way seems stubborn, unreasonable, inconsiderate, and simply impossible to reason with.

Headstrong behavior and the struggle for self-control

If your child seems to be extra-demanding, while ignoring warnings and going way overboard on the quest to meet his or her goals, it's worth looking at that emotion-processing system again. This time, instead of fear or anger, the primary motivation is a goal or reward. What happens when your child wants something he or she can't have in that moment?

- **Emotional responding**: The brain receives a signal: This could be fun!

- **Emotional filtering**: Other parts of the brain weigh in: Can I afford it? Am I allowed?

- **Effortful control**: The rest of the body joins in: Should I take it? Do I need to wait?

- **Emotional awareness**: The brain tells a story about what happened: I want/I need/I'm missing out.

It would be wonderful if your child went through the emotional process like this: feeling tempted at first, then remembering the rule, and getting back on track, without a big emotional reaction. Knowing that not all brains are alike, you might find it helpful to look at this process and see where your child might be getting stuck.

The role of emotional self-regulation in *headstrong* behaviour.

- Some types of rewards or goals might be very powerful for your child, even if they don't seem important to anyone else. It's possible that the emotional responding—in this case, desire— is so strong that your child's self-control (filtering and effortful control) hasn't caught up yet.

- Emotional filtering is where your child's rational thoughts and impulses contend with each other, and the result is a rationale for following one or the other. The rational thoughts don't always win out but they do usually play a role. Interestingly, researchers have found that children diagnosed with ODD pay less information to "punishment information." So, when they are about to make a poor choice, their emotional filtering might not work as well, resulting in less caution and more persistence, even when punishment is imminent.

- When it comes to effortful control, most children who fall into the *headstrong* subtype of ODD have absolutely no problem with this at all...if the motivation is right! They are extremely goal-oriented, even if parents, teachers, or siblings strongly disagree. Again, effortful control for the purposes of self-control can be improved through practice, but if a child has the desire and the willingness to go after that goal, then an improvement in effortful control is not the most important problem to be solved.

- Children who have difficulty with distraction and impulsivity might not be able to say what exactly they wanted, because they probably started doing it before really "thinking about it." Emotional awareness is helpful, especially when planning to avoid temptation and improve self-control, but it is quite an advanced and sophisticated skill set (even adults have a hard time with it sometimes).

Let's return to our earlier examples:

Remember the child who brought home ill-gotten coins, toys, and candy? The first burst of emotional reactivity is hard to argue with, because these items are very tempting. However, the emotional filtering seems to have fallen short. In that moment, the child didn't fully consider how the victim would feel, or how it might feel to be caught stealing. It's also very common for children (and adults) to "discount" the importance of future events in favor of short-term gain. If your child *does* have perspective-taking and understands the consequences of stealing, then you can work together on effortful control and you can ask, "What do we do when we feel like stealing and we know we shouldn't?" Options might include: put your hands in your pockets; give the items to a teacher; look for the owner. Practicing these actions can help boost your child's self-control because it skips the pitfalls of problem-solving.

Remember the child who ignored you when it was time for bed, eyes glued to the comic book? The temptation of the comic book is literally front and centre. The emotional filtering might be a bit limited by the fact that the child is also reading, but rational excuses could include "It's only a few more pages" and "I'm not really tired," while failing to pick up on your obvious frustration. You may notice that simply getting close or gaining eye contact is enough to shift the emotional responding in your favor, or you may find that your child did not give much thought to the etiquette of the situation.

Remember the child who begged for money in the store? The emotional reactivity is hard for your child to avoid, as the colorful displays are exactly positioned to capture your child's attention, and your child's emotional filtering might not be very sophisticated yet. You could probably come up with a few dozen reasons why it makes no sense to put a dollar in a machine to get a stale old gumball, but your child hasn't thought of any yet. Sometimes this kind of dilemma can push you both into another kind of emotional response: anger. In this case, your explanations probably won't carry much weight in answer to the question "WHY NOT?" especially if you have been flexible about this kind of thing in the past.

Helping the *headstrong* child develop self-control without harsh punishment

So, what can a parent do to help a child who seems to be overly focused on goals, and who is willing to ignore the rules to get what he or she wants? First and always: Try not to stress about it or get offended. Yes, it does seem irrational and rude, but if you can stay calm and see the problem through your child's eyes, it will be much easier for you both to find a solution. Remember that self-control is a very difficult goal for both adults and children, and plenty of adults find it hard to stop themselves from eating cookies for breakfast, putting down their phones, and putting aside their favorite activities when asked.

- Describe specific, reasonable limits ahead of time. For example, if you let your child know it's time to leave the playground, and your child wants to swing across the monkey bars one more time, you might be comfortable waiting a few more seconds. However, what if your child decides to swing across the monkey bars *eight* more times? Your child might have wildly overestimated your patience, but by the time he or she notices you glaring and tapping your foot on the ground, it's too late. When you plan out the transition together (describing how you will give the signal, how long you will wait patiently, and what positive feedback he or she can expect to receive when he or she cooperates) your child may be more successful in gathering the necessary "willpower" and less likely to expect "just a little more time."

- Can this desire be met on a clearer schedule? Often, the problem is that the child is trying to get a goal at an impossible time, or hassles you on an unpredictable basis, just in case *this time* might be successful. If you can agree on a specific day, or time of day, and you write or draw that agreement where you can both see it, you may find that your child's self-control improves dramatically. A consistent schedule tells your child exactly when that goal-directed behavior will be successful.

- If you find that your child's persistence is wearing you down, and you are "giving in" to the hassling or arguing every once in a while, you may accidentally be encouraging the *headstrong* behavior. Whenever behavior is rewarded on an unpredictable schedule, even "just this once," children learn that it's always worthwhile to try, just in case. Think of lottery tickets: Most tickets don't win, but there's a chance that your just might. If a player finds that one out of ten purchases gets a pay-off, then the experiment becomes a persistent habit. Communicate a rule in a very clear and simple way—and stick to it.

- If a clear rule with regular access doesn't work to keep your child from trying to satisfy that urge, then you may need add some supervision or limit access. Adding a harsher punishment tends not to work, because your child's emotional filtering may not be very accurate when it comes to predicting the likelihood of the punishment happening again, or how likely he or she is to get caught.

- Can the desire be met in another way? There's probably nothing you can do about the motivation, but if you can work with your child to find a goal that works for both of you, then that energy can be put to good use. For example, if your child is whining for money to buy silly things or even stealing money from you, it's not the money that's the problem. The problem lies in the way he or she is trying to get it. Can you arrange for your child to earn the money, by selling items or performing jobs? Can you look at the need as valid and find a reasonable way to meet it?

- How do you teach those values and beliefs that help emotional filtering? This one takes time, so be patient and creative. Use stories and real-life examples that your child can relate to. Talk about things that happened to your child and remember the powerful emotions he or she felt. Has he or she ever lost a precious toy? Would he or she want someone to take his or her money? When you read books and watch movies, notice when the characters are having a hard time with self-control, and talk about it together. What does your child think? How does he or she think others should make choices?

A powerful strategy to support executive functioning
The importance of "a plan"

Think of a problem you had to solve recently. Did you decide in advance what you wanted to do? Did you imagine what you might say? Did you write out your response, or even practice with a friend?

Your executive functioning skills (such as logical reasoning, prioritizing, planning, switching attention, and self-control) work best when you have time to plan. When we are pressed for time or under stress, we have more difficulty resisting temptation and keeping our priorities straight. This is why we write grocery lists *before* we go to the store. This is why we pack our lunches ahead of time instead of trying to choose the healthy option on a tempting snack menu.

Once you have a plan, you can follow a set of steps and you can simply focus on one thing at a time. The beauty of this strategy is that it takes the focus away from what *not* to do. You are less confused, less tempted, and less vulnerable to distraction, because your attention is limited to a clearly outlined plan. You may still worry about what could go wrong. You might still crave something yummy. However, you can bring your attention back to the plan, pulling your focus away from those impulses.

Parenting with a plan

When parents search for help addressing difficult behavior, it often sounds like this:

"What do I do when my child refuses to get out of bed?"

"What consequence should I use for hitting?"

"If my child calls me names, what should I say?"

Many parents assume that problem behavior is best addressed as it happens. They go looking for the right response or the most effective reaction to stop that problem behavior in its tracks, then wait for the problem behavior to start.

Unfortunately, this reactive strategy puts both children and parents at a disadvantage. When parents try to respond to challenging in the behavior in the moment, they give instructions like "No! Put that down!" or "Stop hitting!" They may be alarmed, frustrated or offended. They are trying to problem-solve, improvise, calm themselves, and support their children, all at the same time. Meanwhile, children diagnosed with ODD seem to have a hard time regulating their own behavior. For these children, it's easier to tune out an alert or a reprimand, and harder to learn from mistakes and put on the brakes.

It's also common for children diagnosed with ODD to have trouble with impulse control. Many of these children are extra-sensitive to the possibility of reward, so they are much better at starting than stopping. This combination creates the potential for plenty of mischief and misery.

When parents are trying without success to use reactive strategies, and they don't know what else to do, they sometimes try *harder*. They shout louder or use harsher consequences. The result is often that children start to avoid their parents, or just learn to ignore the intensity of the parents' protests.

To be successful, to handle transitions and disappointments, to negotiate and problem-solve, your child needs the same kind of support. Challenging behavior is often a sign that your child is struggling to solve problems in a logical way, to switch attention from one thing to another, to decide between competing priorities, and to exercise self-control. However, when you invite your child into the planning process, he or she is better able to use the full complement of his or her executive functioning skills.

Planning can also help to share the vision that is in your own head, so your child can see it too. In a moment of calm, your child might have a chance to see the WHY of a routine or an expectation, even when they are too frustrated or distracted to really get their heads around it in the heat of the moment.

Plans can help your child cope with emotional and practical problems such as:

- getting ready for school

- getting to bed on time

- approaching difficult school assignments
- staying on task while in a store
- responding to teachers
- cooperating with peers
- calming and self-soothing
- asking for help
- coping with disappointment
- preparing for sensory needs
- repairing strained relationships
- recovering from meltdowns.

Once a plan is in place, it keeps working to support your child's executive functioning skills. In situations where desires and fears are so powerful, a plan can be something to hang on to. In situations where stress and frustration are high and self-control is especially low, a plan requires very little thought. Your child can just face the challenge step-by-step.

Plans that support children with emotional sensitivity

For children who struggle with emotional self-regulation, planning ahead can reduce the most common triggers of explosive behavior. Planning avoids surprises and helps children prepare for possible disappointments. Planning also helps children who do not adapt well to new information, so they can prepare a response to potential changes or disappointments, using this extra time to understand expectations, process emotions, and ask questions. In a proactive discussion, children have the opportunity to express their concerns calmly, and advocate for themselves, without a sense of urgency.

Planning with sensitive children could include thinking ahead to situations that might be difficult. Instead of dreading an ordeal, your child can brainstorm with you to think of activities, distractions, and sensory tools that are calming, and find ways to meet sensory needs such as earplugs, options for movement, and alternative spaces to escape to when feeling annoyed or stressed.

Plans that support children who are very goal-oriented

When it comes to children who are more *headstrong* and impulsive, they are experts at scanning for possibilities that no one else could anticipate. They are bold, adventurous, and persistent in achieving their goals. Plans can help you make sure that your goals are aligned with your child's. When you clearly lay out the expectations ahead of time, explaining which options are available and which boundaries are non-negotiable, your child can spend less time testing, exploring, and sprinting toward possibilities that aren't part of your shared mission.

Plans that support executive functioning skills

Extra time and emotional stability do help to boost executive functioning skills, but there are also other tools you can incorporate into your plan to support your children.

For instance, visual schedules and menus can help your child make choices if memory is a struggle. Drawings, photos, or scheduling apps can improve your child's ability to focus. Fidgets and sensory toys can help your child relax and keep busy while you talk and plan together. Lists can help you manage time and set priorities together, which is especially helpful for children who struggle to filter out distractions or remember sequences. Timers can help your child stay on track, exercise self-control, and anticipate changes. Schedules can help children who struggle to switch their attention from one thing to another. Movement and exercise can be included in your plan or even used while you plan, to keep your child feeling alert, focused, and engaged.

Cooperation and collaboration

Best of all, when you plan ahead, you can collaborate with and listen to your child. This helps to make sure that both you and your child feel as if your priorities are included. Your child gets a chance to practice thinking ahead and communicating about needs and wants. You get the opportunity to preview your child's response to the task, so you can make any necessary adjustments, instead of getting stuck trying to carry out a plan that is already not working.

The importance of "practice, practice, practice"

A plan without practice may just be wishful thinking. After all, a plan still requires some mental resources to remember the steps, to follow them in order, to check if you are following each step correctly. If you have ever tried to test a brand new dinner recipe in the kitchen while you are hungry and the kids are running in and out with problems to solve and requests to discuss, you know how hard it is to plan the next step, make decisions, and resist the urge to throw the whole thing in the sink and make pasta (again). Just like you, your child's ability to follow a plan is compromised when he or she is distracted, tired, or frustrated.

The solution to this challenge is simple: practice, practice, practice. As you rehearse your plan, you and your child find it easier to remember each step. You can troubleshoot and test each step without worrying about the consequences. You can role play together, and even switch places so you know each other's lines and can remind each other. You can take as much time as you need. Your memory improves as you rehearse, enabling you to perform more fluently and with less effort.

From thought to action

If you have made plans in the past, had repeated conversations, set intentions, and given reminders, only to watch everything fall apart, you are not alone. It's not easy to learn a new skill or to change an old behavior. Nothing can completely prepare you to go from a plan to "real life," but there are some steps you can take to make progress faster and easier. In the research literature, this process is called Behavior Skills Training (BST). It has been proven to significantly improve skills from gun safety to job performance, with both children and adults.

The following steps might seem silly, embarrassing, or time-consuming to you at first, but think of how much time and effort you have spent explaining what *not* to do. Doesn't it makes sense to invest some extra time in practicing and agreeing on exactly what you would like your child to be able to do?

1. **Put it in writing**: Even if it's crystal clear in your mind, take the time to outline your plan in words. This will allow you to share ideas within your family and review the plan later in case of confusion.

2. **Talk it through**: Describe your plan with the rest of the family. Find out if anyone has questions and fill in any possible gaps.

3. **Act it out**: Physically go through the steps you will perform. Say the words, walk around the house, pick up the toothbrush... whatever it takes so that you are giving a visual example of what

you are asking for. Ask your partner or your child to play your role, so you can say their lines.

4. **Have a dress rehearsal**: Now it's time to try it out. When everyone is smiling and awkward, and you go through the steps in slow motion, that's when learning really starts to happen. You might find that it's very simple, or you might start to see potential pitfalls you didn't notice before, but it's so important to actually walk through the plan. As each member of your family participates, your memory will improve, your commitment will increase, and your chances of success will multiply.

Bringing out the best in you

As you might suspect, planning helps you, too.

When you are trying to solve a problem in the middle of a loud, uncomfortable, or dangerous situation, you may be distracted by the clamor of your own emotional reactivity. You will naturally be much more likely to focus on the negative possibilities, make pessimistic decisions, and remember everything that has gone wrong in the past.

A plan gives you the luxury of time to think, so you can dream up new strategies instead of repeating old mistakes. When you practice the plan, you solidify the events in your memory, which gives you more mental bandwidth for navigating real life, whether that is enjoying the moment or adapting and troubleshooting in small but important ways.

When you are calm, you think differently. You are wiser, more flexible, more sympathetic, and more creative. You are a better problem-solver when your brain is not busy managing stress levels. You are more positive and optimistic, and less likely to come up with defensive or offensive responses. Moreover, thinking about yourself in the future allows you to think differently, considering long-term goals instead of short-term crises, with less emotional distortion or immediate temptation.

Building your child's executive functioning skills: Self-assessment
QUESTIONS FOR REFLECTION

- How often do you notice your child getting distracted or overly focused?

- Do meltdowns tend to happen around transitions?

- Does your child often get into trouble because he or she "just can't help him/herself"?

- Could some of your child's frustration be due to confusion or cognitive overwhelm?

ESSENTIAL SKILLS

- I help my child avoid distraction and make transitions with a plan we practiced together.

- When we make a plan, I put it in writing and we go through all the steps as a team so we know it by heart.

- We have tested and collected tools that help with calming, focus, and planning.

- I've learned to see when my child is getting overwhelmed or confused, so we can slow down and find another solution together.

- I have helped my child understand that we all need help sometimes with our thinking, and I'm honest about tasks that are hard for me.

PRIORITY QUIZ

Does your family struggle with activities that require planning and focus? If you agree with three or more of the following statements, then support for your child's executive functioning skills will help to avoid some of the overwhelm and stress that you are seeing.

- My child often gets stuck on one thing and becomes upset when it's time to stop.

- My child often refuses to get ready to go out.

- Chores and homework are a common source of meltdowns.

- When I ask my child to do something, he or she often procrastinates or gets distracted after a few minutes.

- If I don't keep tempting items out of sight, they might go missing.

- My child has so many last-minute ideas and suggestions that it's hard to stick to a familiar routine.

Where can I find help with my child's executive functioning skills?

STRATEGIES TO TRY AT HOME

Exercise #1

Visual schedules

For children who need extra help with planning ahead, a visual schedule can be a great relief. Visual schedules can be used by children who express anxiety about upcoming changes, or who need help to prepare for transitions. Visual schedules are also excellent for children who are independent and self-motivated, because they reduce the need for reminders and check-ins from adults.

If you have access to a tablet device or even a mobile phone, there are quite a few apps specifically designed to help children with planning and emotional self-regulation. Alternatively, you can simply make your own visual schedules with paper and markers.

Exercise #2

The walkthrough

"Don't forget!" "Be more organized!" These kinds of reminders have no value to a child who is in need of memory strategies or routines to help keep belongings in their place. Children who struggle with executive functioning often don't even know where to start, and don't notice the mistake until the damage has been done (e.g., a toy has been tripped over or broken). When you notice that your child is impulsively racing ahead, getting distracted, or struggling to keep a physical space tidy, it's vital to slow down and create a task analysis or "walkthrough." A task analysis is simply a play-by-play of exactly how to be successful. Make sure each step is small and realistic for your child, and build a small routine.

Write down each step or take photos to make them easier to recall. If memory is part of the problem, remember that memory is not fueled by willpower; it is strengthened by positive experiences, hands-on practice, and cues in the environment. Your child might need extra time or more rehearsal to remember to follow the rules during daily routines or even in social situations. Whenever possible, use proactive preparation for situations that call for executive functioning skills. Your child's lapses are an opportunity to learn and improve, not an occasion for shame and disapproval.

Exercise #3
Connection and calming

When your child is confused, struggling to focus, or distracted, it's hard for him or her to stay calm. Children with executive functioning struggles often express anxiety, sadness, or anger when the world doesn't quite make sense. Similarly, children who have intense emotions will have difficulty using their otherwise adequate executive functioning skills in a stressful or frustrating moment.

Although you may be able to easily see a logical solution to a conflict, make sure to pay attention to your child's emotional state first. If you have a calm-down routine that you can practice together, this will allow your child to be a better problem-solver on his or her own.

Professional support for communication and expectations

If you are not sure how to support your child's executive functioning, you may need some help to set up strategies or to assess how your child is performing. These supports are often recommended for children diagnosed with ADHD but they can also reduce frustration and confusion for children who have difficulty with emotional self-regulation.

- **Trained professionals** who help with executive functioning skills include: Board Certified Behavior Analysts (with specialized training), occupational therapists, and psychologists.

- **Interventions and treatments** that help with executive functioning skills include: psychoeducation assessments to identify cognitive strengths and needs, stimulant medication (as prescribed by a doctor, psychiatrist, or paediatrician), family therapy to support collaborative problem-solving, functional behavior assessment to help identify areas of need and possible replacement behaviors, behavior therapy to practice problem-solving skills, regular cardiovascular exercise to improve cognitive and physical health, support for sleep or nutritional problems. In addition, Dayna Abraham's book *The Superkids Activity Guide to Conquering Every Day: Awesome Games and Crafts to Master Your Moods, Boost Focus, Hack Mealtimes and Help Grownups Understand Why You Do the Things You Do* is written to empower children and help them plan, prioritize and navigate while staying calm and self-regulated.[12]

---

12 Abraham, D. (2017) *The Superkids Activity Guide to Conquering Every Day: Awesome Games and Crafts to Master Your Moods, Boost Focus, Hack Mealtimes and Help Grown-ups Understand Why You Do the Things You Do.* Salem, MA: Page Street Publishing Co.

CHAPTER 9

Understanding Your Child's Values and Motivation

The importance of motivation

As you have worked your way through this book, you've had the opportunity to test out some new emotional self-regulation strategies and build a more positive relationship with your child. You have clarified your expectations and learned more about where your child's cognitive skills might need extra support. You've come a long way, and you've set up a great foundation for cooperation.

Still, there are going to be times when your child's motivation is not in line with your expectations. What can you do?

The more you learn about your child's specific motivation in context, the easier it will be to understand where you are getting stuck, and how to find your next step.

Misconceptions about motivation

Here are some common myths that lead to power struggles and demoralization in families:

Myth #1: If I don't teach her to listen now, she'll never learn.
Fact: Your child's motivation to "listen" isn't going to stay in the on/off position forever. Your child's willingness to cooperate depends on many different things, so the more you know about human behavior, the easier it will be for you to understand why your child wants to do so much or so little of whatever it is that's bothering you.

Myth #2: He needs to learn some respect.
Fact: Your child's ability to follow instructions is not a reflection of his or her love for you. It's easy to take misbehavior very personally, but

if you are attempting to instill "respect" by provoking fear, you may be inadvertently stoking more emotional reactivity.

Myth #3: She should just want to do it.

Fact: While values are important, sometimes children do not share our personal views, or they do not have the long-term perspective to make sense of them. Intrinsic motivation alone isn't required for cooperation, although it helps.

Myth #4: If he doesn't want to do it, I need to figure out how to reward/punish him.

Fact: Your child's resistance or difficulty might not have anything to do with an external reward or punishment. Adding rewards or threatening punishment might not have much effect at all (or it can backfire).

Myth #5: She's just doing it for attention.

Fact: It can be hard to understand what is motivating your child, and attention is just one of many reasons. When you ask your child to stop and she refuses, this may not be a ploy to drive you crazy. There may be something powerful about that particular behavior, so your child won't be terribly motivated to stop unless that need is met or can be met in a different way.

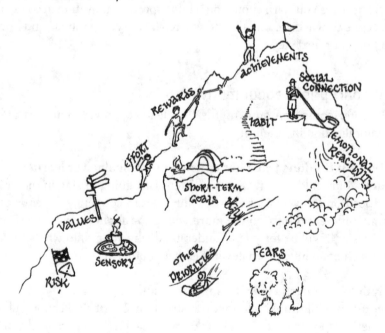

Is my child trying to control me?

When parents ask "What's my child's motivation for all this disruptive, messy, and upsetting behavior?", there are a range of common replies, with one basic theme:

"Don't let him get away with that!"

"If you give her an inch, she'll walk all over you."

"He needs to learn to LISTEN and obey, or he will grow up and run wild."

"Just be consistent, and she'll learn."

"He's just trying to manipulate you."

You have probably heard this message from family members, from teachers, or even from parenting books written by so-called "experts." For many years, most people have assumed that children who failed to follow rules were deliberately and even maliciously disregarding authority, and trying to disrupt the natural order to gain control for themselves.

From an adult's perspective, misbehavior often looks like:

- disobedience

- willfulness

- lack of respect

- spitefulness.

Even the name of the diagnosis, "Oppositional Defiant Disorder," in the *DSM-5*[1] implies that a child's disruptive behavior is a reaction to adult authority. After all, how can a child be oppositional and defiant if there is no one to oppose or defy? In other words, it's all about your child's attitude toward you.

The truth is, there are 101 reasons why children say "no" or behave in a disruptive way. So many of these reasons have nothing to do with the adult in the situation, and when you leap to the conclusion that a child is deliberately trying to steal control from you, you might miss something important.

---

1   American Psychiatric Association (2013) *Diagnostic and Statistical Manual of Mental Disorders (5th edition).* Washington, DC: American Psychiatric Association Publishing.

What's motivating my child?

Now we get to the million dollar question.

The first thing you need to know is this: Motivation is complicated, because humans are complicated. Let's spend some time considering motivation and how it works.

First, think of something you're trying to get done today. Your motivation is probably shaped by of a long list of factors. Some of these factors will make you feel more motivated and some may be discouraging:

- **The task itself**: What exactly are you being asked to do? Is it easy or hard? Generally speaking, the easier, quicker, and more familiar the task is, the more likely you are to do it. When it's awkward, confusing, and inconvenient, your motivation takes a nose-dive.

- **External factors**: How does your situation affect your motivation? Are there rewards or risks? What's in it for you? Your past experience is important too. It's natural to be more motivated to do things that are usually enjoyable, easy, reliable, and rewarding. It's also understandable to be less enthusiastic about repeating uncomfortable, difficult, or possibly pointless activities.

- **Personal factors**: How do your thoughts and experiences affect your motivation? Do you feel hopeful about this task? Is it meaningful to you? In addition to the external pressures or rewards, your own attitudes and beliefs can shape the way you look at a situation, making it more or less appealing. When a task lines up with your values and interests, and when you choose it freely, motivation tends to improve.

- **Emotion and physical resources**: How does your physical state affect your motivation? What about your mood? Think of a time recently when you were feeling really "off," perhaps feeling angry, worried, tired, left out, sick, sad, unsafe, or stressed. Strong feelings, injuries, illnesses, pain levels, or even hormonal changes can have a huge impact. You may find that your usual motivation patterns change completely when you are under stress.

Now think of something that your child is expected to do. Choose something that is simple and observable, like part of a daily routine or coping with a specific situation. Put yourself in your child's shoes.

To really understand what might be happening, you can look at the same factors that might affect your own motivation:

- **The task itself**: Is it easy or hard for your child? Does he or she know when it needs to happen?

- **External factors**: Is his or her effort likely to pay off, or does your child have a history of struggling with this? Will success lead to something valuable to your child?

- **Personal factors**: What does your child think of this task? Is it meaningful and important?

- **Emotion and physical resources**: Is your child easily overwhelmed by emotion? Have you noticed that success depends on mood, sleep, or hunger levels?

Rethinking the meaning of defiance

How often do you break a rule? Let's be honest. Do you ever quietly defy the office rules? Do you ever exceed the speed limit when you drive? Do you ever speak sharply to someone you care about? Do you always take care of your health the way you know you should? Do you always do what you say you are going to do?

As adults, we don't admit this very often but we are often defiant and oppositional in our daily lives. We value our independence. We don't always control our emotions well. We sometimes misunderstand the motives of others or come into conflict with each other. We sometimes eat cookies for breakfast. We like having it "our way."

Even so, as a parent, you probably spend a lot of your day being patient, generous, and cooperative. You have learned how to problem-solve, how to coach yourself through stress, and how to delay gratification. You are at your best when you are thinking of the "bigger picture" and remembering your responsibilities to the people around you. It's not easy, but you're trying.

Now think of what might help you get even better... What would really help you grow as a person? What would make a big difference in your life?

Would you accept help from someone who took the following attitude with you?

"Don't let him get away with that!"

"If you give her an inch, she'll walk all over you."

"He needs to learn to LISTEN and obey."

"Just be consistent, and she'll learn."

"He's just trying to manipulate you."

How would *you* react to being labeled "disobedient" or "disrespectful"? Would you describe yourself as "willful" or "spiteful"?

Here's the bottom line: No one likes to be dominated or controlled. Most people do appreciate having freedom and self-determination. However, our decisions are usually driven by a *combination* of internal and external factors. The same is true for children.

To understand your child's behavior, it's important to look at his or her motivation with curiosity and empathy, not just with resentment and frustration.

Competing goals, needs, and desires

To understand the WHY of difficult behavior, it helps to know if your child has a goal or a need that is in conflict with your expectations.

Purpose and priorities

Children have goals and desires that motivate them, just like adults do. Sometimes these goals and desires lead them "out of bounds." Sometimes a child's goals get priority status over adult expectations. Your child's behavior might be purposeful in trying to get a certain experience, or it might occur with the goal of avoiding something unpleasant.

Often, purposeful behavior is shaped by experience and outcomes. If this type of behavior has "worked" in the past, it's likely to be repeated.

When it comes to children diagnosed with ODD, a conflict over goal-directed behavior can escalate quickly. For children who are more *irritable*, parents might notice a sudden burst of emotional reactivity when these children find that their goals aren't reachable. For children who are more *headstrong*, it can be very difficult to re-orient them and successfully set them on another path, possibly due to the fact that switching attention and inhibiting behavior places a high demand on their executive functioning skills.

Goal-driven behavior can sometimes include deliberate attempts to control other people. When this kind of pressure includes threats or harm, the dynamic can devolve into a coercive cycle, as discussed in Chapter 7.

Reactive behavior

When children are missing something important, they might not know what it is, but they will have trouble with emotional self-regulation or logical decision-making until that need is met.

Sometimes a basic need like food, water, sleep, pain relief, or warmth can put extra stress on your child's emotional self-regulation and executive functioning skills. Perhaps your child has an emotional need that feels depleted, such as the need for security, comfort, belonging, fairness, or control. In this context, you notice a drop in your child's willingness to cooperate with you. You may also see a corresponding increase in aggressive or offensive behavior. This behavior doesn't help to meet the need directly but it does sometimes signal that your help is needed.

You might also see "reactive behavior" erupting when your child is overwhelmed, disappointed, frustrated, or offended. This behavior isn't necessary designed to get a reaction out of you or to meet a particular goal; it's part of a more impulsive, immediate, visceral decision-making process. In this case, the competing need is emotional regulation, as discussed in Chapter 6.

Finding another path

If you can identify the goal or need that your child is pursuing, then you have a number of really helpful options:

For purposeful behavior, you can work with your child to learn how to meet that goal in a way that is not harmful and that works for the rest of the family. Dr. Ross Greene's "Collaborative Problem Solving" process is excellent for helping parents and children come up with solutions in these situations. (You can find more information about it at the end of this chapter.) The ideal outcome in this situation would be for all parties to end up with what they need, and to achieve this outcome you may all need to compromise a little, be flexible, or adjust priorities.

For reactive behavior, you may find it hard to negotiate or set conditions if your child is really struggling with an unmet physical or emotional need.

Here's where many parents face a difficult dilemma: By dropping a demand or providing extra care, parents can help meet their child's needs in the moment, but could this kind of reactive behavior turn into purposeful behavior in the future? The answer is that unfortunately, yes, it's possible.

The solution to this problem is often two-fold: First, provide emotion coaching to help with emotional self-regulation, and help your child access whatever essential needs are unmet. Then, when your child is calmer and able to participate in a collaborative problem-solving process, work together to proactively meet that need next time, or help your child learn how to signal that need in a safer, more socially appropriate way.

Hard-to-understand goals and needs

Some of your toughest behavior struggles probably happen when your child has goals and needs that are hard to articulate, even when they are extremely important for your child's emotional and physical health.

Sometimes these needs are expressed in unusual and perplexing ways. For example, has your child ever done any of the following:

- Sung repetitively or loudly, not stopping when asked?

- Screamed or complained when others made a loud or dissonant noise?

- Refused to wear certain clothes, avoiding clothes altogether or changing clothes often throughout the day?

- Insisted on clothing that was too tight?

- Wore only very loose clothing?

- Hung upside down?

- Stayed constantly in motion?

- Tipped chairs?

- Climbed and hung from furniture?

- Tapped, fidgeted, squirmed, poked, bounced?

Here's what all these behaviors have in common: They are related to *sensory input*. Although these behaviors do seem strange, children have a natural appetite for sensory experiences, and many children seek sensory input with determination and creativity.

What is sensory input and why does it matter?

Sensory input includes the way your child experiences the world with his or her "five senses" (sight, sound, taste, touch, and smell), but your child's nervous system also responds to the sensations caused by movement, pressure, and messages from within the body.

Sensory experiences are often pleasurable, such as a tight hug, a back massage, a sandy beach, a cup of coffee, or a chocolate cake. However, sensory input can interact with behavior in unexpected ways. Sensory input can be painful, or it can relieve pain. It can be invigorating or relaxing. It can be distracting or it can help you focus.

Ideally, your child will enjoy a balance of sensory experiences throughout the day—not too much and not too little. Research on sensory modulation is still in its early stages, but generally speaking, people tend to seek out sensory experiences to help them maintain an ideal "arousal level" (not bored, not vigilant, but engaged and alert).

If your child also has a diagnosis of ADHD, it can be a challenge for him or her get enough sensory input. When you see your child humming, fidgeting, running, swinging, tipping over, climbing, spinning, crashing into things, or thrill-seeking, this might be an effort to get to that ideal level of sensory input. Some sensory input can be unpleasant when it feels too intense, so you might notice your child trying to avoid certain types of clothing, noisy environments, or even strong smells.

Sensory input that calms

Little children often have very obvious sensory calming strategies, including sucking on a pacifier or stroking a soft toy. However, even older children and adults will seek out sensory strategies to calm their bodies and reduce stress. Some of these strategies are socially acceptable, such as yoga, a glass of wine, a long walk, or a massage. Still, most people have a few idiosyncratic habits that they might not even be aware of, like rubbing their temples or massaging their hands. Perhaps adults are more motivated to appear "normal"; they don't want to disturb others, or they simply forget what it feels like to do a handstand or wave their arms like spaghetti noodles. If your child does not have some socially acceptable or easily accessible sensory calming strategies, you might see his or her sensory needs being expressed in an unexpected way (e.g., chewing on clothes, stepping on objects, throwing things around the house, bumping into other people).

"He's just doing it for attention"

Most parents have been cautioned by a well-meaning neighbor or relative who has told them to ignore "attention-seeking" behavior.

However, children seek out their parents' attention as if their life depended on it, because, in a way, it does.

Why social reinforcement matters

It starts at birth. Babies quickly become masters at securing attention from their caregivers. They cry, they gaze, they reach, they babble; and if they are successful, their caregiver will provide what they need: food, warmth, protection, relief, excitement, or help to explore the world around them. As children get older, they learn to take care of some of their own physical needs but they continue to look to caregivers for their social and emotional needs. In addition to food, shelter, and preferred activities, adults provide children with:

- safety and a sense of security and belonging

- congratulations and recognition for success

- consultation and encouragement for setbacks

- important information

- emotional support, validation, comfort, and coaching

- structure and predictability

- fun and companionship.

Seeking appropriate social connection

By the time you reached adulthood, you had developed a range of options for getting social attention when you needed it. You learned how and when to text friends, start up conversations in small groups, get to know your coworkers, ask for help when you needed it, and call out for emotional support when you felt alone or discouraged. Most adults either achieve competence in managing their social needs, or they at least understand what kind of behavior will help them avoid social rejection.

Your child's requests for social attention might be all over the map right now. These requests might take the form of whining, criticizing, teasing, complaining, or insulting. They might even be nonverbal, including pushing, hitting, glaring, destroying property, making loud noises... The list is virtually endless. It can be very challenging to identify when a child is asking for attention, and what type of attention they need most in that moment.

Does your child crack jokes, describe favorite books and video games at length, or fish for compliments? Does your child avoid conversation and eye contact, but sit agreeably side by side? Social interactions can come in so many different forms, and what is an absolute joy for one person is almost intolerable for another. A lack of social skills and emotional intelligence can also place stumbling blocks in front of socially motivated people, so it can be hard to see what kind of social interaction your child really values.

Supporting positive behavior from the outside

Human behavior always depends on context. It's notoriously hard to predict behavior, because sometimes the deciding factor is hard to see from the outside (e.g., a set of beliefs or a personal ambition). However, a decision can also be swayed by more external factors. The more you know about how your child makes decisions, the easier it will be to understand why he or she might be refusing to cooperate.

When you ask your child to complete a task, the answer is probably "It depends."

Specifically, your child's answer might depend on what the task itself is like: *Is it fun? Is it difficult? Is this something I know how to do? Will it take long? Is there anything else that seems more important right now? Will I get hurt?*

The short-term results are also an important motivating factor: *What's going to happen next? What are the odds of success? Will this pay off for me? Will something bad happen if I don't do it? Is this helpful for me? Is this helpful to someone I care about?*

Common sense tells you that your child is more likely to follow an instruction if it seems simple, enjoyable, quick, safe, and convenient; he or she is less likely to agree to do something that is tedious, risky, awkward, or time-consuming.

Your child's expectations are also important, and it's fair to assume that your child is more likely to cooperate if he or she predicts a reliable, immediate, and positive result. If the outcome of cooperation has been unpredictable or negative in the past, your child might be less likely to cooperate.

Can I improve my child's motivation from the outside?

The answer to this question is also "It depends."

Rewards and punishments work...to a point. When researchers in the mid-20th century started to untangle the science of learning and to systematically evaluate the power of rewards and punishment on behavior, the practice of "behavior modification" was born. This was a fairly crude but practical tool. Researchers learned how to manipulate the "carrot" and the "stick," with the purpose of encouraging people to engage in all kinds of desirable behaviors.

If you try to think of every difficult behavior as an opportunity for reward or punishment, you will run into some very awkward side effects, because external consequences are only a part of motivation. Not only that, but your ability to manipulate the environment is limited. In a certain sense, "rewards" and "punishments" can come from many other sources, including natural consequences, not to mention your child's own values and thoughts.

Opportunities for positive feedback and consequences

So, with this humble sense of realism and responsibility, it's fair to look at your child's daily life and ask the questions: How can I encourage my child to work on important skills and treat others respectfully? How can I make sure that his or her best efforts pay off?

If you are thinking of setting up a system of formal rewards, it's best to take advice from an expert who can help to make sure you avoid common mistakes and use enticements in a way that is respectful and helpful. See the resource guide at the end of this chapter for information on where to find this kind of advice.

However, a formal system of rewards is not strictly necessary if you would like to put positive feedback to work in your home. Here are some reasonable and gentle ways to accomplish this:

- Notice the times your child is making an effort and offer sincere praise. It's not necessary to expect perfection. It is enough to recognize those small gestures.

- Look for ways to make hard tasks more inherently enjoyable (e.g., listening to music while tidying up).

- Set some conditions in your home, so that when your child accomplishes some daily chore, there is something to look forward to afterwards (e.g., you might say, "After school, I'd like you to empty your backpack, and then you can turn on the TV.").

- While it's good to offer spontaneous treats "just because," it's also helpful to celebrate big wins. Just make sure you are celebrating the effort, not the outcome. For example: praise the study habits and the perseverance, not the resulting grade.

- If you are going to provide positive feedback or a pleasant consequence, try to tie it to a very specific behavior (not just "Great job!" or "You behaved so nicely") and do your best to offer it as soon as possible. A reward for behavior that happened sometime last week doesn't strengthen a behavior as effectively as one that is delivered promptly.

Important note: While positive feedback and pleasant consequences are often a good way to encourage "good behavior," this approach is more useful when you are working on building a new skill, or increasing the frequency of a learned behavior. Positive consequences may not work so well if you are trying to prevent the challenging behavior from happening or if you would like to see a decrease in a highly reactive behavior (e.g., kicking when very upset). For children who also have a condition such as fetal alcohol spectrum disorder (known in the United Kingdom as fetal alcohol syndrome), or who have an acquired brain injury, a pleasant consequence is appreciated at the time, but this approach is not a very effective a tool for behavior change.

What are the possible benefits of using rewards with your child?

When you start spending more time pointing out your child's successes, and offering your appreciation for his or her cooperation, you might notice a number of encouraging side effects:

- Your own optimism and hope can improve, because you are choosing to pay attention to what is going well (instead of taking successes for granted or being distracted by the struggles).

- Your child's interest in spending time with you is likely to improve, because the ratio of pleasant experiences to power struggles has shifted.

- You may start looking for new behaviors to teach, and begin focusing less on behaviors you would like to decrease.

- If you have been in the habit of using threats to get cooperation, a more positive approach is a tool that can take its place.

- Short-term consequences can help boost motivation for children who might otherwise not be interested in working toward difficult or long-term goals.

- An initial reward might help kick-start a child's interest in an activity that he or she would not otherwise attempt.

- Rewards can encourage your child when he or she is first learning new skills, especially skills that take time and effort to acquire at the beginning but turn out to be useful and easy once learned.

What are the possible risks of using rewards with your child?

Systems of rewards can backfire if not used correctly. Some of the most common unwanted side effects include:

- refusing to meet ordinary expectations without some kind of incentive

- anger and increased disruptive behavior if the reward is not earned

- worrying about not being able to access the reward

- focusing on the immediate reward instead of the long-term importance of the behavior

- lack of cooperation if the rewards offered are not preferred, and loss of interest in preferred activities when they require cooperation

- attempting to negotiate, coerce, or pressure parents to deliver rewards

- parents having difficulty keeping track of rewards promised, leading to missed opportunities for rewarding positive behavior, or accidentally delivering rewards that have not been earned.

Finding a place for rewards in your home

When you think about how you can entice or congratulate your child for meeting your expectations, don't neglect the importance of your child's own goals and needs.

- If you help your child meet his or her own needs regularly, then you can get more cooperation without dazzling rewards, because your expectations are not competing with other important behaviors.

- If you choose to encourage a specific behavior, consider how that behavior will continue to benefit your child, even after the reward is removed. Help your child see the rationale for your encouragement, in addition to pleasing you or earning a treat.

Supporting positive behavior from the inside

Ever heard the proverb "You can lead a horse to water but you can't make it drink"? In this chapter, you will explore your child's motivation from the inside out. Just like the proverbial horse, children are motivated by their own set of values, preferences, and beliefs. Simply offering rewards and delivering punishments is not an effective behavior-changing intervention, because a child's short-term and long-term goals may not be connected to those artificial consequences. Setting expectations without considering your child's fears and desires is going to be an uphill battle indeed.

To build meaningful cooperation, you will need to build on your child's intrinsic motivators. That might sound awkward, but here's the good news: Your child's values, preferences, and beliefs go on supporting his or her behavior, even when you're not in the room (and all throughout his or her life). Long-term behavior change is built on both internal and external motivators.

Finding your child's values and dreams

At first, it might be hard to draw any conclusions about your child's values and dreams, based solely on his or her everyday behavior. For most of the day, your child is occupied with his or her immediate needs or responding to the expectations of other people. He or she might spend time absorbed in video games, social media, Youtube, or talking with friends, and none of it seems to add up to a grand plan or noble cause.

This kind of reactive, short-term decision-making is very common, but that behavior does not mean your child has no values or dreams at all. Most adults will admit that they have aspirations or hopes that lie dormant or get put off until some other hypothetical day. Their daily lives don't reflect their intention to start that weight-loss plan, call friends more often, or read that book. Fears and distractions get in the way, and the same is usually true for children.

Still, if you look closely, you might start to see some patterns. Some children seem fascinated with the idea of being powerful and admired. Other children spend time creating works of art, experimenting with food, learning about other people, or pushing their bodies to find out their physical limits. Some children are explorers, making discoveries on the pages of a dictionary or trying to reach the outer limits of a video game level. These aspirations don't have job descriptions attached to them, but the pursuit of them brings joy.

You might also look at what your child is avoiding. What kind of activities does he or she find hardest to tolerate? Is it boredom? Sitting still? Social pressure? Social isolation? Uncertainty? Control from others? Feeling incompetent? These fears and aversions can shape everyday behavior, and if they become too overwhelming, they can push your child into purely "escapist" behavior. In any case, it is important to know what your child is likely to push against.

Building cooperation based on values

Once you have taken the first step, and you have an idea of some of your child's inner motivators, what do you do with this information?

These values are like the grain in a plank of wood, or the current in a river. You will find it easiest to work with them, not against them.

Attempts to use values as external motivators

Some parents and teachers make the mistake of trying to use a child's values as "leverage." This is essentially a form of coercion, saying, "I'm in control of this. If you don't cooperate with me, you can't have it." This approach can backfire if your child resents being at a disadvantage. Some children learn to sabotage this tactic by responding, "Fine, then I don't want it anymore," or by learning to go behind their parent's' back.

Other people may try to use a more positive approach, and promise, "If you cooperate with me on this unrelated task, then I'll give you what you like." This arrangement is a fairly common one. For example, many employers pay their employees a wage to do things they wouldn't otherwise want to do. However, if the employer stopped paying, the employee would quickly stop coming to work. The same is often true for parents who set up this kind of enticement. It's powerful but it's temporary.

Connecting parental expectations with a child's values

Once you've noticed some of your child's values, you might be tempted to judge them. They might seem silly, trivial, socially awkward, or even antisocial at first glance. However, if you can remember what you learned about the strengths-based approach in Chapter 5, you may recall that a behavior that is inconvenient or unappealing in one setting might turn out to be essential and admirable in the next.

For instance, what if your child wants to be right all the time? If your child insists on getting the last word, gets frustrated by making mistakes, and ignores dissenting opinions, then you might find it difficult to see how this value could ever be compatible with cooperation. However, if you take the strengths-based approach, you might look deeper and see a child who values the truth, logic, and integrity. This might even be a child who would be interested in learning "the right way" to do things, or who would be motivated to tell the truth, even in difficult situations.

If you can approach a value with optimism and respect, you can take an approach that works "with the grain," not against it.

Shaping parental expectations in response to a child's values

Of course, not all of your expectations are going to be in alignment with your child's values. Sometimes this will lead to conflict that is hard to reconcile. If your child values social connection, he or she might be very reluctant to hand over that mobile phone at 8 o'clock in the evening. However, if these boundaries and expectations are very important to you, or your child's safety depends on it, then you will have to resolve this conflict by working through the emotional reactions first, then problem-solving and finding another way for your child to meet his or her needs.

However, sometimes a parent's expectations and a child's values are so at odds that the only solution is to adjust that expectation somehow. Fortunately, you can also take this as an opportunity to teach collaborative problem-solving, flexibility and compromise. Just by recognizing and respecting your child's values, you are teaching a valuable lesson; you are equipping your child to recognize and respect the values of other people.

Other perspectives can motivate

Of course, not everything you do is based on your personal goals and motives. You also make decisions that are rooted in logic, long-term plans, and consideration for others. At this stage, your child may have difficulty agreeing with your expectations if he or she does not see an immediate benefit. He or she may not be a strong logical thinker or planner right now and may have trouble understanding the perspectives of others. However, you can provide that rationale along with your explanation, and in time, your child will be able to see your expectations through that lens.

As your child is better able to regulate emotions and build relationships, it will become easier for him or her to understand why the rules are the way they are. For example, when you give a logical explanation, a child who is distressed may not be able to make much sense of it, but a calmer child can grasp it. When you explain how a situation makes you feel, or how your child's behavior might affect others, a more connected child will have a stronger sense of empathy. If you explain your rationale as it relates to your child's long-term benefit, he or she will be more cognitively prepared to accept it and there will be fewer pressing immediate needs to interfere.

Helping your child stop

In order to help your child behave in a way that is considerate and safe, you may have to ask him or her to stop what he or she is doing. You might even prefer to stop certain behaviors before they start. However, when you've asked your child to stop, you've probably seen plenty of "oppositional" and "defiant" behavior.

This is often where parents feel most helpless. You've probably tried everything you can think of; you've asked politely, you've pleaded, you've reasoned, you've ignored and you've shouted. You've given warnings and delivered punishments, and you've offered incentives to stop in the future.

Nothing appears to work, and even worse, your child's reaction might be more provoking and hurtful than the behavior you were responding to in the first place.

Searching for the root of behavior

At this point, you might be hoping to find a simple, step-by-step, guaranteed guide to stop your child in his or her tracks. However, you have been blessed with a child who is so unique, so determined, so wonderfully inventive, and so expressive that he or she can probably defeat a by-the-book "solution" as easily as winning as a game of tic-tac-toe.

The key to helping your child stop involves understanding why he or she started in the first place. The good news is that if you can find out what he or she wants, you can probably work together and find a better way for him or her to get it. The other news is that discerning the motivator for a behavior can be quite tricky.

Investigating motivation

This section of the book could be a full textbook on its own, but the resource guide at the end of the chapter should help you pick up where this chapter leaves off.

Finding the root of a behavior can be a little like looking for the first domino after the whole set has fallen. Some behaviors are *reactive*, that is, they are impulsive, often emotionally driven, and they might not have an obvious purpose. For example, you might snap at your partner after an especially difficult day at work. The purpose of that behavior is not to intentionally hurt anyone, and it might not get a very pleasant response. You reacted because you felt uncomfortable and depleted, and your partner's careless comment was just another domino to fall. Similarly, your child might shout insults at you when told that the television is not available. The purpose of that behavior is probably not to persuade you to turn the television on, or to make sure you know what a rotten mother you are; it's just a reaction, a brief moment in time where yelling rude words feels great.

Uncovering the reasons for reactive behavior

When your child is especially emotionally reactive, you might feel as if you are walking on eggshells. Any attempt to correct your child's behavior or to give suggestions just escalates the problem. Even your sympathetic questions might not extract a reason for the stormy mood. In emotional processing terms: in the midst of a fight/flight/ freeze reaction, your child's emotional filtering and effortful control is probably not at its best.

You might experience this as a bit of a dilemma: You don't want to take orders and respond to threats; but you worry that if you resist your child's demands or impose a punishment, you will only add fuel to the fire.

Fortunately, your job in these moments is not to *obey* your child or even to *gain control* of him or her. Remember that the basis of your child's emotional reactivity is just a brain signal that is flashing "Something is wrong!" He or she might not know exactly what it is. You can help him or her through this by providing safety, access to basic needs, freedom to use sensory tools to calm himsel or herself, and time. You don't have to argue, teach, or prove anything in this moment. Your own emotional self-regulation will probably be challenged, and your child might even invite you to join in the freak-out by threatening you, destroying things, and pushing your emotional buttons. Feel free to politely decline this invitation. When your child is able to work through that emotional reactivity, then other emotional filters become possible and effortful control is freed up again.

Your child's sensory needs may also drive some types of reactive behavior. Children who experience sensory "under-stimulation" may be especially impulsive and hard to redirect when they are told to calm down and stop wiggling, touching, tasting, climbing, squeezing, and pushing. Children who experience "over-stimulation" may be more physically aggressive, defensive, or disruptive when they are struggling to cope with the sensory input in their environment.

Proactive help for reactivity

After the storm has passed, you can look back to see whether there was something that helped noticeably. Did you see your child's mood improve after a snack? Was there a major improvement when you walked outside? Did your child confide a fear or share a frustration? You can even ask your child to help you pinpoint the earlier "dominoes" in the chain. Once you have a working theory of what your child may have needed (e.g., food, sleep, movement, safety, relief from pain, understanding), you can try providing that to your child proactively, problem-solving it together, and teaching your child to meet that need in an appropriate way before the need turns into a crisis.

Uncovering the reasons for planned behavior

When behavior is planned, it tends to have a more obvious pay-off. It's easier to see the relationship between the behavior and what happens next. Sometimes you can tease out this relationship by observing the pattern and noticing: When did it start? When did it stop? What happens when the outcome changes? Does the behavior change too?

For example, if you notice that your child's loud complaints at bedtime usually result in a visit from a parent, whereupon they stop abruptly, only to start again after the parent has left, then you have a pattern and a hypothesis.

Planned behavior usually persists until it meets the intended need, or until it becomes clear that the hoped-for result isn't available. That's why parents are advised to "stop giving in" and remove the pay-off for the behavior. In this case, some children will give up easily, but others are amazingly optimistic and resourceful, so those children (especially those with *headstrong* tendencies) will seek out and test more effective ways to get the intended result. (Sigh.)

Addressing planned behavior

As you saw in Chapter 7, your child's behavior might be a deliberate effort to pressure you into giving into a demand, or backing off on one of your demands. This tactic can degenerate into a coercive cycle if both sides respond by putting pressure on the other to get their own way.

Instead, you can ask yourself a few questions:

- Can I help to meet my child's need in another way?

- Can my child learn to ask for this in a more reasonable way?

- Can I set up a situation that offers less temptation/distraction/opportunity for this behavior?

- Can I offer my child some information and perspective that would help him or her stop?

- Can I offer my child some "external" motivation that would help him or her stop?

These questions are arranged in a specific order, with the goal of meeting your child's needs as a first priority, and external pressures introduced only as a last resort. As you read in Chapter 7, punishment can have some unwanted side effects, and might not be effective at all if the child's behavior is meeting an important need.

What about punishments?

Since this is a guide for parents and caregivers, and not a textbook, this chapter will use the word "punishment" as it is commonly used: to describe when a parent responds to a child's misbehavior by setting up an unpleasant consequence, ostensibly to encourage the child to comply with the parents' expectations.

Punishments can include:

- reprimands, scolding, criticism, mocking, complaints

- confining or ignoring the child

- excluding the child from a preferred activity or removing preferred objects

- penalties such as removing points, tokens, or money

- inflicting physical pain (e.g., hitting with hand or object, placing soap or hot sauce in the child's mouth).

A punishment can even be a frightening threat if it is done with the intention of controlling behavior. Obviously, some of the punishments listed above are harsh and some are mild. Some are acceptable or even accepted in your culture, and some are frowned upon or forbidden by law. Still, they all serve a similar purpose.

Why use punishments?

Ideally, a punishment is intended to "teach," but the most common purpose is to stop an unwanted behavior or prevent it from happening again.

Of course, there is some logic to this. Adults and children, like all creatures, often learn to avoid unpleasant stimuli. You may have tasted blue cheese or oysters once and thought, "Once was enough. Never again." There are plenty of things you will take pains to avoid. It's just sensible to consider what *didn't work* last time when you are making plans.

Of course, not everyone learns from mistakes. Some people repeat the same behavior and get the same unpleasant results over and over again. If you are asking your child to stop a specific behavior, but no amount of punishment seems to make a difference, then it might be important to understand why.

Less effective types of punishments

Some warnings are extremely effective. When you see a skull-and-crossbones on the label of that cleaning solution, you know that it would be very unwise to drink it. The unpleasant results would be severe, immediate, and more or less guaranteed.

However, when a threat is perceived as uncertain, further away in time, or tolerable, then it will not make much of an impact on behavior. For example, many adults do not floss their teeth, despite their dentist's dire warnings. The threat of a cavity seems distant, possibly unlikely, and maybe not so bad. In the same way, your child may discount the importance of a warning if the consequence is uncertain, distant, or tolerable.

Conflicting goals and needs can override fear

To make a threat "work" proactively, your child must also be able to remember the threat or remember a punishment that occurred in the past, and if this does not occur, then the threat or punishment has no effect on behavior. Even if you are right there to issue a warning, your child must be able to listen and incorporate your reminder into his or her decision-making process. If your child is busy pursuing another important goal, then your threat may not qualify for priority status.

Your child's ability to process "punishment information" and inhibit behavior

If your child is not responding to a threat[2] or a punishment in the way you expect, then it might be important to consider some cognitive differences that make it hard for your child to process that information.

In studies of children with a diagnosis of ADHD, ODD, and CD, researchers noticed differences in the way some children processed and responded to "punishment information."

For example, children and youth in the studies:

- had a harder time resisting impulses and exerting self-control

- needed more time to respond to verbal commands

- had less activation in the parts of the brain thought to be involved in reward and punishment processing

- had a harder time learning from their mistakes, or avoiding situations that had been punished in the past[3]

- showed differences in reward expectation and error correction[4]

- tended to seek out more intense types of stimulation

- had difficulty resisting the lure of an immediate reward, even if it came with a larger punishment.[5]

If your child has been ignoring your corrective feedback, or you have been trying to impose consequences and take away privileges for inappropriate behavior, but nothing seems to make a difference, then it's worth asking yourself whether the message is really "sinking in."

---

2   Viding, E., Fontaine, N. M. & McCrory, E. J. (2012) Antisocial behaviour in children with and without callous-unemotional traits. *Journal of the Royal Society of Medicine*, 105(5), 195–200.

3   Budhani, S. & Blair, R. J. R. (2005) Response reversal and children with psychopathic tendencies: Success is a function of salience of contingency change. *Journal of Child Psychology and Psychiatry*, 46(9), 972–981.

4   Finger, E. C., Marsh, A., Blair, K. S., Majestic, C. *et al.* (2012) Impaired functional but preserved structural connectivity in limbic white matter tracts in youth with conduct disorder or oppositional defiant disorder plus psychopathic traits. *Psychiatry Research: Neuroimaging*, 202(3), 239–244.

5   Van Goozen, S. H., Cohen-Kettenis, P. T., Snoek, H., Matthys, W., Swaab-Barneveld, H. & Van Engeland, H. (2004) Executive functioning in children: A comparison of hospitalised ODD and ODD/ADHD children and normal controls. *Journal of Child Psychology and Psychiatry*, 45(2), 284–292.

This is not a reason to crank up the intensity of the punishments. It is enough for now to understand that you don't need to look for sources of blame (e.g., yourself, others who are "too soft" on your child, your child's stubborn attitude, etc.). Your child may simply experience punishment differently than other children, so it doesn't have the same effects.[6]

Different side effects of punishment for different children

When teachers or family members insist on using punishment as a tool to improve compliance, they may point out that it "worked" for another child. However, the effects of punishment will depend on how your child understands it. If you are trying to get out of the habit of immediately punishing your child, or you are trying to persuade a partner or teacher to change an approach that is simply not working, here are some more possible side effects that are specific to the different "dimensions" within the DSM-5's diagnostic criteria for ODD, specifically, *irritable*, *headstrong*, and *vindictive*.

Sensitive children (with behavior described as *irritable* in the DSM-5 diagnostic criteria) tend to be mistrustful and often perceive the actions of others to be mean or unfair. They struggle with perspective-taking and emotional self-regulation. Your punishment could be completely logical and signaled well in advance, but to your sensitive child in that moment, the punishment can be received quite differently. For instance, a sensitive child who struggles with trust and reasoning might conclude that a punishment is evidence of your cruel intentions or lack of care. Children who are *irritable* are already sensitive to stress and will have difficulty staying calm enough to learn the lesson you are trying to teach in that moment, or even in hindsight.

Determined and goal-oriented children (with behavior described as *headstrong* in the DSM-5 diagnostic criteria) often get into trouble when they break rules, or when they fail to take into account the long-term consequences of their actions. They struggle with impulsivity, planning, and perspective. If you impose a punishment on a child like this in order to teach a lesson, you may see two unwanted side effects:

1. More goal-oriented behavior, including refusal to accept punishment or allow changes, escalated and lengthy protests, extended campaigns to return everything back to its original state.

---

6   Matthys, W., Vanderschuren, L. J., Schutter, D. J. & Lochman, J. E. (2012) Impaired neurocognitive functions affect social learning processes in oppositional defiant disorder and conduct disorder: Implications for interventions. *Clinical Child and Family Psychology Review*, 15(3), 234–246.

2. Minimal effect on future behavior, because *headstrong* children have difficulty predicting the effects of their behavior, so they would not take into account a previous experience, and just forge ahead based on impulse and short-term results.

Children who have difficulty with expressing emotions like anger (with behavior described as *vindictive* in the DSM-5 diagnostic criteria) may look for an opportunity to express anger or discontent through acts of revenge. Even worse, your child might take your attempt at an appropriate parental punishment as permission to mimic your punishment procedures and inflict pain upon others (e.g., "That's what you get" or "You need to learn a lesson").

What actually works to help kids stop?

In addition to the proactive plans that you read about in Chapter 8, here are some strategies you can use *in the moment* instead of yelling, grabbing, and threatening, when your child is carrying on with challenging, disruptive, or dangerous behavior.

Gently capturing attention

If you are in the habit of calling your child from another room, or giving reminders over his or her shoulder, try a different way of approaching your child. Try making sure you are nearby, at eye-level, and close enough to gently tap your child on the arm (if your child is comfortable being touched). Use a soft voice and a friendly expression. This kind of warm, relaxed style of communication tells your child that it's time to switch his or her focus and tune in.

Prevention and supervision

For children who don't look before they leap (or who don't pay much attention to the large flashing signs saying "Warning! Steep Drop Ahead!"), the best offense is a good defense. If you cannot rely on your child to remember rules or predict disaster, you will need to arrange more supervision so you can offer the "common sense" that is currently lacking.

If your child's behavior is especially impulsive, you may also find that you need to keep tempting items and activities out of reach, and instead offer a good selection of enticing activities. In other words, you can keep children out of trouble more effectively if you help them stay occupied with the right kinds of activities.

Prompts that help the child think ahead

Your child may have difficulty seeing the future, but you can ask some leading questions to point the way. By having a conversation and talking through the problem, you can invite your child to make predictions and look for clues. These experiences are the building blocks for strengthening your child's ability to look before he or she leaps.

Instead of giving a lecture or barking out instructions, invite your child to make predictions: "What do you think will happen?" "What will happen next time?" "What happened last time?"

Low-key adult reactions

If your child is not in any immediate danger, you might want to consider taking no action at all. This strategy doesn't usually "work" immediately to stop difficult behavior, but a pause can give you time to stop and think, "Is this behavior telling me something important? Is my child expecting me to run over and jump up and down, as usual? What would happen if I didn't? Is my correction doing more harm than good? What if I keep my cool, wait until this behavior stops on its own, so I can find out more? Will my child try something more appropriate to make a request and ask for attention? Is my child able tell me what is bothering him or her in a different way?"

This kind of low-key response doesn't mean you have to behave like a robot or pretend your child doesn't exist. It's just a way to slow down your usual response so you can quietly observe what might be motivating your child. A pause also allows you to avoid accidentally "rewarding" your child with an exciting, dramatic, or intense reaction that leads to further escalation or an unhealthy pattern of control.

Note: if your child has become accustomed to grabbing your attention this way, the behavior is likely to get temporarily worse instead of better, as your child tries harder to get the desired result. If you can refrain from responding a little longer without increasing your child's risk of physical or emotional harm, that would be ideal. If it's not safe to keep waiting, you can switch to a more proactive strategy and a) offer more attention before that behavior starts next time, and b) brainstorm with your child to select a way to attract your attention that is safer and more courteous.

Total distraction

Many children diagnosed with ODD have trouble switching attention from one activity to another, so you may struggle to quickly capture focus, even by repeatedly calling your child's name or using a loud voice.

Fortunately, you don't have to be forceful. You can get creative instead. Using novelty or humor can quickly grab the attention of a child who doesn't seem to answer to his or her own name. A parent who says the word "Cheeseburger!" or "Transformers!" might prompt a quicker response than a parent who says "Stop that!" This kind of silliness is challenging for parents who are already in a startled or irritated mood, but as with many other questions of how to support children with oppositional and defiant behavior, a mild and creative approach can help to capture attention and prevent a power struggle.

Understanding your child's values and motivation: Self-assessment

QUESTIONS FOR REFLECTION

- How old was your child when you first started to worry about power struggles?

- When you think of your child's behavior as willful and manipulative, does that change how you react?

- Do you always do your very best, or do you sometimes fail by your own standards?

- What kind of sensory input does your child seem to enjoy most?

- Is it possible that sensory input is a strong motivator for your child's challenging behavior?

- What kind of social interaction does your child usually seek out?

- Is it possible that your child's desire for social interaction leads to some challenging behavior?

- If you knew for certain that your child had difficulty processing "punishment information," what would you do differently? What kind of extra support could you offer?

ESSENTIAL SKILLS

- I try to keep an open mind when it comes to understanding my child's motivation.

- I recognize that my goals and values are not always shared by my child.

- In our family, we all have goals and values that are important, so we work together to make sure everyone's needs are met.

- When my child says "no" or breaks the family rules, I look to see if I can understand the underlying need, goal, or value behind that decision.

- When my child doesn't meet my expectations, I look at the context to help me understand why.

- I shape some of my expectations to suit what my child is most enthusiastic about.

PRIORITY QUIZ

Is understanding values and motivation a priority for your family? If you answer "yes" to three or more of these questions, then uncovering what motivates (and discourages) your child will help you avoid some power struggles and learn to collaborate.

- My child's challenging behavior comes out of nowhere and there's no logic to it.

- My child has trouble understanding the logic behind our family rules.

- I set family expectations based on my own values.

- I resent feeling controlled by my child's needs and desires.

- My approach is simple: What I say, goes.

Where can I find help if my child is unmotivated?

STRATEGIES TO TRY AT HOME

Working with your child's motivation (and not against it) is the most effective way to support your child's short- and long-term wellbeing. Even when you are extremely frustrated and you simply want the behavior to *stop*, it's worth asking the questions: Why did my child do that? What was the motivation? What can I learn from this?

Be very careful not to jump to conclusions. Motivation is not always obvious, and you may have to set aside your emotional reactions and existing theories to be truly curious and open-minded.

Exercise #1
Put it on paper

When your child does something surprising or alarming, try writing down as much as you can remember about what happened. You may notice details that escaped you before. When you look at what happened before, you can ask:

- Was my child already stressed, bored, lonely, hungry, confused? In other words, did my child have some extra motivation for something in that moment?

- Was my child getting a lot of something (e.g., attention, stimulation, food, sleep, physical exercise, and had less motivation in those areas)?

- Was there something my child wanted to get away from?

Often, you will find useful information by reviewing what happened immediately before. You may even find that the situation started out gradually (e.g., your child was trying to solve a problem with a sibling, struggling to get the lid off a container, or started to fall behind in a competitive board game).

You won't always be able to offer a detailed play-by-play—especially if you are in another room at the time, or just not paying attention— but some general information about where you were, what everyone was doing, or even just what time of day it was. Sometimes you will remember things that you would rather forget, such as hurtful comments made by you or your child. Be as honest as you can as you re-tell the story. Re-read the words you have written, and see if you can remember anything else, or if any moments seem significant to you.

Filling in the blanks in a format like this may give you a useful way to look at how the problem developed:

- Everything seemed okay when…

- I noticed the first signs of a problem when…

- It got worse when…

- Finally, it started to get better after…

Exercise #2

Re-caption the scene

Sometimes children express their thoughts and feelings in ways that are very hard to hear. They may talk about things that aren't really connected, they may use hateful words, or they may not say anything at all.

Try to think of the scene again, but without the volume. Pretend you can't understand what was said. If you were watching this scene unfold in a movie, what captions might fit? What important thoughts and feelings might be hiding behind the dialogue? Here are some ideas to get you started. If you have already interpreted the dialogue in a way that is hurtful or terrifying, remind yourself that there are other possibilities.

- I'm angry with you right now.

- I'm tired and overwhelmed.

- I'm worried and upset.

- I need to eat a snack before I can make a decision about this.

- My sweater is itching me and I can barely think straight.

- I wasn't expecting you to say that.

- I don't know really know where to start.

- I don't think you're on my team.

- I just can't wait a second longer!

- I don't know what to do with myself right now.

- I had a bad experience with this last time.

- I want to choose for myself.

- I was really hoping for something else.

- This makes me really uncomfortable.

- I don't think anyone likes me.

- I don't know how to calm myself down.

- I don't like this choice and I'm not sure what to do about it.

- I'm worried about what's coming next.

- I don't know how to make you happy.

Exercise #3
Motivation audit

If you are setting an expectation but you are running into the same conflict over and over again, try to put yourself in your child's shoes, and ask what might be motivating (or discouraging) for your child.

Exercise #4
Your child's emotional compass

Just as some children are very reactive when it comes to their emotions, a proactive conversation about emotions can help to shift your child's motivation and attitude. For example, if your child threatens to slap a sibling, you might be tempted to respond by explaining the rules or warning of consequences. However, you may notice that your child has a very different reaction when you gently ask the question "How will you feel if you do that?" You can also use this approach to talk about what happened in the past, or how other people may react in the future.

Exercise #5
Motivational questions about the task itself

Try asking these questions from your child's point of view to look at what might be making a task easier or harder:

- Do I have a plan for when to do the task?
- Is there a reminder to make sure I do it?
- Am I sure I know exactly how to do it?
- Is the task itself enjoyable?
- Is it quick?
- Is there a deadline?
- How difficult is the task?
- Is this task part of a routine, or is it unusual?
- Have I had plenty of practice doing this before?
- What other things are competing for my time and attention?
- Is there a pleasant outcome when the task is completed?
- Am I sure this will work? Have I been rewarded for this in the past?

- Is there a risk involved in this task?

- Have I ever been hurt doing this in the past?

- Is there a risk if I DON'T complete this task?

- Are there people around to help if I need it? Will anyone notice if I DON'T do it?

Exercise #6

Motivational questions about your child's situation

Try asking these questions from your child's point of view to look at what might be making a task easier or harder:

- How am I feeling today?

- Did I get enough sleep?

- Have I eaten?

- Is this a task I chose for myself?

- Is this task personally important to me?

- How does this task make me feel?

- Am I worried about how I will feel if I fail?

- Do I find this task confusing or boring?

- Does this task line up with my personal values?

- Are there are things I would much rather be doing?

- How will I feel when it's done?

- Do I understand why this task is important?

- Do I have the skills and ability required to do this?

- Does breaking this rule help me get something I want?

- Does breaking this rule hurt someone I'm angry with?

- Does breaking this rule help me meet an important need? Does this request match the kind of person I want to be?

- Does this request match the way I want others to see me?

Professional support for aligning values and motivation

If you are looking for more support, or you want to progress more quickly and easily toward your goals, here are some key terms to look for.

- **Trained professionals** who explore values and motivation include: Board Certified Behavior Analysts, coaches and trainers, and teachers of art, music, and drama.

- **Interventions and treatments** that help you align your child's values and motivation include:

  - AIM (Accept, Identify, Move), a behavior analytic program that combines mindfulness, values clarification, goal-setting and positive feedback

  - Values Clarification, an exercise that can help your child express what is most important to him or her

  - Sensory profiling, which when completed by an occupational therapist, can help identify your child's sensory needs and sensitivities, and suggest appropriate ways of meeting those needs

  - Behavior Activation, a cognitive behavioral strategy, which can help resolve problems with mood and motivation, so your child can meet long-term goals and accomplish valued outcomes

  - The Kazdin Method, based on the work of Dr. Alan Kazdin, which works by replacing negative motivational strategies (nagging, complaining, threatening) with calm and simple limit-setting[7]

  - TAGTeach, a playful, flexible, and extremely effective approach to teaching specific skills using positive reinforcement while reducing anxiety and confusion.

---

7   Kazdin, A. E. (2009) *The Kazdin Method for Parenting the Defiant Child.* New York, NY: Houghton Mifflin.

A Final Note

As a parent of a child with oppositional and defiant behavior, I could not have written this without the help of many kind friends and wise professionals.

I did not start out knowing everything I needed to know (despite years of prior experience as a Behavior Analyst with a Master's degree in Applied Disability Studies). I have experienced my share of despair, guilt, depression, and frustration along the way, and I have made many mistakes in my attempts to be a parent.

I am still learning to apply some of the techniques I have written about in this book. My ability to regulate my emotions and maintain an optimistic outlook is a practice that I have to keep coming back to. In other words, I am like you: a work in progress.

It is my sincere hope that this book has helped you to find some insight, compassion, hope, or direction. I have included as many evidence-based expert resources as I could find, because none of us can do this alone.

Amelia

Index

Page references to Figures or Photographs will be in *italics*

Other titles for parents by Jessica Kingsley Publishers

Step by Step Help for Children with ADHD

A Self-Help Manual for Parents

Cathy Laver-Bradbury, Margaret Thompson, Anne Weeks, David Daley and Edmund J. S. Sonuga-Barke

Paperback: £11.99/$18.95 | ISBN 978 1 84905 070 8 | eISBN 978 0 85700 235 8 | 160 pages

Raising a child with ADHD can be distressing and exhausting for the whole family. But given the appropriate knowledge, and the right tools, parents can intervene to manage their child's behaviour, leading to improved relationships at home and, it is hoped, a more successful time at school.

This simple, flexible six-step programme is full of tried-and-tested ideas for parents and professionals supporting families of young children with ADHD. By practicing the techniques and strategies, parents will gain confidence in their parenting and, over time, will improve the child's management of the condition. The programme includes games that will help improve the child's attention, exercises to develop patience and tips for supporting the child in successful self-organization. There are also plenty of useful ideas for developing communication between parents and schools.

Based on research and extensive clinical experience, *Step by Step Help for Children with ADHD* will help families to adapt their parenting to the child, improving relationships and behaviours in the home and at play group.

Cathy Laver-Bradbury is a consultant nurse specializing in ADHD at Solent Community Healthcare, and Pathway Leader for Advanced Clinical Pathway in Child and Adolescent Mental Health at the University of Southampton. **Margaret Thompson** is Honorary Consultant Child and Adolescent Psychiatrist with the Southampton City PCT, an honorary reader in Child and Adolesce nt Psychiatry and Clinical Director in the Institute of Delay, Impulsivity and Attention at the University of Southampton. **Anne Weeks** is a senior nurse, therapist and tutor at the Ashurst Child Development Centre, Ashurst Hospital. **David Daley** is a senior lecturer on the North Wales Clinical Psychology Programme, School of Psychology, Bangor University. **Edmund J. S. Sonuga-Barke** is Professor of Developmental Psychopathology at the University of Southampton where he is Director of the Institute of Disorders of Impulse and Attention. He is also Visiting Professor in the Department of Experimental Clinical and Health Psychology at Ghent University.

Sulky, Rowdy, Rude?
Why kids really act out and what to do about it
Bo Hejlskov Elven and Tina Wiman

Paperback: £9.99/$15.95 | ISBN 978 1 78592 213 8 | eISBN 978 1 78450 492 2 | 192 pages

Children can go through difficult phases - this is a natural part of growing up. Conflicts and arguments are nothing exceptional, but rather a part of everyday family life. The authors of this practical and imaginative book show how parents can create consistent and effective structures, methods and responses, so that children can learn for themselves how to practise self-control and cooperation in a secure environment where they both belong and have autonomy.

Based on years of experience working with children, including those with special needs, the authors structure their methods around the low arousal approach. With many creative suggestions and real-life examples, this book has the potential to change family life for the better forever.

Bo Hejlskov Elvén is a Clinical Psychologist based in Sweden. He is an independent consultant and lecturer on autism and challenging behaviour, and an accredited Studio III trainer. In 2009, he was awarded the Puzzle Piece of the Year prize by the Swedish Autism Society for his lecturing and counselling on challenging behaviour. **Tina Wiman** is a specialist in the field of IT-support for children with special needs. Both Bo and Tina are parents.

Parenting OCD
Down to Earth Advice from One Parent to Another
Claire Sanders

Paperback: £12.99/$19.95 | ISBN 978 1 84905 478 2 | eISBN 978 0 85700 916 6 | 208 pages

When your child has OCD your world can turn upside down and inside out. Claire Sanders has been managing her son's severe OCD for more than 8 years and, although there are no quick fixes, she has learnt a few tips along the way. These cover what is involved in getting a diagnosis, what to expect in therapy, how to cope with panic attacks, how it might affect the rest of your family and how you might feel as a parent. She talks with honesty and humour about these and many other aspects of her son's illness providing practical advice and insight from one parent to another.

This is a must-read for any parent or carer who has a child with OCD. It is the equivalent of a comforting chat with a friend who has been through it all before and can reassure you that you are not alone.

Claire Sanders is the mother of a teenage son who has had severe OCD since the age of 6. She had no previous interest in medicine or mental health and worked as an advertising and website copywriter until everything changed and she involuntarily became an expert in dealing with an OCD child. Claire now provides 24 hour care to her son and lives in Hampshire, UK with her family.

Stay Cool and In Control with the Keep-Calm Guru
Wise Ways for Children to Regulate their Emotions and Senses
Lauren Brukner
Illustrated by Apsley

Paperback: 12.99/$19.95 | ISBN 978 1 78592 714 0 | eISBN 978 1 78450 300 0 | 136 pages

Meet the Keep-Calm Guru, our expert guide to the art of staying cool, calm, and in control in the face of overpowering feelings!

This illustrated book introduces wise ways for children to recognize and cope with anxiety, anger, frustration, and other difficult emotions. Using everything from yoga poses and pressure holds, to deep breathing and relaxing coloring activities, the Keep-Calm Guru shows kids how to take back control and feel cool, calm, and just right.

Suitable for children with sensory and emotional regulation difficulties aged approximately 7-14 years.

Lauren Brukner is a Senior Occupational Therapist who lives in New York City with her husband and her three children. Lauren has appeared as a guest on The Autism Show, The Manhattan Neighborhood Network's School-Home Connection, and the Matt Townsend Show on Sirius XM Radio. Her award-winning books have been listed as resources on websites such as Real Simple Magazine, Inc. Magazine, Marie Claire, Everyday Health, AOL's Health and Wellness, MSN Health, Mothering. com, About.com, and Friendship Circle, as well as numerous school district curricula around the world.

More Creative Coping Skills for Children

Activities, Games, Stories, and Handouts to Help Children Self-regulate

Bonnie Thomas

Paperback: £19.99/$29.95 | ISBN 978 1 78592 021 9 | eISBN 978 1 78450 267 6 | 256 pages

This collection of fun and adaptable activities, games, stories and handouts is a complete resource for supporting children coping with stress and difficult emotions. From engaging arts and crafts, to interactive stories and relaxing meditations, all the interventions and activities are thematically structured so that each chapter contains the means for building specific skills or overcoming behavioral issues. Each chapter contains suggested goals, positive affirmations and photocopiable handouts to enable a child to continue practising and learning new life skills outside of sessions with parents or professionals.

The activities in this book are ideal for use with children aged 3-12 to help them rebalance and gain a strong grasp on their emotions.

Bonnie Thomas, LCSW is a child and family counselor who lives on the coast of Maine with her husband, her son, a pug, and a chihuahua. She has a passion for creative expression, arts and crafts, nature based activities, and playful living. She is also the author of *Creative Coping Skills for Children*, *Creative Expression Activities for Teens*, and *How to Get Kids Offline, Outdoors, and Connecting with Nature*, all published by Jessica Kingsley Publishers.